The Quakers in America

The Columbia Contemporary American Religion Series

Columbia Contemporary American Religion Series

The spiritual landscape of contemporary America is as varied and complex as that of any country in the world. The books in this new series, written by leading scholars for students and general readers alike, fall into two categories: Some titles are portraits of the country's major religious groups. They describe and explain particular religious practices and rituals, beliefs, and major challenges facing a given community today. Others explore current themes and topics in American religion that cut across denominational lines. The texts are supplemented with carefully selected photographs and artwork, and annotated bibliographies.

—

Roman Catholicism in America
CHESTER GILLIS

Islam in America
JANE I. SMITH

Buddhism in America
RICHARD HUGHES SEAGER

Protestantism in America
RANDALL BALMER AND LAUREN F. WINNER

Judaism in America
MARC LEE RAPHAEL

THE QUAKERS

in America

Thomas D. Hamm

COLUMBIA UNIVERSITY PRESS

NEW YORK

COLUMBIA UNIVERSITY PRESS
Publishers Since 1893
New York, Chichester, West Sussex

Library of Congress Cataloging-in-Publication Data

Hamm, Thomas D.
    The Quakers in America / Thomas D. Hamm.
        p. cm. — (Columbia contemporary American religion series)
    Includes bibliographical references and index.
    ISBN 0-231-12362-0 (alk. paper)
        1. Society of Friends—United States.   I. Title.   II. Series.

    BX7635.H26   2003
    289.6′73—dc21

                                                                    2002041422

⊗

Columbia University Press books are printed on
permanent and durable acid-free paper.

Printed in the United States of America
c 10 9 8 7 6 5 4 3 2 1

CONTENTS

PREFACE

This is a book that I did not expect to write. I am a historian who has sometimes opined that nothing really interesting has happened since about 1900. When I finished my last book, a history of my own Earlham College that focused mostly on the twentieth century, I was determined to escape to the relative safety of the nineteenth century, where no one could contradict my findings by saying: "I was there and it didn't happen as you have written." Yet when James Warren approached me about the possibility of a volume on contemporary American Quakerism, I accepted the offer without a second thought.

Such a book appealed to me, in part, because of the unevenness of scholarship on Quakerism. For a relatively tiny group, Quakers have attracted considerable scholarly attention, drawn in large part by the prominence of women in Quaker history and the appeal of Quaker commitments to religious freedom and opposition to slavery. Quakers themselves have been prolific writers. We have an abundance of thoughtful and articulate books offering their authors' view of what Quakerism is or should be. Yet there was no recent scholarly work that tried to describe and explain contemporary American Quakerism in its considerable diversity.

That is what I have tried to do in this volume. As a historian, I believe that history is important, so about a fifth of the book is devoted to the history of American Quakerism. That history begins in England. Like Roman Catholics, Quakers cannot be studied in isolation from Friends abroad. On one hand, in that history one certainly finds commonalities of faith and practice that virtually all American Friends share. On the other hand, one also finds a series of splits and separations in the nineteenth century whose implications American Friends still face. Quakers today span the whole spectrum from fundamentalist to New Age universalist. Readers may find my continual qualifications of absolute statements by referring to that diversity frustrating, but to ignore it would be to draw a sketch that was less than completely true to life.

I bring to this task both the blessings and the handicaps of being an insider. I am myself a lifelong Friend with family ties that go back to the beginnings of the Religious Society of Friends. I grew up in a pastoral meeting in which I still worship, but I have also spent several years in unprogrammed meetings. I teach at a Quaker college that sees its Quaker heritage as the heart of its identity. Earlham is in many ways a kind of Quaker crossroads, with students and faculty who come from almost every Quaker stream. My sixteen years there have given me opportunities for contacts with a variety of Friends that inform much of what I have written. I have tried to be conscious of how my Quaker commitment might color what I was writing. Still, any reader should be aware that this depiction of contemporary Quakerism is one with which a number of contemporary Quakers probably will not agree.

In my research, I was fortunate to have the help of a number of Friends/ friends and colleagues. Margery Post Abbott of Portland, Oregon; Paul Anderson of George Fox University; Martha Paxson Grundy of Cleveland Heights, Ohio; and Evan Farber, Paul Lacey, and Jay Marshall of Earlham read the entire manuscript and made numerous corrections, clarifications, and helpful comments. Joanne Warner, currently the Clerk of the Friends Committee on National Legislation, and Emma Lapsansky of Haverford College read portions as well and were equally helpful. J. William Frost of Swarthmore College commented on the proposal and manuscript and shared unpublished papers on simplicity and sexuality. Alan Weinacht, superintendent of Indiana Yearly Meeting; Curt Shaw, superintendent of Western Yearly Meeting; J. Stanley Banker, pastor of Indianapolis First Friends Meeting; Paul Anderson; Wayne Evans, area superintendent for Evangelical Friends Church—Eastern Region; and Mary Ellen McNish, executive secretary of the American Friends Service Committee, all were generous in agreeing to be interviewed. The Earlham College Professional Development Fund provided funds for telephone interviews and travel to yearly meetings in the summer of 2001. Finally, as always, my wife, Mary Louise Reynolds, was my gentlest and most welcome reader and critic.

T.D.H.
9th Mo. 2002

The Quakers in America

CHAPTER ONE

Meeting for Worship
and Meeting for Business

"Plain" is a word that resonates with many meanings for Quakers, but the Stillwater Meetinghouse near Barnesville, Ohio embodies most of them. Approaching it from the west, one might not immediately realize that it is used for religious purposes. Outwardly, it appears to be an unusually solid red-brick barn, or a small warehouse or Victorian factory. But coming closer, one notices the tombstones in the graveyard (none more than two feet high) alongside, and a sign that identifies this as the site of a Friends meeting.[1]

Inside, the lack of ornamentation, of anything that most visitors would perceive as denoting "sacred space," is striking. Shades of gray paint set off the walls and woodwork. The only concessions to modernity are the electric lights and the plywood that lines the high ceiling. Across the center of the room, east to west, runs a divider, its middle part now open, remaining from the era when men and women Friends held separate business meetings and the shutters in this partition would have been closed. Three rows of tiered benches line the west side of the building. They have railings on top of the back, a reminder of the day when recorded ministers—not ordained pastors but congregants with a gift for speaking—would have sat on these "facing benches" and would have grasped the railings when they rose to speak. Now only the south end of the meeting house is in use. In the center of the aisle separating the facing benches is an antique table, with two people seated behind it. The man is in blue jeans; the woman beside him wears a white cap and a plainly cut dress such as Amish women might wear. They are, respectively, the reading and presiding clerks of Ohio Yearly Meeting of Conservative Friends. On the bench below them sit three other Friends.

As others come into the room, they greet and chat quietly with each other. Most are dressed casually, indistinguishable from any other group of white, middle-class Americans. But a few stand out, men in pants with suspenders and blue work shirts wearing straw hats that they do not remove, a woman in a cap and dress similar to the presiding clerk's. Without any prearranged signal, the fifty or so people present settle into a long period of silence, broken only by the sounds of the breeze through the trees and the buzz of insects coming through the open doors. Then a few Friends rise to speak. Their themes are emphatically scriptural—the New Birth, the Wheat and the Tares, the Cross—with long passages of the New Testament recited from memory.

After half an hour or so, one of the three Friends on the middle facing benches rises and says, "If Friends are willing, perhaps we can attend to the business of the meeting." Another calls on those present to move up from the back benches: "As we're getting smaller, we need to get closer together." Business does not begin with an invocational prayer; instead the presiding clerk reads a passage from the Bible. Then the meeting proceeds. It is considering answers to the queries, the questions on spiritual life and administrative matters that each monthly and quarterly meeting must ad-

Stillwater Friends Meetinghouse. JAMES & BERTHA COOPER/COURTESY OF *FRIENDS JOURNAL.*

dress; for example, have new meetings been established, or is care taken for the education of children of members? Summaries of the answers have been proposed. As the clerk reads them, Friends respond with statements of approval, like, "I am glad for that summary." Most of the business consists of committee reports. The clerk concludes the consideration of each by reading a minute indicating that the report has been considered and approved by the meeting. Never is a vote taken; it is for the clerk to discern the will of the meeting, which for Friends is the will of God.

"Deliberate" is the method here, an intense desire to act, not according to human wisdom but instead in the confident expectation that God, through the Holy Spirit, will be present to guide Friends. One Friend tells how she felt led to visit another yearly meeting a few years earlier, but once she was there, God gave her nothing to say during its sessions. In one discussion, a Friend expresses a fear that the yearly meeting is moving too quickly toward a conclusion, "in our own wisdom," rather than under God's guidance. Ultimately, the matter is held over to the next day for further discussion, when a different course does strike the meeting as the correct one.

Ohio Yearly Meeting of Friends (Conservative) is aptly named. It represents the strand of American Quakerism that has been most resistant to change and has clung most tenaciously to the old ways. Friends of other bodies journey to Barnesville, Ohio to experience its unique atmosphere, aware that it retains something that virtually all other Friends have given up. Its customs and practices are, in large part, those that most Americans vaguely associate with Quakers. At least a few of its members see it as the last truly Quaker body left in the world, since the overwhelming majority of American Friends have chosen very different directions. One sees that clearly by traveling about one hundred miles north.

At first glance, one might not recognize the building as a church. It looks like a new suburban school, and entering it, if you take a wrong turn, you find yourself going down long corridors with classrooms and offices. The largest space would certainly do any junior high school credit as an auditorium or gymnasium—the stage, the sound system, the lines on the hardwood floors laying out basketball zones, the screen for projections and Power Point presentations, the long rows of moveable plastic seats. But the signs and posters on the bulletin boards are all religious, and the literature gives information on opportunities for various Sunday School classes, missionary activities, and sports ministries.[2]

The large auditoriumlike room is the "Multi-Ministries Center." In one sense, it evokes the Stillwater Meetinghouse: little about it suggests a traditional church. But then the music begins. The master of ceremonies introduces the "Son Tones" from the Mount Gilead Evangelical Friends Church. Immediately the quartet launches into harmony, a bouncy gospel song. Many in the choir seated on the stage around them begin to clap, and many out in the audience join in. Applause comes at the end of each number. Now the quartet launches into an *a capella* "Swing Low, Sweet Chariot." Then the harmony shifts to a medley of Christian songs, the four men trading lines and responding to one another and blending their voices. Midway through their performance, much as would any rock group, they introduce their keyboard player to the audience, inviting applause. There is nothing stiff here—the heartfelt joy of the certainty of salvation and eternal happiness through Jesus is almost overwhelming. Occasionally, someone among the hundreds of people in the audience punctuates the performance with a cry of "Praise God!" or a "Whoo!" just as one might hear in a more secular setting when the performers sweep up the audience with their rendition of some favorite number.

The Son Tones are the beginning of an hour of enthusiastic worship. Most of it is musical—singing choruses, the words of which are projected onto the large screen at the front of the room; numbers by the choir; a few solo performances; all interspersed with prayers. Marks of evangelical faith are everywhere—greetings of "brother"; spontaneous amens; the persistent use of the title "Pastor." Most of those present carry Bibles. When the music stops, the main speaker of the evening, Dr. John Williams, Jr., takes charge. One part of the program is a service of dedication for new area superintendents. They kneel for prayer at a specially constructed rail at the front of the room, surrounded by the pastors of the yearly meeting. Williams's address is tightly focused on the Bible, with the expectation that the audience will follow along in their own copies. The message is reiterated by the Scripture verses projected onto the screen. Williams urges his listeners to expect the impossible through their faith in Jesus. And that faith is apparent in every song, every prayer, every speaker. Even an evidently bored teenager's doodling is an elaborate "Jesus Saves" design of the cross.

The place is the Canton, Ohio, First Friends Church. It is a new building, in use only about a month in July 2001. It proclaims itself "The Miracle on 55th Street." The people present are members of the Evangelical Friends Church–Eastern Region, gathered for their yearly meeting. Although they usually do not call themselves Quakers (they prefer "Evangelical Friends" both because it is scriptural and because it distinguishes them from other groups of Friends), they represent an important and aggressive strand of American Quakerism today.

The McCoy Room on the campus of Wilmington College in Wilmington, Ohio would in many other places probably be called a chapel. The A-frame construction, the light fixtures, and the woodwork all bespeak popular models of church construction in 1962, when, a plaque indicates, the McCoy family made possible its construction. Yet this room lacks the paraphernalia we would usually associate with a church or chapel. There is no altar. The only musical instruments are pianos. A single decoration hangs on the walls, a banner from the United Society of Friends Women International (USFWI) Triennial recently held in nearby Cincinnati. A basket of flowers on an antique table at the front of the room provides the only other bit of color.[3]

At 8:40 on this Friday morning in July, sixteen people are present when a well-dressed, enthusiastic woman announces that she would like to lead the group in singing hymns. At first the grand piano drowns out the voices, but over the next few minutes others enter the room, until about forty people are present. Some of the hymns would be familiar to most Protestants: "Joyful, Joyful, We Adore Thee," or "To God Be the Glory." A touch of sectarianism is provided by "The George Fox Song":

Walk in the light, wherever you may be
Walk in the light, wherever you may be!
In my old leather breeches and my shaggy shaggy locks
I am walking in the glory of the light, said Fox!

As the singing concludes, the group settles into a period of silence, the purpose of which is not explained; everyone understands. Then it proceeds to business. The presiding officer is a friendly, middle-aged man; in a reversal of common roles, however, his assistant is a woman while a man takes the minutes. The college president makes a long report, ranging from the achievements of outstanding students to the formation of a committee on the Quaker identity of the institution. Then those present stand and applaud the retiring superintendent of the yearly meeting, Rudy Haag, who has left the hospital to be present for his final report. Succeeding reports are dispatched briskly and indicate both happiness and concern. Statistics are worrisome; of the yearly meeting's total membership, for example, only 43 percent attend worship any given Sunday. And while the yearly meeting has set up a fund to make grants to local congregations for special projects, little interest has been shown in making use of it.

The afternoon session opens with a presentation by a youth group. These young people, in their shorts and T-shirts, are indistinguishable from the teenagers seen at any mall across America, save perhaps that all are white. They stage a skit: one of the participants is stuck in the "Box of Sin." Others—an alien from another galaxy, a greedy television evangelist, a tree-hugging hippie Quaker—appear to propose various solutions. Finally, the solution comes: to accept Christ.

The contrasts between the 110th annual session of Wilmington Yearly Meeting of Friends in Wilmington, Ohio and the Evangelical Friends meeting in Canton are obvious. The style is different, and so, if inquired into, are some points of doctrine and theology. The worship is more subdued. An "Amen!" does occasionally burst forth from someone present, but such affirmations are not the dominant motif. These sessions are, for the most part, implicitly rather than explicitly religious. Yet reading the written reports and hearing the prayers of those present leaves no doubt that these Friends share the Christian identity and commitments of their neighbors to the east. Wilmington Friends represent another important strand of contemporary American Quakerism.

Young Friends at Wilmington Yearly Meeting, 2001. COURTESY OF WILMINGTON YEARLY MEETING.

Many of those present in the auditorium at Bluffton College in northwestern Ohio have the look of people familiar with a college campus. Dress is casual. The cars in the lots of the dormitory where many are housed bear bumper stickers for National Public Radio, peace, ecology, and feminism, along with not a few faded ones for Gore and Lieberman. Gay men and lesbians are present and are welcomed and affirmed in their identities, as informal conversations and the presence of the Friends for Lesbian and Gay Concerns group show. When the roll call is taken, it is striking how many answer from college towns in Ohio and Michigan: Ann Arbor, Athens, Granville, Kent, Kalamazoo, Oberlin, and Wooster. Bluffton is a Mennonite school, but these Quakers are comfortable with the hospitality of another of the historic peace churches.[4]

The meeting opens with worship, those present sitting in silence, speaking when they feel led to. The evening closes with silence but also with sadness. As the official record of the gathering puts it: "Our concluding worship has been touched by the knowledge that while we have been meeting this evening the state of Ohio has murdered Jay D. Scott," referring to the execution of a convicted murderer. Such matters are on the minds of many of those present. Later in the sessions, the group will record its moral support for members who engage in "war tax resistance," will denounce the death penalty, and will pointedly criticize President Bush's "missile shield" program.[5]

This is a group that also values discussion, on every possible subject and involving people of all ages. The "Middle School Epistle" reports "a discussion about the Loch Ness monster, and green alien cats that built the pyramids. We talked about dinosaurs and how they became extinct, and evolution vs. Creation. We talked of ethics and politics. We discussed prayer and Meeting for Worship. The class discussed cults. We discussed what God is like."[6]

But while these Friends may be intensely political, they are also intensely spiritual. A highlight of the five-day yearly meeting is an address by Marty Paxson Grundy, a Cleveland Friend and the yearly meeting's recording clerk. Its point is simple: individuals must be in balance with their meetings, and they achieve that through their relationship with God. It seamlessly blends history, theology, and psychology, citing a variety of Friends from the seventeenth to the twentieth centuries as well as the Bible. As are the messages heard in the other yearly meetings, it is a call for people to come into a deeper, closer relationship with God. But in contrast to them, it is not definitely Christian. For many in Lake Erie Yearly Meeting, to be a Quaker is not necessarily to be a Christian.[7]

Barnesville, Canton, Wilmington, and Bluffton represent, in rough geography, four corners of the state of Ohio. The Quaker gatherings that they host also represent the four major divisions of American Quakerism. Ohio Yearly Meeting, the smallest, represents the three yearly meetings of Conservative Friends left in the United States. Eastern Region is part of the group that calls itself Evangelical Friends International. Wilmington Yearly Meeting was one of the founders of the largest international Quaker group, Friends United Meeting. Lake Erie Yearly Meeting, the youngest of the four, is part of Friends General Conference. All four yearly meetings, and all four groups, have roots in the Quaker movement that began in England in the 1640s. All claim to be anchored in that heritage. Yet the surface differences that the casual visitor observes reflect profound theological diversity with some common strands of understanding.

These Friends obviously worship in different ways. At first glance, those of Ohio and Lake Erie seem similar. For both bodies, worship is what Friends call "unprogrammed," not having any preordained order, with no one person appointed or hired as the main speaker. Ohio Yearly Meeting, however, recognizes that some Friends have a gift for speaking in meeting, and has a process for recognizing this by "recording" it—making a record that the Friend, whether male or female, has "a gift in the ministry." Such recorded ministers are simply people with a gift for preaching, not pastors. Lake Erie, on the other hand, like most yearly meetings in Friends General Conference, does not record ministers. Wilmington (although it contains a few unprogrammed meetings) and Eastern Region are "programmed" yearly meetings, meaning that the congregations have pastors, with orders of worship similar to those in most Protestant churches. Both hold to the conception of the ministry found in Ohio, however, in that neither "ordains" ministers. Ordination implies that human agency gives some power or validity to ministry. Instead, Friends simply recognize that a divine gift is present. But even the general labels of "programmed" and "unprogrammed" can embrace considerable diversity. The hymn singing and preaching at Wilmington are rather staid compared to the exuberance and demonstration in Eastern Region. And, as will be seen, the silent worship in Ohio and Lake Erie often proceeds from very different theological bases.

All of the Friends attending these yearly meetings have been drawn by some kind of spiritual yearning or commitment. In each of these groups are some Friends who are "birthright," a Quaker shorthand for Friends who were born to Quaker parents and grew up in a Friends meeting.[8] Each contains "convinced" Friends as well, converts to the Quaker faith. For those in Wilmington, Ohio and Eastern Region, that faith is explicitly Christian. Christ is always at the center of their worship. They would vehemently reject any intimation that they, because of their differences with other Christians, are not Christian themselves. At Lake Erie, the Christian identity of Quakerism is more problematic. Many there see themselves as Christians, but others argue that Quakerism should not be limited in that way. And even among self-identified Christian Quakers, there are different understandings of Christ. Some, especially among Evangelical Friends, emphasize the historical Jesus who was born to the Virgin Mary in Palestine two thousand years ago and through whose atoning death on the Cross they claim salvation. Others see Christ as the Son of God and Savior, but are not disturbed by those who express doubts about the Virgin Birth. Still others see Christ as Inward Teacher, a spirit or light that can be experienced by all humanity. For Friends in Lake Erie, this idea of the Inner Light, or "that of God in everyone," shared by all people is the cornerstone of faith. Ohio Friends, and probably most in Wilmington, would link it more explicitly to Christ but also see it as a foundation of Quaker distinctiveness. But Eastern Region Friends are on record as rejecting the "so-called Inner Light" as unscriptural and dangerous.

Similar differences are found in understandings of God. Many of the members of Lake Erie Yearly Meeting say that God can be experienced by many names and in many ways—Krishna, Allah, Jehovah, Great Spirit, Gaia, Goddess. Some object even to a reference to God as "He" or "Him." Some at Wilmington and in Ohio Yearly Meeting, even if they do not embrace such a vision themselves, find it tolerable. But others in the three other yearly meetings, especially at Canton, see it as unsound doctrine, possibly putting its holders in danger of eternal damnation and not to be sanctioned in any way.

Neat categories for these Friends are difficult to create, and labels can be confusing. Those in Eastern Region call themselves Evangelical Friends to signify their unity with non-Quaker evangelicals on doctrines like salvation through faith in the Atoning Blood of Christ and the authority of the Bible. Some go further and describe themselves as fundamentalists, emphasizing a strict and literal reading of the Bible and suspicion of anything that suggests doctrinal compromise. Many Friends, however, in Wilmington and some in Ohio are comfortable with such labels as well. In turn, probably many Evangelical Friends see themselves as doctrinally and socially conservative, but not in some of the ways that one finds at Barnesville. On the other hand, some Friends in Wilmington and Ohio, and most in Lake Erie, accept a description of their theology as liberal, by which they usually mean that they do not always feel bound by historic intepretations of the Bible and tend to emphasize the inclusive love of Christ in their faith. And in Lake Erie, many Friends describe themselves as universalists, who believe that Quakerism is not necessarily Christian and that all religions may hold important truths. (Chapter 5 will explore these distinctions in greater detail.)[9]

The names that these Friends use for themselves, their organizations, and the buildings in which they worship also tell us something about them. In Lake Erie and Ohio yearly meetings, the local congregations are called "meetings" rather than churches. This harkens back to the early Quaker view that the "church" is the universal body of all believers. "Meeting" signifies the gathering of a body of believers for worship together. Similarly, the label that Ohio, Lake Erie, and Wilmington use for the larger body of which they are a part, "Religious Society of Friends," reflects that theological stance. For many Friends, however, that view has lost its resonance and relevance. Some Wilmington Friends would still hold to it and would call their congregations meetings. But just as many talk about the "Friends Church." And among Eastern Region Friends, "meeting" and "society" were abandoned over a century ago as outmoded. All of their congregations are churches.[10]

All four of these entities still reflect the business structure that arose among Friends in the seventeenth century. The basic unit was the monthly meeting, gathering, as the name implies, once a month to transact business. It would own property, receive and eject members, and see to the normal business of congregations. To handle matters beyond the local level and facilitate communication, two or more monthly meetings would make up a quarterly meeting, gathering four times annually. At the top of the structure was the yearly meeting, holding its sessions once a year, the ultimate authority for faith and practice among Friends within its bounds. Today, Wilmington, Lake Erie, and Ohio yearly meetings still hold to that structure. Eastern Region, in contrast, while it is still a yearly meeting, no longer has monthly or quarterly meetings. Instead, it is based on local congregations and districts.

All four bodies also reflect their ties to the Quaker past in their decision-making methods. Friends believe that in their business sessions, if they are prayerful and sensitive, the Holy Spirit will come among them, or the Inner Light will manifest itself, so that the will of God on a particular matter will become clear. Thus Friends do not make decisions through voting, as they do not believe that the will of the majority is always the will of God. Instead, objections from a principled minority can be enough to stop action until the meeting finds unity to proceed in some way. Friends often call this point of agreement "clearness"—clearness of any sense of hesitancy or fundamental disagreement, clearness that the Divine Will is manifest on the matter. It has become common in recent years for Friends to refer to their business methods as "consensus decision making," although this label draws protests from other Friends who believe that consensus is secular. In their view, instead of seeking consensus, Friends properly seek unity, which is a divine gift and not a human achievement. Presiding over the business meeting is a clerk. Most meetings separate the offices of presiding and recording clerks—the former oversees the business procedures while the latter produces the written record of business. But, as we have seen, Ohio Conservative Friends still hold to the traditional practice of combining the two offices.

The clerk's responsibilities in a Quaker meeting for business are heavy. He or she has the duty of judging the "sense of the meeting," based not only on spoken comments but also on nonverbal cues and his or her own sense of the motions of the Spirit in the meeting. Two favorite words of Friends in these circumstances are "discernment" and "weight." While Friends believe that any speaking to a matter should come only from a clear conviction that the Spirit is leading the speaker, they recognize that human nature often asserts itself and a clerk may be faced with diametrically opposed views on an issue. One way that Friends have traditionally dealt with such differences is to acknowledge that Friends are usually at different levels of spiritual maturity. A clerk will judge individual comments by their "weight," whether they manifest signs of a divine leading and a good spirit. Friends whose words usually bear such marks are often known as "weighty." Thus a good clerk will have the gift of discernment, the ability to find commonality among differences and to combine differing views into a solution that might embrace elements of a variety of positions, the insight to shape a decision in a way that is somewhat different from all of the positions that have been heard and yet is satisfactory to all. And constantly, amid the human voices in the meeting, the clerk needs to be sensitive to his or her own experience of the Spirit and the Light and where they lead. Evangelical Friends, like those in Eastern Region, have compromised this older belief somewhat by allowing, under certain circumstances, a vote to help determine "the sense of the meeting." But most Friends, while seeing themselves as thoroughly democratic, still eschew voting, confident their traditional method will lead them in the direction in which God wants them to move.

Finally, all of these Friends see themselves as called to live out their beliefs in ways of life that manifest their faith to the world. Friends call these manifestations "testimonies." Quaker author John Punshon calls testimonies forms of communication, proclaiming "how the world ought to be, and thus, by implication, what other people *ought* to do."[11] They may be verbal statements. They might be written addresses to others, such as Lake Erie's statement on the death penalty, living out what those Friends see as the Quaker Peace Testimony. The Friends in Barnesville in Amishlike dress see their lives as displaying the Quaker testimony of simplicity. Friends in Canton see their exuberant worship as a testimony to their experience of salvation through Christ and their commitment to share it with others.

These Friends disagree among themselves about how much they have in common. Certainly there are Friends in each group who question, if not deny, the Quaker *bona fides* of at least some in the other groups. Many unprogrammed Friends dispute that pastoral Friends are real Quakers. Friends who see themselves as evangelical argue that no one who has not had a saving experience of Christ is a real Quaker. In politics, doctrine, relations with other denominations and with the ecumenical movement, and relations with one another, Friends are strikingly diverse. The differences are all the more striking when one realizes that they exist in a group that has around 100,000 adherents in the United States today, about the same as the number of Roman Catholics in a single medium-sized diocese like Belleville, Illinois. Yet, as noted above, all have common origins in what was, until the 1820s, a relatively united religious movement. Some knowledge of Quaker history is necessary to understand how this remarkable Quaker diversity arose.

CHAPTER 2

The Origins of American Quakerism, 1640–1800

The story of American Quakerism begins, as do the stories of many American faiths, on the other side of the Atlantic. The first Friends were English men and women, visionaries caught up in the tumult of the political, religious, and social upheavals of the 1640s and 1650s in the British Isles.

It was a "world turned upside down," in the words of one contemporary. These were men and women suffering from inner torment, trying to work out for themselves, and seeking others who could help them answer, what seemed to be the most important question that anyone could ever confront: How do I know the will of God for my life? They were plain folk—shepherds, cobblers, farmers, what their neighbors called "goodmen" and "goodwives." Their search took them into marketplaces and shops, barns and houses, and, most of all, onto the desolate moors and dales of the north of England. The answers that they ultimately found are the foundations of Quakerism.

The eruption of Quakers from the moors and market towns of Yorkshire and Lancashire and Cumbria into the rest of the land was one of the strongest indications of that era's dislocation. From their experiences in the lonely country in the north of England they drew the inspiration for one of the most distinctive and radical of all Protestant faiths.

George Fox and the Children of Light

Religious movements begin by appealing to individuals, who, drawn together, form ties and find a common identity. Thus it is always dangerous to generalize too much from the experiences of one person. Yet, allowing for all of the disparate individuals and influences, understanding the rise of Quakerism means coming to terms with George Fox.

Fox was born in Leicestershire, in the Midlands of England, in July 1624. Almost all of what we know about his early life and the first years of the Quaker movement comes from the autobiography that he composed in the 1670s. He entitled it a *Journal*. As is the case with any autobiography, historians find evidence of selective memory, choosing the incidents that reflected well on his abilities and those of his followers, omitting those that were embarrassing or might even become dangerous with the passage of time. Yet with all of these limitations, Fox's *Journal* is an extraordinarily vivid portrayal of a gifted and driven personality.[1]

His family was Puritan in its views, meaning that they sympathized with those who saw the Protestant Reformation in the Church of England as incomplete, and longed to see the Church purified according to what they understood as New Testament principles. By the early 1640s, Puritans seemingly had the upper hand in England. The civil war between king and Parliament that broke out in 1642 was in large part over religion, with Puritans identified with Parliament. The overthrow of royal military power by 1645 allowed Puritans to move to impose their vision of reform. But the downfall of the old established Church released energies that were too great to be confined. Dozens of competing groups appeared. Some, such as Presbyterians and Baptists, already had considerable support. Others, ranging from Muggletonians to Brownists to Familists to Fifth Monarchists, were more marginal but acquired followings in certain parts of the country.[2]

In this world George Fox came of age. By his own account, the young George was an unusually pious and serious young man. He reproved other teenagers for wasting time in taverns. Still, the competing claims of Presbyterians, Independents, Baptists, and other sects that each represented the true Christian church deeply troubled him. How was he to know who was right? So in 1643 he set off on a kind of pilgrimage, searching for answers. Fox's journey took him across the south and middle of England. "I was tempted almost to despair," he recorded, "and some years I continued in that condition, in great trouble." Fox visited a variety of clergy and laypeople of different sects, but none seemed to have the answers that he sought. Returning home, he felt "dried up with sorrows, grief, and troubles, which were so great upon me that I could have wished I had never been born."[3]

In the spring of 1646, Fox resumed his lonely wanderings. They took him farther from home, now up into the north of England, onto the moors of Yorkshire and Lancashire. Along the way, Fox encountered others who shared his fears for their souls and disenchantment with the competing sects and churches around them. Talking with these like-minded seekers, and in his own ruminations, Fox worked out certain conclusions about the nature of Christianity. One of the first was that "being bred at Oxford or Cambridge was not enough to fit and qualify men to be ministers of Christ." Another was that "God, who made the world, did not dwell in temples made with hands, . . . but in people's hearts. . . . His people were his temple and he dwelt in them." Realizing how different these ideas were from those of any of the priests or preachers he encountered, Fox became even more certain that truth was not to be found in their churches.[4]

Finally, later that year, Fox had the pivotal experience of his life. Still tormented by doubts about his course, "when all my hopes . . . were gone, so that I had nothing outwardly to help me, nor could tell what to do, then, Oh then, I heard a voice which said, 'There is one, even Christ Jesus, that can speak to thy condition,' and when I heard it my heart did leap for joy."[5]

This experience led Fox to a series of what he called "openings," or what we today might call revelations, times when he was certain that God was speaking directly to him. As he wrote later, "the Lord did lead me gently along, and did let me see his love, which was endless and eternal, and surpasseth all the knowledge that men have in the natural state, or can get by history or books." Over the next three years, these "openings" would lay the foundation for the movement that would become Quakerism.[6]

At the heart of Fox's experience was the Light of Christ. As he put it, "every man was enlightened by the divine light of Christ; and I saw it shine through all, and they that believed in it came out of condemnation and came to the light of life, and became the children of it, but they that hated it, and did not believe in it, were condemned by it, though they made a profession of Christ." Fox's understanding of this Light, the Inward or Inner Light, as Friends have come to call it, was complicated, and his writings and the writings of other early Friends lend themselves to varied interpretations. What is clear is that Fox and other Quakers agreed that all people had within them a certain measure of the Light of Christ. If they heeded it, that Inward Light would show them their sinful conditions and their need for Christ, and would lead them to salvation. But if they ignored it or failed to heed its admonitions, they would be lost and ultimately damned. This experience was not limited to those in Christian lands. Pagans who had no knowledge of the historical Jesus could still experience the Inward Light of Christ, and, if obedient to it, could be saved without ever having heard Christian preaching or knowing the Bible.[7]

Fox's experiences also led him to argue for the possibility and necessity of immediate revelation: God speaking directly to humanity without any intermediary. For many of his contemporaries, this was frightening doctrine. They saw in it the potential for complete religious anarchy. Fox responded that no such harm could ever come from obedience to God. Others accused him and other Quakers of devaluing the Bible, placing it below their Inward Light. To be sure, a few notorious incidents did take place in the 1650s in which Quakers burned their Bibles, seeing them as "outward" stumbling blocks in the way of real religion. Fox, however, always denied any hostility toward the Bible; one of his contemporaries said he knew the Scriptures so well that if somehow all of the Bibles in the world should be destroyed, the text could be reconstructed from George Fox's memory. Most early Friends were steeped in the Scriptures. Fox's argument was that the same Spirit that had inspired the writers of the Bible was still available to humans, and that past written work of that Spirit, while it should be valued, should not be placed above the Spirit itself.[8]

Yet another of Fox's experiences that shaped the early Quaker movement came in 1648. "Now was I come up in spirit through the flaming sword into the paradise of God," he wrote. "All things were new, and all the creation gave another smell unto me than before, beyond what words can utter. I knew nothing but pureness, and innocency, and righteousness, being renewed up into the image of God by Christ Jesus, so that I say I was come up to the state of Adam which he was in before he fell." Such an experience would not be unique to Fox: "And the Lord showed me that such as were faithful to him in the power and light of Christ, should come up into that state in which Adam was before he fell." In other words, Fox was claiming the possibility of perfection, freedom from all sin. This was in sharp contrast to the teachings of most of the sects and churches around him, which argued that due to the Original Sin of Adam and Eve, humans were sinful beings who must always strive to overcome their sinful natures through the grace of God but would never completely succeed.[9]

For Fox, all of these experiences culminated in what he called "the Lamb's War." "The Lamb," of course, is one of the titles given to Christ in the New Testament. As Quaker historians Hugh Barbour and J. William Frost have observed, for Fox "the Lamb's War" was a "fusing of personal experience and social ethic" into "a cosmic world-view." Fox called all Christians to struggle with the experience of the Light, and fight the Lamb's War against evil within themselves. At the same time, they would struggle against it in the larger world. Many early Friends had a sense of apocalyptic urgency; they and many others in England in the 1650s were convinced that the physical return of Christ, the Lamb, was imminent. At times Fox fancied that he would play a special role in the army of the Lamb in the final battle of Armageddon against Satan and his followers.[10]

Fox shared these experiences with others, preaching in separatist congregations. Significantly, one of the first people, if not the first, to embrace Fox's teachings was a Nottinghamshire woman, Elizabeth Hooten, who became a Quaker leader. As Fox's biographer Larry Ingle notes, Fox was flexible in the labels he applied to the movement that was developing around his message. He preferred "Children of the Light," but used other terms as well: "People of God," "Royal Seed of God," and "Friends of the Truth," which became the basis for the name that later became general and official, "Religious Society of Friends." In the autumn of 1650, Fox found himself before the court of quarter sessions in Derby, charged with blasphemy for his claims of Adamic holiness and infallible guidance. His confrontation with the justice, Gervase Bennett, was dramatic. Fox exhorted Bennett to "tremble in the fear of the Lord." Bennett replied by scornfully hurling back at Fox the insult, "And quake, thou quaker, before the majesty of the law." Bennett was using an insulting nickname that apparently was already being commonly applied to the Friends. As a result of the confrontation, Fox spent almost a year in the Derby jail.[11]

Released from jail, in 1651 and 1652 Fox sought hearers in Yorkshire and Lancashire. He won important converts, mostly farmers and former soldiers with Puritan sympathies. A critical experience, which many see as the foundation of Quakerism as a definite movement, happened in May 1652. In Lancashire, Fox felt led to climb Pendle Hill. There he had another opening to "sound the day of the Lord. . . . And the Lord let me see . . . in what places he had a great people to be gathered." In nearby towns and villages Fox found many sympathizers, and he addressed a crowd of a thousand on Firbank Fell. Most important, that summer took him to Ulverston in Lancashire, where he was a guest at Swarthmoor Hall, the home of Thomas Fell, a judge with Puritan inclinations, and his wife Margaret. Fox came into the Ulverston church, and, as Margaret Fell later recounted, he

> opened us a book that we had never read in, . . . to wit the Light of Christ in our consciences, and . . . declare[d] of it that it was our teacher, that we should believe in it, and turn our minds to it. . . . "You will say, 'Christ saith this, and the Apostles say this'; but what canst thou say? Art thou a child of Light, and hast walked in the Light, and what thou speakest, is it inwardly from God?" I saw that we were

all wrong, and that we were but thieves that had stolen the Scriptures. . . . And I sat down in my pew and wept . . . for I saw that all that we had done before was worth nothing.

Margaret Fell would prove to be perhaps the single most important convert to early Quakerism. Swarthmoor Hall became the organizational center of the movement, a clearinghouse for correspondence and a refuge for traveling Friends. Fell's gentry standing would also provide Friends with access to people of influence at critical times over the next two decades.[12]

The Quaker Movement, 1652–1660

In the next decade, Quakers attracted thousands of converts. Although numbers are difficult to ascertain, some estimates put them at about fifty thousand by 1660. Yet Friends also faced considerable opposition and persecution, both legal and extralegal.[13]

From its early strongholds in the north, Quakerism spread south and east. By 1660, Friends had congregations in every county in England, a considerable following in Wales, and a foothold in Ireland, albeit only among English colonists in Ulster and the counties around Dublin. Scotland remained almost completely immune to the Quaker message. London by 1660 had become a major Quaker center, although the northwest of England was the area where Friends were most concentrated.[14]

Quakerism's growth was all the more impressive in the face of considerable hostility to the movement. Contemporary opponents saw it as the most pestiferous of all of the heresies to emerge from the Civil War. As early as 1653 Francis Higginson, a Puritan minister in Westmorland, published a little book entitled *The Irreligion of the Northern Quakers*, the first of dozens of anti-Quaker tracts to appear before 1660. Quakers found themselves mobbed and run out of towns. Individual Friends faced accusations of witchcraft, treason, and being secret agents of the pope. Many were imprisoned on charges of vagrancy and blasphemy.[15]

Why did Friends arouse such ferocious opposition? One reason is that the early Quakers challenged myriad theological and social conventions. They also played a powerful role in creating a sense of a world being turned upside down.

Consider, for example, the centrality of women in the Quaker movement. Fox and other early Friends argued that women were the spiritual equals of men and had as much right to minister as men. To be sure, the early Quakers accepted most of the standard socially prescribed distinctions between men and women. But to say that a woman could be the equal of a man as a minister of the gospel was a radical idea. It was reinforced by the leadership of women like Margaret Fell and Elizabeth Hooten. Quaker women traveled widely to spread the Quaker message. The first Quaker to visit North America, for example, was Elizabeth Harris. Another woman Friend actually traveled to Constantinople in 1657 with the goal of witnessing to the Muslim Sultan of the Ottoman Empire! Quaker language, moreover, often expressed spiritual life in feminine terms. In Quaker eyes, "Mothers in Israel" were the spiritual equals of fathers, and many found this threatening.[16]

The very name "Quaker" denotes the incredulity the early Friends inspired in many of their contemporaries. Consider this description of Quaker worship by Francis Higginson:

> . . . many of them, sometimes men, but more frequently women and children, fall into quaking fits. . . . Those who are taken with these fits fall suddenly down, as it were in a swoon, as though they were surprised with an epilepsy or apoplexy, and lie groveling on the earth, and struggling as if it were for life. . . . While the agony of the fit is upon them their lips quiver, their flesh and joints tremble, their bellies swell as though blown up with wind, they foam at the mouth, and sometimes purge as if they had taken physic. In this fit they continue sometimes an hour or two, sometimes longer, before they roar out horribly with a voice greater than the voice of a man, . . . greater sometimes than a bull can make.

Higginson was an outspoken critic of Fox, and perhaps prone to exaggeration, but he doubtless recorded what many others believed.[17]

Friends heightened their threatening aura with behavior that was, even by today's standards, bizarre. Fox, for example, implied in some of his early writings that he was Christ himself returned to earth and could perform miracles, and rumors of such claims spread. Quakers commonly interrupted the services of other denominations, commenting on the sermons and trying to point congregations to what they saw as the truth. Those subjected to such invasions objected, often violently. Quaker rhetoric could be ferocious. Consider, for example, Mary Fell, daughter of Margaret, writing to the priest of her parish: "Lampitt, the plagues of god shall fall upon thee and the seven vials shall be poured out upon thee and the millstone shall fall upon thee and crush thee as dust beneath the Lord's feet how can thou escape the damnation of hell." Mary Fell was eight years old! Quakers felt called to strange public witnesses. Most notorious were a few Friends who felt led by God to "go naked as a sign." This meant appearing unclothed in some public place, as a sign of either the spiritual innocence of the Friend or the spiritual nakedness of their opposers.[18]

A turning point for Friends, and probably a damper on some of the more extreme manifestations of Quaker enthusiasm, came in the autumn of 1656 with the case of James Nayler. Nayler was a Yorkshire farmer and former soldier who had become one of the most effective and influential of early Quaker preachers; some historians argue that in the early days of the movement he was at least Fox's equal. In 1655, Nayler had gone to London to help lead the movement there. He became involved in a dispute centered on Martha Simmons, an articulate Friend who often preached in meetings. Simmons began to criticize leading London Friends and even challenge Fox. Nayler, who may have been passing through some kind of mental breakdown, sided with her, and with a group of sympathizers set off for Bristol, another Quaker center. Simmons and her sympathizers decided that Nayler

James Nailor Quaker fet a howers on the Pillory at Westminster whiped by the Hang man to the old Exchainge London, Som dayes after, Stood too howers more on the Pillory at the Exchainge and there had his Tongue Bored throug with a hot Iron, & Stigmatized in the Forehead with the Letter:B: Decem: 17: anno Dom: 1656:

Contemporary images of James Nayler. FRIENDS COLLECTION, EARLHAM COLLEGE.

was Christ returned to earth. When they entered the city they re-created Christ's entry into Jerusalem on Palm Sunday, hailing Nayler as Christ. (Whether Nayler agreed is unclear.) The whole party promptly found themselves clapped into jail on a charge of blasphemy; the case became so notorious that the House of Commons itself tried Nayler and condemned him to be branded and imprisoned. Other Friends quickly disavowed Nayler and his followers. The Nayler case was a turning point, after which Friends became more cautious about such individual "leadings."[19]

The decline of public displays, however, was not enough to make Quakers acceptable to authorities or to most of the people of England. As the Quaker movement solidified, other peculiarities became firmly situated as foundations of the movement, peculiarities that heightened the perception of Friends as threatening.

Foremost was Quaker worship. Friends had no priests or official pastors. They believed that God, through the Holy Spirit, could move anyone to speak, that all Christians could and should be ministers. Their worship involved no predetermined liturgy or ritual; Friends gathered and waited in silence. To be sure, silence was not the rule. The early movement was founded on the energetic and effective preaching of Quakers like Fox, Nayler, and Hooten. But they were not designated as pastors or ministers of particular congregations, which led to a perception of spiritual anarchy.[20]

Equally radical was the Quaker view of the sacraments. For Friends, they were purely spiritual. Thus Quakers did not take physical communion with wine and bread, nor did they baptize with water. Friends argued that true communion was the fellowship of believers in the presence of Christ in a gathered meeting for worship, while the only true baptism was that of the Holy Spirit. To outsiders, of course, this meant that virtually all other Christians had misunderstood these vital matters for sixteen hundred years, until the Quakers came along to set them right.[21]

Particularly threatening to the English upper classes was the Quaker belief in spiritual equality. This did not mean that Friends were committed to overturning the entire social order as they found it; they accepted that some would be governors and some would be governed. But they opposed the displays and manifestations of social deference and respect that were the foundations of virtually all of European civilization. For example, Friends refused to use titles such as "Your Honor" or "Your Lordship" or "My Lady," instead addressing all people simply by their names. Similarly, it was the custom of the time to use "thee" and "thou" when addressing an inferior or close friend. "You" was, under the grammatical conventions of the time, the plural of "thou," and was appropriate when talking with more than one person *or* with a social superior, rather like the "royal we." Friends insisted on addressing all people as "thee" and "thou," which to many seemed rude and disrespectful.[22]

Finally, Friends took certain portions of the Bible quite literally. Like many other religious groups, they were averse to public displays of vanity. Thus Quaker clothing was plain and unornamented, although it did not take on distinctive features until the end of the century. More problems were posed by two distinctive readings of the New Testament. One was the Quaker understanding of Jesus' injunction in Matthew, "Swear not at all." This meant that Friends refused to take any kind of judicial or legal oath. They responded to such demands by asserting that Christians should speak the truth at all times and under all circumstances, and that an oath implied a double standard. This meant, however, that Quakers were often faced with contempt of court and other legal penalties for their refusal. Fox and other Friends also read the New Testament as forbidding Christians to fight. Thus pacifism became identified with Quakerism early in its history, although there is evidence that some Friends rendered military servuce until the end of the century without penalty from their meetings.[23]

By 1660, Friends had established themselves as an important, and to many, threatening, presence in the British Isles. Some Friends were led to carry the Quaker message elsewhere. It was natural that some would be drawn to the New World.

Friends in the New World

Scholars are agreed on the identity of the first Friend to arrive in North America. She was Elizabeth Harris, who traveled in the Chesapeake region as early as 1655 or 1656, arousing interest among Puritans in both Virginia and Maryland. By 1662, nearly sixty Friends had visited the two colonies, and several Quaker meetings had been established. Maryland proved relatively tolerant of Quakers after 1660. Virginia was a different case. There Friends faced imprisonment because of their refusal to attend the services of the established church and pay tithes to it. At least one Virginia Friend died in jail. Such treatment encouraged others to move south into the swamps of Albemarle Sound, establishing a small Quaker presence in what is now North Carolina by the 1670s.[24]

In 1656, English Friends made a more concerted effort to attract converts in North America. When two women Friends, Ann Austin and Mary

Fisher, arrived in the Puritan colony of Massachusetts, authorities in Boston immediately seized and imprisoned them, burning their Quaker books and examining them for marks of witchcraft before putting them on a ship to Barbados. Other Friends who arrived soon after received similar treatment, and the provincial legislature passed a law fining ship captains who brought Quakers to the colony. Undaunted, in 1657 English Friends built their own small ship, the *Woodhouse,* and, depending on divine leading (since none had any knowledge of navigation), set off for New England, arriving safely.[25]

Between 1656 and 1659, at least thirty-three Quakers visited Massachusetts. All were expelled, often accompanied by brutal punishments: whipping, branding, and other mutilations. Converts received similarly harsh treatment, being subjected to banishment and confiscation of their property. Authorities in Salem actually ordered that two children of a Quaker couple there, Lawrence and Cassandra Southwick, be sold as indentured servants in the Caribbean, but failed when they could find no ship's captain who would carry out their ruling. Finally, in 1659, Massachusetts passed a new law imposing death on any Quaker who returned to the colony after having been twice banished. Such laws and persecution only attracted Friends, who saw opportunities to suffer for Truth and expose the wickedness of their persecutors. Nevertheless, Massachusetts authorities did not back down. In 1659 and 1660 they hanged four Friends—Marmaduke Stephenson, William Robinson, and William Leddra from England; and Mary Dyer, who had left Massachusetts twenty years earlier in another theological dispute.[26]

Puritans saw in Quakerism an almost unimaginable threat to the society that they were trying to build in the American wilderness. Quaker views on direct revelation, the Bible, the sacraments, and ministry seemed to them blasphemous, and Puritans saw extirpating blasphemy and heresy as God-given duties. But Quakers also aroused haunting specters of disorder. Their refusal to defer to authority, the power and public roles of Quaker women, and their opposition to oaths all seemed direct challenges to the Puritan social order. The seemingly irrational compulsion of Friends to flock to the places where they faced the most opposition seemed to some evidence of demonic possession. Only a change of government in England and a royal order in 1661 brought the hangings in Boston to an end, although harassment in other ways continued. Ultimately, Friends in Massachusetts were few, confined mainly to Salem, what is now Maine, and areas on and around Cape Cod.[27]

Not surprisingly, Rhode Island, the one New England colony founded on religious toleration, proved most open to Quakers. It had attracted a wide variety of nonconformists and dissenters, many of whom embraced the Quaker message. To be sure, toleration did not mean acceptance; when George Fox himself visited in 1672, Roger Williams, the founder of the colony, challenged him to a public debate. Fox could not remain, but other Friends agreed to meet Williams in August 1673. The collision was a raucous affray in which Williams claimed that the Friends in the audience constantly interrupted him with groans and jeers. Friends dismissed Williams as "the bitter old man"; Williams characterized them as "set on fire from the Hell of Lyes and Fury!" Nevertheless, Quakerism flourished in Rhode Island, where Friends became a major force in politics.[28]

Friends also reached the Dutch colony of New Netherland in the 1650s, although their appeal was almost entirely to English settlers on Long Island. Governor Peter Stuyvesant was no friendlier to them than his Puritan counterparts, and ordered the arrest and imprisonment of Quaker missionaries and those who sheltered them. Quaker sympathizers, especially in Flushing, protested, and eventually the Dutch government, encouraged by authorities back in the Netherlands, adopted a policy of not harassing Friends so long as they remained peaceable. This policy continued when the English seized the colony in 1664 and renamed it New York.[29]

Thus, by the 1660s, Quakers had established a foothold on the North American continent. The great influx of Quaker migration to North America, however, would come after 1680, and as the fruit of developments in England.

Change, 1660–1689

Great Britain underwent another revolution in 1660, with the overthrow of the Commonwealth government and the restoration of the monarchy under King Charles II. This political upheaval had profound effects on Friends.

The Restoration Parliament was full of vengeful royalists who associated religious dissent with political subversion. They had no love for Quakers. An abortive uprising in London early in 1661 by the Fifth Monarchists, another group of radical dissenters, heightened their fears. Between 1661 and 1664 Parliament enacted a series of laws that effectively proscribed Quaker worship. One statute, the Quaker Act of 1662, specifically outlawed gatherings of Friends. Quakers faced additional hardships when they refused to pay tithes, the taxes for the support of the legally established

Church of England. Finally, paranoid about subversion, the Restoration government saw loyalty oaths as a bulwark of legitimacy. Friends, even when they bore the government no ill will, refused to demonstrate their allegiance in such ways. The result was extraordinary hardship. Between 1661 and 1689 thousands of Quakers were imprisoned or fined; Fox, for example, was in jail almost constantly between 1663 and 1668. At least five hundred died in the horrendous prisons where they were confined.[30]

The Quaker response to persecution was complex. While some fell away, most Friends remained constant. Fox and other leaders urged them to keep up public worship even when it meant certain arrest. A favorite Quaker story is about the children of Reading, who continued to gather for worship even when all of their parents had been imprisoned. Friends apparently garnered considerable public sympathy through their devotion to principle.[31]

Quakers also resisted persecution. One means was by attempting to use the legal system to their advantage. That meant, for example, that they worked to find technical defects in indictments and writs. They also petitioned Parliament for the repeal of intolerant laws and approached the king personally to ask for the release or pardon of Friends. The executions in Massachusetts came to an end through a royal order that Friends procured in 1661. Friends also tried to find alternatives to oaths that would be acceptable both to Quaker consciences and to the authorities. Ultimately this was resolved by allowing them to affirm the truth of the statements they made in court, rather than swearing. This distinction was vital to Quakers.[32]

Friends also tried to prove their loyalty to the new government by disavowing any interest in political subversion or revolution. In January 1661 Fox and other leading Friends in London issued a long letter that was the first formal expression of what Friends came to call their Peace Testimony. The document began with an explicit acknowledgment that it was intended to clear Quakers from accusations of "plot and fighting" and demonstrate "their innocency." It went on to proclaim: "All bloody principles and practices, we . . . do utterly deny, with all outward wars and strife and fightings with outward weapons, for any end or under any pretence whatsoever." Some historians have argued that Fox and some other Friends, in order to escape suspicion, perhaps codified what had been contested among Quakers earlier. Pacifists could hardly be seen as potential participants in an armed uprising. On the other hand, Fox and other Friends had clearly been moving in this direction before 1660.[33]

Quakerism itself changed after 1660. As Larry Ingle puts it, Fox took "a sharp right turn, moving away from the millenarian pronouncements and challenges to the status quo that had together marked his public ministry." Public demonstrations like interrupting church services and going naked as a sign faded away. The Lamb's War no longer looked toward political and social apocalypse. The basic framework of Quaker belief— the ministry of all believers, spiritual equality, direct revelation, waiting worship—remained the same. But it would be less exuberant, more structured.[34]

One indication is the organizational system that Friends created in the 1660s. Partly in response to persecution, partly for greater and more effective disciplinary control of members, they organized themselves into the structure of monthly, quarterly, and yearly meetings that most Friends follow to the present day. In some ways, this was similar to the presbyterian system of church government that many Puritans had embraced, but Friends gave it a unique twist. At the monthly and quarterly meeting levels there were separate meetings of men and women, each for the management of the affairs of their own sex. To be sure, the men's meetings had more powers, but to empower women even to this extent was virtually unknown otherwise at the time.[35]

Finally, a new generation of Quaker leaders emerged after 1660. Fox lived until 1691 and remained the single most powerful Friend in the world until his death. But, with the exception of Margaret Fell (whom Fox married in 1667), almost all of the other central figures of the 1650s were dead by 1663. Those who took their places were different in significant ways. An good example is Robert Barclay, who in 1676 published what most Friends regard as the single most influential statement of early Quaker faith, *An Apology for the True Christian Divinity*. Barclay was a Scottish laird who had been educated at a Jesuit college in France before embracing Quakerism. The very attempt to compose a systematic Quaker theology spoke eloquently of the new direction.[36]

Even more influential than Barclay was another convert of the 1660s, William Penn. Penn, born in 1644, was of the elite—the son of a Commonwealth admiral who had agilely changed allegiance to the king in 1660, wealthy, an Oxford man. Running the family estates in Ireland, however, Penn encountered Friends, and by 1667 had joined them. He became an indefatigable propagandist for Quakerism, publishing numerous pamphlets and books and preaching eloquently. He also gave Friends an entrée into circles where they previously had had little influence, even with King Charles II himself. Penn ultimately used that influence in ways that would have a crucial impact on the future direction of Quakerism.[37]

William Penn as a young man. FRIENDS COLLECTION, EARLHAM COLLEGE.

The Holy Experiment

Given the persecution and hostility that they faced in England, it was not surprising that Friends, like other religious dissenters in Europe, looked toward a colony in the New World as a possible haven. William Penn played a key role in making such hopes a reality.

Friends had attempted to create a Quaker colony in western New Jersey in the 1670s, but the major Quaker colony would be Pennsylvania. It came to Penn as a royal grant in 1681. As sole proprietor, Penn had absolute power over the colony and the form that its government and settlement took. Not surprisingly, he framed it according to Quaker principles, making it the first society in the world to be so established. Penn was confident that if properly constituted, Pennsylvania and its capital, Philadelphia (Greek for "City of Brotherly Love"), would be a model for the rest of the world. Thus Penn's "Frame of Government" provided for complete religious freedom and did not include governmental support for any church, including Quakerism. (Penn did limit office holding, however, to Christians.) Quaker marriage practices and opposition to oaths were provided for, and there was no provision for any kind of militia or military establishment. The criminal code was enlightened compared to England's, with capital punishment provided only for treason and murder, not the numerous offenses that brought the death penalty in England.[38]

Penn also wanted to model Quaker principles of peace and fair dealing in his relations with the native peoples of Pennsylvania, mainly the Lenni Lenape or Delaware. He instructed his commissioners to obtain title to lands at fair value, and by all accounts the Indians saw him as treating them equitably and with respect. In contrast to the warfare that seared the frontiers of nearly every other colony over the next seventy years, Pennsylvania would remain at peace.[39]

Penn was in debt for most of his life, so he also saw Pennsylvania as a money-making venture. Thus he tried to encourage settlement by making land available on easy terms. He also encouraged the migration of families, rather than the young single male adventurers who caused problems in other colonies like Virginia. At the same time, he realized that many immigrants would come as indentured servants, working for room and board for a master for a limited time in exchange for the payment of their passage. Servants who completed their terms would also receive land.[40]

Friends in the British Isles found Pennsylvania attractive. Migration began in 1681, and by the end of 1683 more than three thousand Friends had arrived. They quickly replicated the system of monthly, quarterly, and yearly meetings that George Fox had established earlier. Thus later Quaker arrivals were easily assimilated into the new Quaker meetings. While travel and correspondence kept these Friends closely tied to London Yearly Meeting, they were technically independent of its authority. The first sessions of Philadelphia Yearly Meeting were held in the fall of 1681.[41]

By any standard, Pennsylvania was a success. The combination of relatively fertile soil and thrifty, hard-working farmers made it literally a land of plenty. The excellent port of Philadelphia provided easy contact with the rest of the world and a ready market for meat and grain from the farms of Bucks and Chester counties. The colony attracted growing numbers of immigrants. By 1700, its population was probably twenty thousand, a majority not Friends. This growth and prosperity would continue until the American Revolution.[42]

Material prosperity did not always produce political harmony. Penn had provided for an elected assembly, but he saw himself as a benevolent autocrat with final authority in virtually all matters. Since he was in England most of the time, he entrusted the government to a series of lieutenants, who found themselves facing an increasingly restive population. Even worse for Penn, the "Glorious Revolution" of 1688 removed his friend King James II from the throne, and Penn was suspected of treason against James's successors, William and Mary. For Friends, however, the Glorious Revolution was a forward step, since it finally brought to England legal religious toleration and the end of persecution. By 1700, Pennsylvania had settled into the pattern it would follow for decades, of a popularly elected assembly that Quakers dominated and a governor appointed by William Penn or his sons.[43]

Quietism

By 1700, Quakerism was in its third generation. Virtually all of the early leaders were dead—George Fox in 1691, Margaret Fell Fox in 1702, Robert Barclay in 1690. Penn remained active, but increasingly plagued by ill health and political problems. With the passing of the first two generations of Quaker ministers and leaders, Friends settled into an age of what historians have labeled Quietism. They became more inward looking, more focused

Early meeting house at Burlington, N.J. FRIENDS COLLECTION, EARLHAM COLLEGE.

on the maintenance of good internal order, and less confident about pros-elytizing or making converts.[44]

The roots of Quietism go back to the foundations of Quakerism. The goal of all consistent Friends had always been obedience to the will of God as He revealed it to them. For Friends after 1700, that revelation of divine will came largely through introspection, silence, emptying their minds of all distractions, and totally crucifying and eradicating any evidence of hu-man will, or what Friends called "creaturely activity." Friends desired that they would never do anything that was according to their own inclination, wisdom, or inspiration. For a few, even saying a simple prayer or reading the Bible had to be under a divine leading. Silence became more pervasive in meetings for worship, as even those recognized as having a gift for preaching became increasingly fearful of speaking without divine leading and struggled before they broke the silence. Such caution was reinforced by the developing roles of elders, Friends who were charged with nurturing ministers and silencing those whose speaking in meeting was not edifying.[45]

Quietism also shaped the Friends' vision of how salvation was achieved. It came not in a single, transforming experience. Instead, the Inward Light constituted a kind of seed. If Friends were obedient to its guidance, the seed would grow and flourish, guiding and eventually taking control over their lives. Thus nurtured, it led believers into an experience of holiness, or sanctification, which fitted them for heaven. This process was strength-ened by experiences that Friends called baptisms, seasons of divine visitation that often took the form of suffering or depression. Friends believed that such ordeals, "bearing the cross," purged the soul of impurity. Thus Quak-ers looked askance at the Great Awakening that swept through the English-speaking world between 1740 and 1770, with its calls to immediate expe-riences of salvation. For Friends, this suggested an easy way to heaven instead of the long, tried process that they believed God really used.[46]

Other developments strengthened this trend toward introspection. One was the recognition of birthright membership. Before 1700, Quaker under-standing of membership was rather hazy. Friends knew who belonged and who did not. They also agreed that the children of members who married within the group and otherwise conformed to the rules were members. By the 1720s, however, this haziness was causing problems, first in England and later in America. Friends usually took responsibility for impoverished members, and increasingly they found themselves faced with poor people claiming to be Friends. So they moved toward more careful record keeping and toward formally recording the children of members in good standing as having a right of membership by birth.[47]

A Friends meeting for business, ca. 1700. Friends Collection, Earlham College.

The Quaker Reformation

Developments in the mid-eighteenth century strengthened the tendency of Friends to isolate themselves from larger trends in the spiritual world. After 1740, a new generation of young Quaker leaders emerged, both in Great Britain and in North America. They were committed Quietists, but they also sensed that material prosperity and the end of persecution had mired most Friends in lives of ease. These Friends saw reform, a tightening of discipline and further protections from the blandishments of an enticing world, as required.

Certainly the reformers could make a case. On both sides of the Atlantic, Quaker thrift, moderation, and reputation for fair dealing had brought considerable wealth. In England, families such as the Gurneys and Darbys were building fortunes in banking, insurance, and early industrialization, especially textile and iron manufacturing. The great Quaker merchants of Philadelphia, such as the Pembertons, Norrises, and Drinkers, were among the wealthiest families in the colonies. Many of these well-to-do Friends were at ease in the non-Quaker world, especially as political leaders. Typical was John Kinsey, who served as both speaker of the Pennsylvania assembly and clerk, or presiding officer, of Philadelphia Yearly Meeting. This ease was reflected in the clothing they wore, the mansions that they built, and the slaves whom they imported and purchased. Less affluent Friends showed signs of declension in other ways, such as marrying non-Quakers, dealing in goods seized by military forces, or deviating from the plain dress and language.[48]

The reformers responded with proposals to return Friends to primitive purity. Many involved tightening the Discipline, the body of Quaker rules and regulations for corporate and personal conduct: giving more attention to plain dress and speech, moving against those who attended services of other denominations, and especially dropping from membership, or "disowning," Friends who married "out of meeting," either to non-Quakers or to fellow Friends in a non-Quaker ceremony. Meetings also became less tolerant of married couples who had engaged in premarital sex, which was not uncommon in eighteenth-century America. Such reformers looked askance at leading Friends who combined spiritual leadership with political power. They saw the latter as generally antithetical to the former.[49]

Events in Pennsylvania in the 1750s strengthened the reformers' case. Relations with the Indian peoples had deteriorated for at least two decades. William Penn's sons, who still controlled the colony, were no longer Quakers and were not as scrupulous as their father had been. Growing immigration had also brought large numbers of Scots-Irish immigrants from Ulster, who did not share Quaker pacifism. Open warfare broke out in 1755, and the Friends who controlled the Pennsylvania legislature found themselves, for the first time, with the responsibility of defending the colony. Faced with the choice of upholding the Quaker Peace Testimony or retaining power, many Friends chose the former. Enough withdrew from the legislature to give non-Friends a majority. And so Pennsylvania faced its first war.[50]

By the 1770s, the Quaker reformers had made a considerable impact. The number of disownments for violations of the Discipline was growing steadily. Friends who combined political power with spiritual leadership were the exception rather than the rule, even in colonies like Rhode Island and Pennsylvania, where Quakers had been leaders for a century. Paradoxically, however, Friends were also becoming more publicly visible, even as they tried to heighten the "hedge" between themselves and "the world."[51]

Quaker Benevolence

Ultimately, neither the number of adherents (perhaps 100,000 out of a population of 3 million in North America in 1775) nor distinctive beliefs and practices made Quakerism important to the larger American society. Friends came to have an influence out of proportion to their relatively small numbers because they were leaders in certain humanitarian causes, especially in race relations. Even as they gave up political power, Friends showed a growing interest in protecting the rights of American Indians. Friends also were pioneers in the crusade against slavery.

Quakers had prided themselves on their fair treatment of Indians, which they continued even after they gave up control of the Pennsylvania government. To try to retain some influence for good, Philadelphia Friends, with the support of sympathetic German Mennonites and Moravians, formed The Friendly Association for Regaining and Preserving Peace with the Indians by Pacific Measures. The Friendly Association was unprecedented in two respects. It marked one of the first times that Friends had formed any kind of organization outside their meeting structure to carry out their testimonies. More important, it was the first time that white people in the colonies had organized to defend Native American rights. The success of the Friendly Association was mixed. It did play a critical role in persuading some of the Delaware to cease hostility against the English in 1757. But Quaker attempts to control exploitation by white traders and to turn the Delaware into farmers on the white model were unsuccessful. Friends continued to be interested in Indian rights and affairs, virtually alone among English colonists.[52]

Probably more important in the long run was the emergence of a Quaker stand against slavery. Slavery had existed in North America since 1619, and some early Friends there joined their European neighbors in holding both Indians and Africans as slaves. Some Quaker merchants in Newport, New York, and Philadelphia were actively involved in the slave trade. Quaker planters in Virginia and the Carolinas held slaves to work their plantations. Between 1700 and 1750, a growing number of Friends in New Jersey and Pennsylvania became slave owners. Indeed, some evidence indicates that Friends there were more likely than non-Quakers there to purchase and use slaves.[53]

Some Friends, to be sure, challenged slavery. Dutch and German Quakers in Germantown, Pennsylvania sent a memorial, or protest, against slavery to Philadelphia Yearly Meeting in 1688, and other individuals voiced antislavery sentiments. But they had limited impact before 1750.[54]

After 1750, however, Quaker opinion turned decisively against slavery. The Quaker reformers united in condemning it. They saw in slavery harm to both the slave and the slaveholder. Slavery meant denying people the liberty to be obedient to the leadings of the Inward Light. As for the slave owners, they found themselves constantly beset by temptations to laziness, violence, and exploitation, all of which were antithetical to the achievement of the holiness that brought salvation. Critical in this change was a Friends minister from Mount Holly, New Jersey, John Woolman (1720–1772). Traveling as a minister, he insisted on paying the slaves of his hosts when they served him and confronted slave owners individually to try to convince them of the evil of slavery. His little book, *Some Considerations on the Keeping of Negroes*, had considerable impact on both Friends and non-Quakers. Woolman worked quietly but persistently to move Philadelphia Yearly Meeting toward an antislavery position, which it finally embraced after his death. The posthumous publication of his *Journal* in 1774 heightened his reputation; it has attained the stature of a spiritual classic. As historian David Brion Davis has noted, "when all allowances are made for cultural trends and climates of opinion, one must ultimately come down to the men who precipitated change. If the Western world became more receptive to antislavery thought between . . . 1746 and . . . 1772, the self-effacing Quaker was a major instrument of the transformation."[55]

Although Friends moved steadily against slavery, progress was uneven. By 1750 six yearly meetings existed in North America—New England, New York, Philadelphia, Maryland (later Baltimore), Virginia, and North Carolina—and they proceeded at different rates. Philadelphia was the largest and most influential, however, and after 1753 it began to act. First it authorized the printing of Woolman's *Some Considerations*. In 1758, it ordered that Friends who bought or sold slaves should be "labored with"— they would not be disowned, but could not attend meetings for business or contribute money. By 1770, New England Yearly Meeting had ruled that all its members who owned slaves must emancipate them. Philadelphia Yearly Meeting had followed suit within six years, and by 1784 all of the American yearly meetings had ruled that members who owned slaves must make arrangements to free them or lose their membership. And some Quaker slaveholders, to be sure, chose the latter.[56]

Quaker opposition to slavery had its limits. It did not necessarily imply a commitment to racial equality or immunity to the racist beliefs that were endemic among the white population. Friends came to the decision in the 1780s to receive black members only after considerable debate. Even then the handful of black Quakers often found themselves segregated. But Friends led in organizing antislavery societies, petitioning legislatures to abolish slavery, and rescuing freed blacks who had been kidnapped and forced back into slavery. The end of slavery north of Maryland by 1800 was in large part a Quaker accomplishment.[57]

Friends and the American Revolution

The debates leading up to independence, and the war years from 1775 to 1783, were difficult times for American Quakers. Most were deeply skeptical about revolution; many were outspoken in loyalty to the Crown. A complex of factors produced this outlook. More than most colonists, Friends were closely connected with their coreligionists in the British Isles, who constantly warned their American brothers and sisters against anything that smacked of treason. Independence meant war, which was of course against firmly held Quaker beliefs. And when Friends looked at the leaders of the independence movement in colonies like North Carolina and Pennsylvania, they saw politicians who for other reasons had been at odds with Quakers for generations.[58]

Some Friends, to be sure, favored independence. Several signers of the Declaration of Independence had Quaker ties. Ironically, one of them, Stephen Hopkins of Rhode Island, had been disowned only a few years before for holding a slave. Others enlisted in the Continental Army or served in the new state militias. In Philadelphia, a few Friends broke away and formed a splinter group known as the Free Quakers.[59]

Such rebel Quakers were exceptional. For most Friends, the achievement of independence brought hardship. Leading Philadelphia Friends found themselves exiled to the back country of Virginia as security risks. At least one Philadelphia Quaker was hanged by American authorities for aiding the British when they occupied the city in the winter of 1777–1778. Many states enacted laws requiring oaths of loyalty that disavowed any allegiance to the Crown, oaths that yearly meetings urged Friends not to take; Virginia authorities even seized the records of monthly meetings to search for evidence of treason. And of course there were the usual hardships of wartime for Friends—the fines for refusing to bear arms or drill with the militia. Several Revolutionary battles, particularly Germantown, Brandywine, and Guilford Courthouse, were fought in the midst of Quaker neighborhoods.[60]

When the war ended and independence was a fact, virtually all American Friends came to terms with the new government. Their political power was gone. Most continued to vote, and a few would hold office. But the days when Friends controlled whole legislatures were over. And for Quaker reformers, this loss of political power was a good thing, moving Friends away from "the world" and its enticements. Quakers in 1800 were very different from what they had been a century earlier. And the next century would bring even more dramatic changes.

CHAPTER 3

Their Separate Ways:
American Friends Since 1800

In the spring of 1828 the Quaker settlements in Henry County, Indiana were still new and raw. Friends had been there about ten years, most of them migrants from North Carolina, some with roots in the Delaware Valley by way of eastern Ohio. Only for two years had they had their own monthly meeting, called Duck Creek. Those two years had been occupied mainly with dealing with errant Friends who married out of meeting or danced or drank to excess. But in April the Duck Creek Friends found themselves confronting an unprecedented problem. William Bond, a life-long Quaker who had been active in meeting business in both North Carolina and Indiana, was "complained of" for uttering these words: "Elias Hicks is as good a man as Jesus Christ and a certain approved minister aught to be killed!" Friends debated William Bond's case before concluding to disown him in August. But by that time, Bond and his sympathizers had left behind the larger group of Duck Creek Friends to form their own meeting.[1]

William Bond was unusually violent in his language, but his experience, and the experience of the Quakers of Henry County, Indiana, was one that Friends would repeat over and over in the nineteenth and twentieth centuries. In 1800, American Friends were a united group, bound together by a common heritage, by intervisitation and communication, and by a common set of rules and values. Although six yearly meetings existed, all looked to Philadelphia and London as centers of Quaker thought and leadership. More important, these Friends shared a common theology: the distinctive doctrines of the Inward Light of Christ, immediate revelation, unprogram-med worship, pacifism, and separation from "the world" manifested in plainness and peculiarity.

By 1900, the Quaker world was dramatically different. The number of yearly meetings naturally increased as Friends followed the general move-ment westward across the continent. But American Friends were now di-vided into three main streams of thought: Hicksite, Gurneyite, and Wil-burite. A majority had eschewed the traditional Quaker peculiarities. And divisions were bitter, as each tended to dispute the legitimacy of the other two Quaker outlooks.

A century later, these divisions had not, for the most part, healed. Attempts to bring about reunions were successful in some quarters but in others caused new separations, as did the emergence of new issues. By the end of the twentieth century, American Quakers were probably fewer in number than they had been in 1800. And they now spanned the spectrum of American religion, from committed Christian fundamentalists to uni-versalists who disputed that Quakerism was necessarily Christian or even theistic.

The Great Migration

In 1800, American Quakers were unevenly distributed across the landscape. The Quaker impulse toward separation from the world and the need for oversight of members encouraged Friends to cluster in certain neighbor-hoods. Friends in New York, for example, lived mainly in enclaves on Long Island and in two counties on the east side of the Hudson. Even when they spread west, they continued to settle near each other in a few places. Sim-ilarly, the overwhelming majority of Friends in Philadelphia Yearly Meeting were in one county in New Jersey and five around Philadelphia. In North Carolina, which had become an important Quaker center, three counties in the northeastern part of the state and four in the central part of the state embraced most Friends.[2]

The nineteenth century saw considerable change in Quaker population patterns. Friends in rural New England followed the general pattern of migration toward towns and cities or to the west, especially upstate New York and Michigan. Friends in the Delaware Valley headed west, particu-larly into eastern Ohio. Southern Friends followed a somewhat different pattern. In contrast to most southerners, who went either due west or south and west, Friends from Virginia, North and South Carolina, and Georgia headed over the Ohio River into Ohio and Indiana, drawn to territories where slavery was banned. By 1821, two new yearly meetings, Ohio and Indiana, had been established. This pattern continued into the trans-Mississippi west. Friends avoided slave states like Missouri and Arkansas in favor of Iowa and Kansas. By the 1880s, Friends were reaching the Pacific coast.[3]

This westward migration had a profound impact on older Quaker communities. Friends virtually disappeared from South Carolina and Georgia, and many meetings in North Carolina and Virginia were laid down, the Quaker term for dissolved, because almost no members were left. The same was true to a lesser extent in New York and New England. Nantucket Island, for example, which had hundreds of resident Friends in 1800, was home to only one a century later. Philadelphia remained a major Quaker center, but in spite of tremendous growth in the city in the nineteenth century, the number of Friends in the area declined.[4]

The Hicksite Separation

Not all of this decline was the product of westward migration. The bitter separations that came about between 1827 and 1880 also took their toll.

The most important of these separations, which had effects on Quak-

Marcus Mote, *Indiana Yearly Meeting of Friends, 1844.* The Orthodox body. FRIENDS COLLECTION, EARLHAM COLLEGE.

erism that endure down to this day, took place in the 1820s. At its heart was an elderly minister from Long Island, Elias Hicks (1748–1830). Recorded a minister in the 1770s, Hicks had traveled widely among American Friends and was well known and respected. Only as he approached age seventy did he become a focus of controversy.[5]

At issue were Hicks's views of Christ and the Bible. In his sermons, and in letters to both supporters and opponents, Hicks made statements that some Friends found disturbing, if not heretical. Compounding the problem was the fact that Hicks was not a systematic, or even consistent, theologian. At times he said and wrote different things to different people, and thus one could pick and choose to cast him either as a stalwart defender of traditional Quakerism or as a dangerous opponent of truth.[6]

Hicks was consistent in one respect. As he looked at the Quaker world in the 1810s and 1820s, he found much to disturb him. Too many Friends, especially well-to-do ones in Philadelphia and New York City, were becoming overfond of "the world." Forming ties with non-Quaker evangelical Protestants in business and in philanthropic enterprises such as Sunday schools and Bible and missionary societies, Friends had drawn closer to them. Thus non-Quaker ideas and concepts were making their way into the Society of Friends. The evidence was abundant: declining standards of plainness, growing sympathies for the work of non-Quaker "hireling ministers," and especially, views of the nature of Christ and the authority of the Bible that seemed at odds with Quakerism as Hicks understood it.[7]

Although he was often charged with denying the divinity of Christ, Hicks was emphatic in asserting that he did believe in it. Hicks understood Christ, however, in a different way than most other Christians and many Friends. Simply put, Hicks argued that Jesus was not *born* as the Christ. Instead, he *became* the Christ, the Son of God, because He had been the only human being ever to live in perfect obedience to the Divine Light that was within Him. Thus, while Jesus was unique, He was the model of the life that all Christians ought to lead. Similarly, Hicks said that he believed in the Virgin Birth, but that such belief was not essential.[8]

Hicks's view of the Bible was similarly nuanced. "As respects the Scriptures of truth, I have highly esteemed them from my youth up, have always given them the preference to any other book, and have read them abundantly more than any other book, and I would recommend all to the serious and diligent perusal of them," he wrote in 1829. Hicks qualified this statement, however, by concluding that their greatest value was that "they have instructed me home to the sure unchangeable foundation, the light within."

Elias Hicks. FRIENDS COLLECTION, EARLHAM COLLEGE.

Here was the crux for Hicks. While the Bible was a valuable record of God's past revelations, such revelation continued, through the leadings of the Holy Spirit and through the Inward Light. Moreover, God had given humans reason to use in their religious growth as well. Thus Hicks adamantly rejected any suggestion that the Bible was the sole authority for Christians. "Is it possible that men can be guilty of greater idolatry, than to esteem and hold the Scriptures as the only rule of faith and practice, by which they place them in the very seat of God and worship them as God?" he asked in 1820.[9]

Many Friends found these views to be sound, traditional Quakerism. But Hicks horrified others, and by the early 1820s his critics, especially in Philadelphia, the intellectual and spiritual center of American Quakerism, were so unhappy that they sought to silence the Long Island minister. They received important support from a series of ministers from England who visited North America between 1819 and 1827.[10]

Hicks's opponents eventually became known as Orthodox Friends. Hicks's backers had no trouble finding the source of their opposition: the Orthodox were really crypto-Episcopalians or Presbyterians, overly influenced by their ties to these denominations, usually in the pursuit of economic or political power. Many historians have found considerable merit in this critique, while others have accepted the Orthodox vision of themselves as traditional Friends defending Quakerism against the inroads of Unitarianism and skepticism.[11]

Orthodox Friends put forth a vision of Christ and the authority of Scripture that echoed those of other Protestants. For them, Christ was conceived and born as the Savior, the Son of God, come to earth for the purpose of redeeming humanity. He did this through His atoning death on the Cross. His sacrifice, giving His life and shedding His blood for the sins of humanity, made salvation possible for all people. As for the Bible, the Orthodox agreed with Hicks that it should not be put above the Spirit that gave it, and that the Spirit must be the ultimate authority. But they feared Hicks's statements about overreliance on the Bible, which diminished its unique inspiration and indicated a pride that could derive only from the temptations of the evil one.[12]

Tensions between Hicks's opponents and supporters built steadily between 1819 and 1827. Historians have found other factors involved as well. In Philadelphia Yearly Meeting, for example, the Orthodox may have been the more economically successful Friends, those better adjusting to the emerging Industrial Revolution. Similarly, in that yearly meeting, rural Friends were more sympathetic to the Hicksites and urban Friends to the Orthodox. Questions of power and relations among monthly, quarterly, and yearly meetings, as well as the authority of elders over ministers, became entangled in the theological debates. And personalities were intertwined in all of these problems. Hicks and his supporters could scarcely conceal their disdain for Orthodox leaders like the Philadelphia elders Jonathan Evans and Samuel Bettle and especially for English ministers. The tensions reached a head in Philadelphia Yearly Meeting in April 1827, when the Hicksites, despairing of fair treatment from the Orthodox leaders who controlled the meeting, decided to leave and set up a "reformed" yearly meeting. Probably two thirds of the yearly meeting's membership followed them, so that now two Philadelphia Yearly Meetings existed. The other yearly meetings had to decide which was the legitimate body, so similar separations followed. In New York and Baltimore, Hicksites were an overwhelming majority, and in Ohio Yearly Meeting they were close to half. In Indiana Yearly Meeting, however, they formed only about a fifth of the membership, and only a few New England Friends endorsed Hicks. Virginia and North Carolina yearly meetings sided completely with the Orthodox. Most important, London Yearly Meeting, which Friends had traditionally considered the final arbiter in such matters, also repudiated the Hicksites and firmly endorsed the Orthodox. In all, the Hicksite Separation probably left about 60 percent of American Friends with the Orthodox and 40 percent with the Hicksites.[13]

The wounds of this separation were deep and lasting. The rhetoric of both sides was ferocious. "Hicksism," wrote one Orthodox minister, was "the great leviathan, the monster of human reason and human wisdom, who is endeavouring to lay waste the atoning blood of Jesus Christ . . . . It is a dark delusive spirit; . . . in the mystery of iniquity it lives." Hicksites, preached another Orthodox minister, were "evil men and seducers," allied with Antichrist. Hicksites were equally fierce in denouncing the Orthodox. "What can be more clear than that it is the natural tendency of orthodoxy to subvert every important principle of Quakerism?" asked a Hicksite journal in Philadelphia. "If our civil government should admit of it," preached a Hicksite minister, "the kennels of the blood hounds of religious persecution should be ransacked, . . . and those scenes of cruelty that have disgraced the page of history again should be realized." Almost fifteen years after the Separation, wrote one Baltimore Hicksite, the Orthodox "manifest[ed] no abatement of their hatred."[14]

Thus both Orthodox and Hicksite Friends emerged from the split deeply scarred. Both drew lessons from their experiences, lessons that did not serve them well over the next three decades.

Hicksites After 1827

Hicksite Friends after 1827 were a diverse, if not motley, group. They embraced three persuasions of Friends. One, probably the most numerous, was conservative and viewed Orthodox Friends as innovators, leading Quakers away from traditional beliefs. A second persuasion consisted of Friends who, on a number of doctrinal questions, probably were closer to Orthodox Quakers than they were to Elias Hicks. These Friends sided with the Hicksites, however, for a variety of reasons. Some were apparently alienated by what they saw as the arrogance of the Orthodox leaders; others simply acquiesced in what was majority opinion in their meetings. The third group of Hicksites was made up of incipient liberals. These Friends, especially strong around Philadelphia, in upstate New York, and in parts of Ohio, were open to ideas from the larger American society, particularly those connected with Unitarianism. They also were suspicious of authority that tried to limit their freedom in ministry or association. Given such diversity, conflict among Hicksites was inevitable.[15]

The immediate impetus for splits among the Hicksites came from outside the Society of Friends, in the radical reform movements that appeared in the 1830s. Three of these—antislavery, women's rights, and nonresistance—had an understandable appeal to many Friends, since they coincided with long-held Quaker beliefs. When the American Anti-Slavery Society was formed at a meeting in Philadelphia in December 1833, for example, about a third of those present were Friends, most of them Hicksites. The early women's rights movement was closely linked to antislavery, as some women abolitionists were led to see similarities between the status of free white women and slaves. Not surprisingly, the most prominent and visible female abolitionists in the country in the 1830s and 1840s—Sarah and Angelina Grimke, Abby Kelley, and Lucretia Mott—were all Friends. Mott was one of the most powerful and talented ministers among Hicksites. Thus the call for the first women's rights convention in American history, at Seneca Falls, New York in July 1848, was issued by five women, three of them Hicksite Friends and another a former Quaker. James Mott, Lucretia's husband, presided over the gathering. Nonresistants were absolute pacifists who looked toward a world in which all governments based on coercive force would wither away and humans would live directly under the Government of God, according to the principles of the New Testament. Many Hicksites embraced this movement as well. In the 1840s, some became involved in a series of utopian communities that tried to live according to nonresistant principles.[16]

Such radical reforming Hicksites were a minority, however. For those who had separated from the Orthodox to uphold Quaker exclusivity against outside influences, such associations were dangerous. "As the Israel of God we must dwell alone," preached one leading minister of Philadelphia Yearly Meeting. More conservative Hicksites also feared that reformers "acted in their own wisdom," rather than depending on the leadings of God. "By keeping in everlasting patience, we will do more for the cause of the slave than if we were to speak volumes," wrote a Quaker woman from Long

Island. Still other Hicksites argued that radical reformers were tainted by infidelity and false religion. They especially feared incipient feminists. "What did woman want in the name of rights, but liberty to roam over the country from Dan to Beersheba, spurning the protection of man?" asked George F. White, probably the most prominent conservative Hicksite.[17]

Conflict was inevitable. It surfaced in the late 1830s and burst into the open in 1841, when conservative Hicksites in New York moved to disown three leading abolitionist Friends there. Ultimately, the radical reformers in New York, the Philadelphia area, and Ohio and Indiana Yearly Meetings all left the main Hicksite body to form new associations that they called Congregational or Progressive Friends. In many places, such as Michigan and parts of upstate New York and eastern Ohio, their departure left but a shell of Hicksite Quakerism remaining. Once separated, the Congregational Friends set about reforming Quakerism. They abolished traditional offices such as elder. They discarded most of the Discipline. By the 1850s, music was becoming part of Congregational Friends' worship, and they were welcoming ministers of other denominations, a striking departure from the traditional Quaker antipathy to "hireling priests." The various Congregational yearly meetings issued public addresses and petitions to state legislatures and Congress advocating the abolition of slavery, equal rights for women, and an end to the army and navy. Early in the 1850s, many Congregational Friends were drawn into Spiritualism, attempting to commune with the spirits of departed loved ones and historical figures. After 1860, most either joined other denominations or returned to the larger Hicksite body.[18]

In 1850, the victory of more conservative Hicksites, who wished to purge their society of all outside influences, seemed complete. Yet within two decades, the Hicksite yearly meetings had embraced most of the causes that appeared so controversial in the 1830s and 1840s. The sources of this transformation are unclear. They may have been cultural, as Hicksite Friends became tied more closely to the larger American society through education, books, and periodicals. "The changes wrought in the entire social fabric by the marvelously multiplied abundance of letters defies computation," one Ohio Hicksite Friend noted in 1886. One example: Quakers had traditionally been intensely suspicious of colleges, yet in 1860 Hicksite Friends began the discussions that would found Swarthmore College four years later. Part of the change may simply have been generational. Almost all of the conservative ministers and elders who had led the attacks on reformers in the 1830s and 1840s were dead by 1870, while some of the leading radicals, most notably Lucretia Mott, were still alive and active.[19]

By the 1880s, Hicksite Friends had achieved a new consensus about their faith, albeit with dissent from a few elderly Friends of Quietist views. They openly described themselves as *liberals*, in sympathy with Unitarians and liberal movements in other Protestant denominations. For Hicksites, liberal Quakerism had several features. One was a commitment to toleration of dissent and freedom of thought. Few Hicksites would tell another what to believe. A second feature was devotion to the Inner Light as the source of religious authority, above the Bible or written doctrinal statements. Another was rejection of doctrines important to most other Protestants, such as Atonement through the blood of Christ or even the existence of Satan or hell. Finally, Hicksites increasingly spoke of continuing or progressive revelation. As one Philadelphia Friend put it: "Truth is continually changing, and we must acknowledge it and change accordingly." In Hicksite minds, Christians had to accommodate themselves to the new findings of science and scholarly criticism of the origins of the Bible.[20]

An important manifestation of Hicksite openness to new ideas was the founding of new institutions. In 1859, a Hicksite Friend in Reading, Pennsylvania opened what he called a First Day School, the Hicksite equivalent of a Sunday school. By the 1880s, First Day Schools were part of almost every Hicksite meeting, and Hicksites were holding national conferences to discuss ways to strengthen them. Hicksites also showed a new openness to outreach to the larger American society. In 1869, the Hicksite yearly meetings had agreed to undertake humanitarian work among American Indians under the administration of President Ulysses S. Grant. Although this came to an end in the late 1870s, it laid the foundation for regular conferences on other subjects, such as prison reform, temperance, and the rights of African Americans. Finally, in 1893, the Hicksite yearly meetings held a conference to exchange views on strengthening their meetings. In 1900, these efforts were joined under one organization, known as Friends General Conference, which thereafter held gatherings to bring together Hicksite Friends from around North America.[21]

In 1900, Hicksite Friends numbered about 20,000, probably half of their numbers in the 1820s. Decline would continue in many rural areas. But they felt relatively confident about their future, committed to their vision of Quakerism. They had changed. While they retained unprogrammed worship and a nonpastoral ministry, most had ceased to wear the plain dress or to use the plain language outside their families. The changes among Hicksite Friends, however, were modest compared to those that had taken place among the Orthodox.[22]

Orthodox Friends, 1827–1860

In many ways, Orthodox Friends were more united than Hicksites after the separation. They shared a common view of the divinity of Christ. The experience of schism made them even more committed to protecting what they saw as a fragile Quaker structure. Unfortunately, these views and experiences were not enough to preserve their unity. By 1860, they had divided into two groups, Gurneyite and Wilburite.

At the heart of this strife was the ministry of an English Friend, Joseph John Gurney (1788–1847). Gurney was born to privilege: he was the son of a wealthy banker in Norwich, England; his mother was a descendant of Robert Barclay, the late seventeenth-century Quaker leader. Although as a religious dissenter he could not enter an English university, Gurney studied at Oxford under private tutors, obtaining the equivalent of a degree. After some internal struggle, in his twenties he committed himself to a life of humanitarianism and service to Friends.[23]

Much of Gurney's influence grew out of his personality, which all regarded as charming, even captivating. He was a gifted public speaker. He was tireless in his work for education, prison reform, and the abolition of slavery, causes that led him to form close ties with non-Quaker reformers, mostly of evangelical views. He was also one of the few Friends of his era who had studied Hebrew, and thus possessed scholarly credentials that only a handful of other Quakers had. In the 1820s and 1830s, Gurney produced a series of books in which he envisioned a fundamental reshaping of the foundations of Quakerism.[24]

Gurney believed that the first two generations of Quaker leaders, including his ancestor Robert Barclay, had erred on certain points. One was the doctrine of the Inward Light. Gurney argued it could not compete with the Light imparted by the Bible. Comparing the two was like comparing noon and twilight, he argued. Similarly, Gurney argued that justification, or acceptance by God, and sanctification, or the achievement of holiness, were separate experiences. Justification came first, an instantaneous experience through faith in the power of the Atonement of Christ. Sanctification followed it as a gradual experience. Finally, Gurney argued that while Friends should retain their commitments to unprogrammed worship, simplicity, the ministry of women, and pacifism, they should not fear work with other evangelical Protestants in good causes.[25]

By the 1830s, Gurney had become the dominant voice in London Yearly

Joseph John Gurney. From J. B. Braithwaite, ed., *Memoirs of Joseph John Gurney* (Philadelphia, 1862).

Meeting, resisted only by a few Quietists. From 1837 to 1840 he traveled in North America, visiting almost every Orthodox Quaker community. Most Orthodox Friends found him irresistible. But some, especially in New England, eastern Ohio, and Philadelphia, were troubled. The most vocal of these critics was a minister from Rhode Island, John Wilbur (1774–1856). When Gurney arrived in America, Wilbur considered it his duty to warn Friends against what he saw as Gurney's serious errors. Most New England Friends approved of Gurney, however, and they turned on Wilbur, first dissolving his monthly meeting and then disowning him. Outraged, in 1845 Wilbur's supporters separated from the larger body in New England Yearly Meeting, taking about 10 percent of the yearly meeting with them.[26]

Wilburite Friends saw in Gurney "an overactive, restless spirit" that threatened the foundations of Quakerism. They resented his criticism of the writings of early Friends. They were suspicious of his ties with non-Quakers. But most of all, they saw Gurney departing from traditional Quaker doctrine. To them, Gurney's emphasis on the authority of Scripture placed the written record of the Holy Spirit's previous revelations above the Spirit itself. Even worse, they perceived, was Gurney's separation of justification and sanctification, an easy way to heaven. Friends had traditionally seen the achievement of salvation as a long, tried process. Now Gurney offered a way "to avoid the painful endurance of the baptism of fire and the Holy Ghost."[27]

The separation in New England forced other Orthodox Friends to decide which was the legitimate New England Yearly Meeting. Most yearly meetings sided with the larger Gurneyite body. But two were badly split. Ohio Yearly Meeting was hopelessly deadlocked until 1854, when it split into Gurneyite and Wilburite bodies of roughly equal size. Philadelphia Yearly Meeting avoided separation in 1857 only by cutting off all official contact and correspondence with other yearly meetings, although most of its leaders clearly sympathized with Wilbur.[28]

Thus, on the eve of the Civil War, in 1860 American Friends found themselves fractured. Hicksite Friends had lost a significant minority when the Congregational Friends left them in the 1840s. Orthodox Friends were divided into Gurneyite and Wilburite groups. Gurneyites were definitely the largest, probably 50,000 to 60,000 of the roughly 100,000 American Quakers. While Wilburites would for the rest of the century attempt to maintain an unyielding commitment to the old ways, Gurneyite Friends would prove much more open to the larger American culture. After 1860, that would produce a revolution.[29]

Gurneyites and the Great Revival, 1860–1900

In 1875, a Methodist minister decided to pay a visit to the sessions of Indiana Yearly Meeting in Richmond, Indiana. One might expect that a Methodist would find Quaker ways strange and unfamiliar, but what he encountered made him feel right at home. "It resembled one of our *love feasts* at a *National Camp Meeting* more than anything else to which I could liken it," he wrote. Worship opened with a rousing hymn. Then the presiding minister called for those present to testify about their experiences of salvation and sanctification, and dozens responded. Finally, an altar call was issued, and dozens more came to the front, seeking to be "born again." It was a scene that would have been almost inconceivable twenty years before but now was becoming increasingly common among Gurneyite Friends. In fact, the service in Richmond was restrained compared to other Friends meetings being reported.[30]

How did Friends come to embrace such radical change? The roots go back to Gurney's time; although he never anticipated such departures from Quaker tradition, his influence was critical. He epitomized the willingness of some Friends to form ties with the larger American society, particularly evangelical Methodists, Presbyterians, and Baptists, in various good works and reforms. For forty years, Gurneyite Friends had read their books and periodicals, worked with them in Sunday schools and missions, and, in some cases, had attended their schools and colleges. It was inevitable that they would absorb some of their ideas.[31]

Just as important, Gurney's theology opened Friends to such influences in other ways. Friends now shared with non-Quaker evangelicals a common vision of how to achieve salvation, in an instantaneous conversion experience. It was probably inevitable that they would experiment with some of the methods that other denominations used to produce conversions. And those were the methods of revivalism.[32]

Change developed gradually. In the 1850s and 1860s a new generation of Gurneyite leaders emerged, especially in Indiana Yearly Meeting, now the largest in the United States. They advocated a renewal movement. These Friends, while wishing to preserve practices such as unprogrammed worship, pacifism, the ministry of women, and a plain lifestyle, also wished to see reform. They proposed to renew Quakerism by banishing what they saw as anachronisms, such as the prejudice against higher education, the rules against marrying non-Quakers, and the tendency of Quaker ministers to preach in a high-pitched, chanting style that was known as the "singsong." They encouraged all Friends, not just recorded ministers, to speak during meetings for worship. They even urged Friends to eschew their sectarian image, opening themselves to ties with even Unitarians and Hicksites.[33]

The Civil War was traumatic for all Friends, but especially for Gurneyites. Southern Friends were virtually all staunch Unionists who found themselves the target of considerable hostility from the new Confederate government. The problem was different in the North. There hundreds of young Friends, faced with a choice between upholding the Union peaceably and fighting in what they saw as an antislavery war, chose the latter. For the first time, some monthly meetings simply looked the other way as young members rendered military service. The leaders of Gurneyite reform were equally committed to the Union but did not wish to sacrifice the Peace Testimony. So, first beginning in Indiana Yearly Meeting, but in other Gurneyite yearly meetings as well after 1867, they began holding what were called general meetings. These were teaching meetings spread out over three or four days, intended to bring Friends a better understanding of basic Quaker doctrine. Important ministers and yearly meeting officials were in charge. The meetings always included times of worship, however, and gradually these came to dominate. Therein lay the roots of revolution.[34]

That revolution in the 1870s came about when a group of young Quaker ministers seized control of the general meeting movement and used it to forward new teachings. These ministers, most notably David B. Updegraff and John Henry Douglas in Ohio and Esther Frame, Dougan Clark Jr., and Luke Woodard in Indiana, shared a common experience of instantaneous holiness or sanctification. They were part of a powerful interdenominational movement in post–Civil War America that argued that all Christians should have two experiences. The first would be conversion, or being "born again." The second would be sanctification, in which all tendencies to succumb to the temptations of sin would be eradicated through faith and the influence of the Holy Spirit. As Updegraff wrote of this attitude, which became known as "holiness Quaker," toward the original general meeting movement:

> Many could not see that the blessing of God rested upon an attempt to convey to perishing sinners "accurate *information*" about our "distinctive *tenets*." I was one of that number and joined with others in imploring that "the dead" might be left to "bury the dead" and that we might unite in preaching the gospel and in getting converts to Jesus. In the providence of God such counsel prevailed, and then it was that our General Meetings became "Revival Meetings."[35]

So what became known as "The Great Revival" began.

The revivalists proved brilliant in their use of traditional Quaker language and ideas to justify radical departures from the practices of two hundred years. Friends had always believed in the liberty of anyone to speak in a meeting for worship. Revivalists used that to advocate their ideas.

DAVID B. UPDEGRAFF.

David B. Updegraff. From Dougan Clark and Joseph H. Smith, *David B. Updegraff* (Cincinnati, 1895).

Friends had always justified their opposition to water baptism by empha-sizing the baptism of the Holy Spirit. Revivalists identified that with sanc-tification. Friends had long had traveling ministers. Revivalists followed in that tradition as they went from place to place holding revival meetings. Most of all, they used the long-standing Quaker commitment to the pos-sibility of experiencing sanctification or perfection. With all of these bases, and although they believed that they were simply returning to the fervor of the early Friends, they were still revolutionaries. They were convinced that the techniques of Protestant revivalism were the most effective in pro-ducing conversions and sanctifications, and so they brought them into

Friends meetings: altar calls, mourners' benches, hymn singing, prayers for the conversion of specific individuals, outbursts of fervent emotion. "You cannot understand it here," an Indiana Friend told London Yearly Meeting in 1878. "No one can without seeing it. Our meetings were shaken as by a vast whirlwind."[36]

The fruits of this revival were significant. It affected all of the Gurneyite yearly meetings except Baltimore, from New England south to North Carolina, from New York west to the Pacific coast. It brought thousands of converts into Friends meetings, most of them with little prior exposure to Quakerism. This, in turn, produced a growing demand for pastoral care and regular preaching, and by 1890 many Gurneyite meetings were calling ministers to serve as pastors, with responsibility for regular preaching. Thus most Gurneyite meetings moved toward programmed worship, with only short periods of silence and a regular schedule of prayers, hymns, and a sermon. By 1890 musical instruments were being introduced. Many Friends meetings adopted the name "Friends Church." Most of the old peculiarities, such as the plain dress and plain language, were discarded as unnecessary or dangerously separating Friends from other Christians. In 1878, Ohio Yearly Meeting actually repudiated the doctrine of the Inward Light as unscriptural. By the 1880s, some revivalists began employing water baptism.[37]

Such radical innovations inevitably produced a reaction. Some Gurneyite Friends, especially in Indiana, Iowa, and Kansas, could not accept them, so between 1877 and 1883 another round of separations took place, after which these Conservative Friends, as they became known, gradually forged ties with older Wilburite bodies. Other, more moderate Gurneyites, many of them the renewal movement reformers of the 1860s, seeing good in many of the innovations, chose to remain and try to blunt the radicalism of the revivalists. Their solution was to attempt to restore order by finding some common platform on which all Friends could stand. This movement reached its height in a conference in Richmond, Indiana in the fall of 1887, attended by representatives of all of the Gurneyite yearly meetings as well as sympathetic Friends from Philadelphia, England, and Ireland. The main goal of the Indiana Friends who called the conference was to halt the drift toward tolerating water baptism. Their instrument was a "Declaration of Faith," which became known as the Richmond Declaration. It affirmed traditional Quaker understandings of the sacraments, peace, and the ministry of women. It equivocated between older and holiness understandings of the nature of sanctification. It was deeply evangelical on matters such as the divinity of Christ and the authority of Scripture, taking stands that virtually all evangelicals would have affirmed. Though it was intended as a unifying document, the lasting impact of the Richmond Declaration was uncertain. Some yearly meetings endorsed it, but others saw in it a dangerous step toward creedalism. And the most committed revivalists saw its condemnation of water baptism as an infringement on their liberty of conscience.[38]

As the nineteenth century came to an end, Friends in the Orthodox tradition were divided and changed. A minority, the Wilburites, perhaps 10,000, were still committed primitivists, trying to preserve Quakerism unchanged from the practices of the eighteenth century. But most Gurneyites, about 80,000 in number, had accepted change. Most of them, although not all, were now in pastoral meetings, no longer outwardly different from their neighbors. For them, the "Friends Church" was separated from its Protestant neighbors by only a few minor points of doctrine. Quaker distinctiveness was at a low ebb. By 1900, however, a reaction was developing, one that had profound consequences.

The Quaker Search for Order

The early years of the twentieth century saw all persuasions of Friends—Wilburite, Hicksite, and Gurneyite—looking for ways to bring their yearly meetings closer together to work on behalf of common causes and interests. The three groups took this impulse in different directions, reflecting their history and different attitudes toward centralized authority.

Wilburite Friends, who after 1900 came to call themselves Conservative Friends, were naturally the most cautious. They contented themselves largely with issuing a common doctrinal statement in 1913 and with the ties that their young people formed in their boarding schools. A Philadelphia Yearly Meeting fund helped build new Conservative meeting houses. Overwhelmingly rural, Conservatives saw their numbers dwindle drastically in the first half of the twentieth century, as their young people left Quaker neighborhoods and did not return. Two Conservative yearly meetings, Kansas and Western, declined so much in numbers that they were laid down, in 1929 and 1962, respectively.[39]

Hicksite Friends were more aggressive in attempting to work together through Friends General Conference (FGC), as their branch came to be called. An attempt to impose a central authority on the various elements of the conference—the First Day School, Young Friends, Philanthropic, and Religious conferences or unions—through the formation of an Advancement Committee failed. FGC did establish a central office with a secretary. Between 1904 and 1951 two men held the position, Henry W. Wilbur and J. Barnard Walton, assisted by a much-loved Philadelphia Friend, Jane P. Rushmore. By the 1920s, the Hicksite label had largely given way to Friends General Conference.[40]

One of Wilbur and Walton's priorities was reversing the long decline in Hicksite membership. Between 1840 and 1900 it had gone from about 35,000 to about 20,000, and it continued to slide in the 1920s, when it reached 17,000. Ohio Yearly Meeting was laid down in 1919, and Hicksite yearly meetings in Indiana, Illinois, and upstate New York dwindled to a few hundred members. By the 1930s, however, new FGC meetings were being founded in cities and university towns like Cleveland, Pittsburgh, and Ithaca, and by 1946 the membership of Friends General Conference had stabilized.[41]

The theological outlook of the FGC yearly meetings in the first half of the twentieth century was continuous with the liberalism that had developed in the last half of the nineteenth. The doctrinal statements of the groups still identified them as Christian. In 1926, Friends General Conference proposed a Uniform Discipline, which almost every one of its yearly meetings adopted in some form. Tolerance was its most striking keynote; old statements condemning denial of the divinity of Christ disappeared. Worship continued to be unprogrammed. Marking the growing emphasis on religious democracy, most yearly meetings stopped recording ministers in the 1920s.[42]

Gurneyite Friends followed a different course. They were bolder in attempting to form a central organization. Ironically, they were also the most contentious and strife-prone of the three major traditions in the first half of the twentieth century.

Gurneyites followed the Richmond conference of 1887 with conferences in Indianapolis in 1892 and 1897. At the latter, they embraced a proposal for a national organization composed of the Gurneyite yearly meetings with a Uniform Discipline and legislative authority over the yearly meetings. The drafting of the Uniform Discipline was entrusted to Rufus M. Jones, editor of the Philadelphia weekly *American Friend*, and James Wood, the long-time clerk of New York Yearly Meeting. By 1901, all of the Gurneyite yearly meetings except Ohio had endorsed the framework that Jones and Wood produced, and so the national organization, dubbed the Five Years Meeting, held its first sessions in 1902.[43]

The achievements of this new Quaker body were real, but not as far-reaching as its projectors had hoped. They envisioned an organization that would provide "unification, compactness, strength, solidity, power of resistance, and an effective wielding of our forces" by bringing all of Gurneyite Quakerism to bear on deviations from sound doctrine and practice. A small central office was established in Richmond, Indiana, and Jones's *American Friend* was made the new organization's official organ.[44]

The Five Years Meeting's most important accomplishments were in the support of Quaker missions outside the United States. These dated back to the 1870s, when Indiana Friends had sponsored a Quaker missionary in Mexico. As was the case in other Protestant organizations, women took the lead in supporting overseas work. The Women's Missionary Union of Friends in America (now United Society of Friends Women) dated from 1882. By 1910, the Gurneyite yearly meetings were supporting Quaker enterprises in China, India, Mexico, the Caribbean, and Alaska. Most important ultimately would be the Quaker work that began in Kenya in 1902. Kenya is now home to more Quakers than any other country in the world. With the exception of the missions under control of the pastoral Ohio Yearly Meeting (now Eastern Region), this missionary work became a function of the Five Years Meeting.[45]

The Five Years Meeting did not produce the unity that many Friends sought, however, because events overtook it—most important, the rise of a modernist movement among Gurneyite Friends. The central figure was the coauthor of the Uniform Discipline, Rufus M. Jones.

Jones was the commanding figure in American Quakerism in the first half of the twentieth century. Born in Maine in 1863, he was educated in Quaker schools and at Haverford College, whose faculty he joined in 1893. A year later, he became editor of the newly formed *American Friend* and embarked on a lifelong crusade to unite all Quakers. He saw himself as battling two extremes, the very conservative Wilburites who still dominated Philadelphia Yearly Meeting (Orthodox) and the holiness revivalists who, in Jones's view, had almost eradicated real Quakerism from their churches. In the 1890s Jones formed strong ties with young English Friends who were drawn to theological modernism and thus were rebelling against the evangelicalism that had dominated London Yearly Meeting since Gurney's day.[46]

The larger modernist movement in Protestantism had three beliefs: that religious ideas must be adapted to changing conditions and circumstances; that God is immanent, to be understood through human cultural development; and that the world is fitfully but definitely improving, moving toward realizing the Kingdom of God. Jones endorsed all of these ideas in his

Rufus M. Jones. FRIENDS COLLECTION, EARLHAM COLLEGE.

writings, which by 1910 included several books and hundreds of editorials and articles in the *American Friend*. He gave them a Quaker flavor, however, by adapting them to fit what he saw as Quaker needs, drawing on Quaker history as he understood it. Thus he emphasized continuing and direct revelation to argue that modern scholarship that challenged traditional understandings of the Bible was simply a continuation of the Quaker past. Similarly, he endorsed the Social Gospel movement, which sought to reform American society between 1900 and 1920 by applying Christian principles, seeing in it the Quaker tradition of philanthropy. Finally, he, more than any other Gurneyite, brought back to Quaker consciousness the old Quaker belief in the Inward or Inner Light. Indeed, Jones saw real Quakerism as a kind of mystical experience based on direct experience of the Light.[47]

Jones found many followers after 1900, among both pastoral and non-pastoral Gurneyites. Many were associated with the colleges that Friends had founded in the nineteenth century. Through the *American Friend*, Jones had a medium to spread his vision, and he won a considerable following among English Friends. Hicksites, who were moving in a similar direction as Jones, found him congenial. Jones enthusiastically cultivated ties between Hicksite and Orthodox Friends. Probably the best example was in 1917, when he took the leading role in founding the American Friends Service Committee, the best known of all Quaker organizations. Originally established as a mechanism for Quaker conscientious objectors to render alternative service during World War I, in the 1920s it expanded its vision to try to apply Quaker methods of humanitarianism and peace making to trouble spots both within the United States and abroad. This, of course, was consistent with the Social Gospel vision of Jones and the other Quaker modernists.[48]

Not all Gurneyite Friends approved of Jones or his vision. By 1900, many of the surviving leaders of the Great Revival, such as John Henry Douglas, Esther Frame, and Luke Woodard, were strong critics. They perceived Jones and his sympathizers as unenthusiastic about revivalism and prone to overintellectualizing religion. "Jesus said feed my sheep, not my giraffes," was the trenchant comment of one Quaker woman in New England. The most important opponent of Jones, however, was of his generation: J. Walter Malone.[49]

Malone was born into an old Quaker family in southwestern Ohio in 1857 and moved to Cleveland as a young man, where he achieved considerable success in business. He and his wife Emma had become converts to holiness Quakerism, and in 1892 decided to use their wealth to found a Bible college, or "training school for Christian workers," as they called it, which eventually became the Friends Bible Institute. Their school was designed to be different from the Quaker colleges. It offered no liberal arts or scientific courses, only classes that would prepare its students to be pastors, missionaries, Sunday school teachers, or other kinds of religious workers. The Malones and all of the teachers at Cleveland were deeply suspicious of Quaker modernism. By questioning the inerrancy of Scripture, it threatened the authority of the Bible. By emphasizing the Inner Light, it seemed to minimize the need for definite experiences of conversion and sanctification. By stressing social service and reform, it seemed to suggest that humans could save the world, rather than looking to the Second Coming of Christ. And by dwelling on the mercy and love of God, it seemed to ignore His judgment. In 1902, Malone began publishing a journal, the *Soul Winner*, to advance his views. In 1905 he changed its name to the *Evangelical Friend*, which became increasingly outspoken in its attacks on Jones and other modernist Quakers. Malone and his coadjutors were consciously part of the larger movement in American Protestantism that would become known as fundamentalism.[50]

For the next two decades, modernists and holiness Friends struggled for the control of the Five Years Meeting and its yearly meetings. The

J. Walter Malone. COURTESY OF MALONE COLLEGE, CANTON, OHIO.

battle had at least three fronts. One was the personnel of the Five Years Meeting—its central office staff and its missionaries. Central to this struggle was the *American Friend*, the official organ. In 1912, Jones severed his connection with the journal and it moved to Richmond, Indiana, with the Five Years Meeting assuming ownership. But the succeeding editors, S. Edgar Nicholson and Walter C. Woodward, were just as sympathetic to modernism. The second front was the Quaker colleges. Holiness Friends did their best to exclude modernist teachings from schools like Earlham in Indiana, Whittier in California, Pacific in Oregon, Friends in Kansas, and Penn in Iowa. The results were uneven. For over a decade, holiness Friends in Indiana tried to force modernist Bible professor Elbert Russell out of Earlham, and when he left for other reasons, actually conducted the equivalent of a heresy trial aimed at his successor. They failed, and Earlham became a modernist bastion. They had more influence at Friends, Penn, and Pacific. Finally, the battle was fought in dozens of Friends meetings, usually over the preaching and views of individual ministers. By the 1920s, Friends had a clear sense of which meetings would be likely to call a pastor of modernist views and which would prefer someone educated at Cleveland.[51]

These tensions reached a climax early in the 1920s, a time when conflict between modernists and their fundamentalist opponents divided most Protestant denominations in the United States. Holiness Friends now openly identified with the larger fundamentalist movement in American Protestantism. The more intensely evangelical Friends wanted the Richmond Declaration of Faith and George Fox's 1671 Letter to the Governor of Barbados, which enunciated what they saw as basic evangelical doctrine, made part of the Uniform Discipline, without qualifications that had previously been adopted. To avoid the threat of separation, the 1922 sessions of the Five Years Meeting largely did this. Nevertheless, these actions did not lead to the dismissal of officials like Woodward whom fundamentalist Friends found offensive. In 1925, Oregon Yearly Meeting left the Five Years Meeting. Small separations followed in Indiana, Western, and Iowa yearly meetings. In 1937, Kansas Yearly Meeting followed Oregon in departing from the Five Years Meeting, as did many fundamentalist Friends in California. In 1956 Nebraska Yearly Meeting "set off," or transferred, most of its membership into the new Rocky Mountain Yearly Meeting, to accommodate those who wished to leave the Five Years Meeting as well.[52]

These fundamentalist-leaning Friends gradually developed their own institutions and associations. Friends Bible Institute, now Cleveland Bible College, remained central, but Quaker Bible colleges were also founded in Indiana, Kansas, Oregon, and California. Various journals, such as the *Friends Herald* in the pastoral Ohio Yearly Meeting and the *Friends Minister*, affiliated with the Union Bible Seminary in Indiana, provided communication. In 1947, these Friends held the first of a series of national conferences that eventually led to the founding of a new organization in 1963, the Evangelical Friends Alliance. Thus a fourth strain of American Quakerism, parallel to Friends General Conference, the Five Years Meeting, and the Conservative yearly meetings, was institutionalized.[53]

Reunion, Diffusion, Growth, and Decline

The history of American Quakerism between 1945 and 1970, a time of general growth in American Protestant churches, was one of paradox. Many of the old yearly meetings saw declines in membership, sometimes dramatic. Yet this decline paralleled the founding of hundreds of new Friends meetings, churches, and worship groups, as Quakers expanded into areas where they had previously been unknown. In some regions, old divisions were healed, as Hicksite and Orthodox, Gurneyite and Wilburite yearly meetings reunited. However, other theological strains became worse.[54]

A growing interest in trying to heal old wounds and cooperate had been apparent in some quarters since the early twentieth century. Some Hicksite and Orthodox Friends began worshiping together. Some new meetings chose not to affiliate with a yearly meeting in order to avoid taking sides. Friends Council on Education was founded in 1933 to provide a way for Hicksite and Orthodox schools to work together. Another sign of healing was the establishment of the study center Pendle Hill in Wallingford, Pennsylvania, outside Philadelphia, in 1930. One of its goals was to bring together Friends of different views.[55]

The reunions came in the eastern yearly meetings. The first took place in New England in 1943, when the little Wilburite yearly meeting and the larger body affiliated with the Five Years Meeting combined. This move, however, led to new strains, as at least two pastoral meetings in Rhode Island judged the new Discipline adopted by the yearly meeting to be insufficiently evangelical. By 1951, both had departed to join Evangelical Friends.[56]

More momentous were the reunions of Hicksite and Orthodox Friends in New York, Philadelphia, and Baltimore yearly meetings. In all three areas, both bodies had experienced declines in membership, and reunion appealed to a sense of economy and efficiency. More important, the old theological divisions had, for the most part, faded with time. By the 1920s, reunion had begun at the local level, as some meetings that had been divided since 1828 began worshiping together again. Nearly all were comfortable with modernism—many pastors in New York Yearly Meeting were enthusiastic proponents of reunion. The process was complete in New York and Philadelphia by 1955, while Baltimore was not completely unified until 1968. New York and Baltimore yearly meetings affiliated with both the Five Years Meeting (Friends United Meeting after 1965) and Friends General Conference. As the Orthodox Philadelphia Yearly Meeting had never joined the Five Years Meeting, reunion there meant that the new body affiliated only with FGC. The reunion in Philadelphia also brought the merger of the two oldest American Quaker periodicals, the Orthodox *Friend* and the *Friends' Intelligencer*, founded by Hicksites in 1844, into the *Friends Journal*. It remains the major voice of unprogrammed Quakerism in North America.[57]

Reunion in some yearly meetings coincided with chronic tensions in others, and at least in the case of Friends United Meeting, created new ones. All of the pastoral yearly meetings in FUM contained significant numbers of fervently evangelical Friends whose views were much the same as those of members in the Evangelical Friends Alliance. The reunions in New York and Baltimore and changes in New England Yearly Meeting, as well as the establishment of new yearly meetings affiliated with both FUM and FGC, brought into FUM unprogrammed Friends whose theology was fervently modernist, sometimes even disputing that Quakerism was necessarily Christian. These differences made FUM the most contentious of Quaker bodies in the last half of the twentieth century.[58]

By the end of the twentieth century, the number of Friends in the United States was roughly what it had been one hundred years earlier. Their distribution, however, was strikingly different. The yearly meetings that in 1900 had been overwhelmingly rural, such as those in the Midwest, had lost over half of their membership, as Quakers left the land and old Quaker farming communities broke up. A good example was Walnut Ridge Quarterly Meeting around the town of Carthage, Indiana. In 1900 it had about 1,700 members. A century later the total was about 300. Yearly meetings such as Indiana, Western, and Iowa now had most of their membership in meetings in small towns or medium-size urban areas. The decline of rural Quakerism dramatically affected the Conservative yearly meetings, with the same results. This also was true in the Quaker farm communities around Philadelphia, although the migration of Friends out of the city into new suburbs replacing the farms compensated to some extent, and in some cases fueled significant growth. Friends United Meeting, concentrated in the Midwest, has especially suffered numerical decline in its North American affiliates because of social change, as have the evangelical yearly meetings on the Great Plains.[59]

Even as many older meetings declined, new ones were founded. These fell into two categories. One was made up of unprogrammed meetings and worship groups, nearly all of them in urban centers or university towns. Such meetings had begun to appear in the 1920s and 1930s, but they exploded in number after 1950. They usually came into existence when a Quaker family moved to a place where no meeting existed. Friends, through an advertisement in *Friends Journal* or less formal contacts, found others interested in Quakerism. This core group would begin to meet either in a private home or in some other facility, often a Protestant church. Dozens of such meetings have been formed in the last half century, although not all have survived. In Chicago, for example, where in 1920 only two Friends meetings existed, there are now six. California had only two unprogrammed meetings in 1900; now more than forty exist. Today, there is an unprogrammed meeting in every state of the union. In some cases, these new meetings affiliated with older yearly meetings. In Iowa and North Carolina, for example, they joined Conservative yearly meetings, giving them a paradoxically liberal cast. In others, they formed new yearly meetings, some affiliated with FGC, some independent.[60]

The other side of growth came mainly in the Evangelical Friends Alliance, which after 1960 became aggressive in planting new Friends churches. The original yearly meetings (Ohio, Oregon, Kansas) changed their names to reflect their expansion into adjacent states. Evangelical Friends pointed proudly to statistics that showed steady increases in attendance in some yearly meetings. Some Friends churches, such as in Canton, Ohio or Yorba Linda, California, have members and attenders in the thousands. Evangelical Friends show special interest in the Sunbelt, with Eastern Region (formerly Ohio Yearly Meeting) expanding into Virginia, North Carolina, and Florida, and Southwest (formerly California) opening new churches in Arizona.[61]

Thus, almost two hundred years after the first of the separations that rent them, American Friends remain divided and relatively few in numbers in proportion to the whole population of the United States. Few Quaker leaders foresee a day when all of the diverse strands of Quaker belief will again be united into a single fabric. But for all their diversity, certain common threads are still visible in virtually all Quaker bodies. They will be our next subject.

CHAPTER 4

Quaker Faiths and Practices

Generalization about American Quakers today is almost impossible. The process of division that began in the 1820s has carried them down divergent paths. Sometimes these paths are close enough that communication among them is possible. Friends move from one to another, occasionally even making dramatic changes in course. At times in the last thirty years, hopeful Friends have seen differences lessening. For example, in 1986 a Philadelphia Quaker wrote confidently that "the spiritual realities which underlie the division within the Religious Society of Friends are the same and . . . if divested of the superstructure the Spirit would be free to unite us." Other Friends have been less certain; a decade earlier Jack Willcuts, the long-time editor of the *Evangelical Friend*, had opined about the various persuasions of Friends that "all we have in common are some exciting ancestors." Yet even Willcuts wrote movingly of the common spirit that he found.[1]

In this chapter, I will argue that, even conceding the wide range of beliefs found among American Friends, certain ones are still almost universally shared. Five stand out: worship based on the leading of the Spirit; the ministry of all believers; decision making through the traditional Quaker business process; simplicity as a basic philosophy of life; and a commitment to education as a manifestation of Quaker faith.

Worship

All Friends affirm the importance of worship. While they see individual or private worship as vital, they agree that it is essential for Quakers to gather with like-minded people for corporate or group worship. "Worship is always possible," according to the *Faith and Practice* of Philadelphia Yearly Meeting, "alone or in company, in silence, in music or speech, in stillness or in dance," but this handbook states uncompromisingly that "the meeting for worship is the heart of the Religious Society of Friends." Many Friends still use the traditional label of "meeting for worship" for these occasions, but most pastoral Friends use the terms popular with other Protestants, such as "the service" or simply "church" or "worship."[2]

Today, American Quaker worship is exceedingly diverse. Outwardly, unprogrammed meetings, without a pastor or set order of hymns, sermon, and prayers, are closer to traditional forms, yet even they show considerable diversity and, in most cases, are very different from Quaker meetings before 1860. Programmed meetings are outwardly similar to services in other Protestant churches, but they also include a wide range of practices. Pastoral Friends, moreover, often argue that theologically their Christ-centered worship is closer to that of the early Friends than many current unprogrammed meetings.

All of these ways of worship, however, have certain commonalities. Wilmer Cooper, a pastoral Friend who grew up in a Conservative family, argues that Quaker worship should have four common elements: silence, communion, ministry, and fellowship. The differences come with the emphasis that Friends give to each; pastoral meetings tend to have less silence and more ministry, for example. A North Carolina pastoral Friend argues for another commonality, the belief that any speaking in a meeting for worship, whether it be by the pastor or any other member, must come from a sense of divine call and obedience to it. Rufus M. Jones summed up this understanding: Quaker worship is "a vital discovery of divine Life revealing itself here and now in and through a group of persons who are bent on transmitting that life."[3]

Friends comprehend one of these common elements, communion, in a way that separates them from virtually all other Christians. Friends do not observe communion through physical elements of bread and wine. Instead, they believe that the true communion that Christ enjoined on His followers is spiritual, when they gather and share and worship in harmony and love. Friends find various grounds for this. Considerable energy has gone into biblical exegesis to prove that Jesus did not intend that physical communion would become a rite in His church. Quakers point out, for example, that there is no mention of the bread and wine in the Gospel of John's account of the Last Supper, which other Christians see as the basis for their understanding of communion. One long-time Quaker pastor observed that "in the Bible . . . when God plans any kind of an institution in which things material have a part, He is most diligent to give full details about it." Since we do not find full details on the method of taking communion (or baptism for that matter) in the scriptures, these two ordinances cannot be necessary for salvation. Some Friends think that true communion is found in a simple fellowship meal. Many liberal Friends argue that all of life should be sacramental, that "insofar as we are faithful in our testimonies, our very lives may thus serve for others as the outward and visible evidence of inward and invisible communion." Others argue that true religion is by its nature spiritual. Thus outward observances, like physical communion and water baptism, while they may be comforting to some, are not necessary, and may even be distractions. As Paul Anderson, an influential Evangelical Friend, puts it: "Friends believe in the sacramental work of the Present Christ so strongly that they refuse to reduce it to a symbol or ceremony."[4]

While, as will be seen, Friends often have radically different ideas about how much vocal ministry should take place during worship, who should present it, how long it should be, and what its themes should be, they agree that it should come from a sense of divine leading. One influential Quaker writer argues that this is a manifestation of what he calls the first principle of Quakerism, that "Jesus Christ has come to teach His people Himself." An Evangelical Friends pastor wrote in 1994 that "the Spirit is no respecter of persons. He may choose to speak through *any* surrendered worshiper, and when He does, the message has the delightful quality of the unexpected and unpredictable." John Punshon, an English Friend who spent a decade teaching at the Earlham School of Religion, concludes that revelation directly from God "comes to every single human being without exception." Liberal Friends agree. They express this belief by breaking the silence of an unprogrammed meeting or speaking out of the "open worship" of a pastoral meeting.[5]

Since an unprogrammed Quaker meeting is so different from virtually all other forms of Christian worship, Friends have put considerable energy into explaining it to themselves, to newcomers, and to outsiders. For some, its very *differentness* is part of its appeal. As Quaker writer Chuck Fager notes, Protestant worship is "typically only another expression of an already noisy world." Meeting for worship is a contrast, a New England Friend has argued, "the only radical alternative form of Christian worship where each is personally responsible for one's own spiritual journey and which can only be grown and nourished in corporate gathering." One Friend calls the unprogrammed meeting "an experiment in religious anarchy," a gamble that "more will be brought out of the room than was brought in—more depth, more insight, more truth, more knowledge, more growth, in each and among all."⁶

What do Friends think, or hope, will happen in a meeting for worship? One Illinois Friend stated simply that "Meeting for worship is a time I choose to spend in the presence of God. Silent worship is about becoming Friends with God." Quaker educator Paul Lacey sees many things taking place; it can be "a time when our sense of the rightness of things, the gathering up of those recollections of joy, the gathering of those impulses which are so deep that their sources are unremembered—though we know they can be trusted—the gentle leading of our affections, all these bring us to serenity." Another Friend wrote that in worship we are "doing the most important thing we ever do . . . seek[ing], individually and collectively, to come into the living presence of God, opening ourselves to the leadings and promptings of God's spirit." Not all Friends come for such an experience. A Philadelphia Quaker, a self-professed atheist, wrote that "for me, Friends don't hold meeting for *worship*, but meeting for meditation, for thinking, for comfort, for stimulation, for joy, for love." But atheist Friends are exceptional; most members and attenders of unprogrammed meetings agree that they come seeking some experience beyond human existence.⁷

The unprogrammed Quaker meeting house gives expression to this vision of worship. As Howard Brinton, one of the most influential Friends of the twentieth century, wrote fifty years ago: "At first sight, it might appear that the meeting can only be described by negatives—there is no altar, no liturgy, no pulpit, no sermon, no organ, no choir, no sacrament, and no person in authority." The lack of ornamentation is usually striking. A few meeting houses have pictures on the walls, usually on a Quaker theme—a favorite is English Quaker artist J. Doyle Penrose's *The Presence in the Midst*, showing Christ appearing during a meeting for worship—but many others do not. Stained glass is still eschewed. Older meeting houses often retain the facing benches where once the recorded ministers and elders sat looking out over the congregation. Only a few Conservative meetings retain the old practice of seating men and women on different sides of the meeting house. In newer meeting houses, a less hierarchical pattern is common, arranging benches around a center area, so that there is not a clear sense of front and back. In most unprogrammed meetings today, casual dress is typical, although others, especially older Friends, still feel that more formal attire is appropriate. All types of meetings, however, will have

Friends appointed to "head" the meeting, signaling when the time has come to end or "break" it. Then those present will shake hands with and greet each other.[8]

Physical attendance at meeting is not enough, all Friends agree; one must arrive prepared to worship to reap the maximum benefit. A number argue that preparation begins before arrival, with prayer at home. At the meeting house, one of the unwritten rules (sometimes made explicit in brochures attempting to explain unprogrammed worship to those new to it) is that however much conversation and visiting may take place outside, silence is to be preserved in the meeting room. Once seated, Friends will begin to "center." This is a kind of spiritual focus that has a variety of elements. Some Friends view it as a kind of relaxation, a suspension of "analysis and judgment." John Punshon sees it as "adopting a discipline of detachment: severing the bonds from whatever the unreflective part of ourselves tries to bend to its use to prevent the soul from opening itself to God." Friends seek a kind of passivity, a denying of any sense of self. Many draw on Jungian or even Buddhist meditation techniques. At one time, a sign hung at the front of the Cambridge, Massachusetts meeting house: "Don't Just Do Something—Sit!" Openness is also key; one must be prepared for the possibility that God may send thoughts or messages that will lead to new and unexpected actions.[9]

Most striking, of course, is the quiet of meeting, or what one Friend

Unprogrammed: Amawalk, N.Y., Meetinghouse. FRIENDS COLLECTION, EARLHAM COLLEGE.

Unprogrammed: Cambridge, Mass., Meetinghouse. © Skip Schiel.

Unprogrammed: Providence Meetinghouse, Media, Pa. Friends Collection, Earlham College.

calls "a descent into silence." "Silence is the most powerful sign of inward dependence on God," writes John Punshon. "Words, from whatever source, are human and are inevitably adulterated by our worldly ways. Silence, on the other hand, is a reflection of purity. . . . In worship, it means that we wait, expectantly and patiently, for what God has to say to us." For him, the end of silence is not just the absence of noise, but stillness, a distance from the world that brings complete openness to God. As Quaker philosopher D. Elton Trueblood put it, "it is not sufficient, for creative silence, merely to abstain from *words*. We must also . . . abstain from all of our own thoughts, imaginations, and desires." Such stillness, as Patricia Loring, who has written extensively on Quaker spirituality, concludes, can come only with divine assistance. Another Friend sees stillness, however, as opening us not to a force that is outside us, but rather to "the 'still small voice' that dwells within each of us—the voice of God that speaks to us and that we express to others through our deeds." Friends acknowledge that adjusting to the silence can be difficult, requiring practice and self-discipline.[10]

Friends admit that often worship fails to measure up to these standards. As one Philadelphia Quaker has acknowledged, silence can be worshipful, but it can also be empty, uneasy, or even perfunctory. A Friend from California points out that "learning to handle an hour of silence is tough. We fidget and get restless. . . . An hour can be a very long time, and it can be too quiet one week and too noisy another." A scholar who has extensively studied Quaker worship and procedures has concluded that what Friends call a "covered" meeting, one in which those present sense real spiritual power and influences, is rare. Sixty years ago, Rufus Jones wrote that "silence itself has no magic. It may be just sheer emptiness, absence of words or noise or music. It may be an occasion for slumber, or it may be a dead form." For newcomers it can be especially disconcerting. Some Friends criticize those who prefer all meetings to be silent, with the stillness rarely broken, as worshiping the silence as an end rather than a means. Silent worship can be a challenge especially for small children. Most unprogrammed meetings deal with this by having children attend the first fifteen minutes or so of worship, then dismissing them for First Day School (the unprogrammed Friends' equivalent of Sunday school) or a similar activity. Some Friends argue, however, that this deprives children of both an opportunity to learn to worship and of possible ministry that they might share with the adults.[11]

Unprogrammed Friends freely admit that they pass the silence in a variety of ways. One problematic element is music. While there is no

"Skyspace" interior, Live Oak Meetinghouse, Houston, Texas. © ROBERT BALDRIDGE.

previously arranged congregational singing, many meetings now have a time of music and singing before worship begins. Some meetings have a piano in the worship room if someone feels moved to play. It may happen that someone will feel led to sing, or suggest that the meeting join her or him in a song. Some meetings have copies of the FGC hymnal available for this purpose. Some attenders spend part of meeting reading the Bible or other spiritual books, although others argue that this is inappropriate. Some close their eyes to try to block out all distractions, although others feel that this is all too often a concession to sleepiness. Thoughts often stray into matters ranging from grocery lists to work to personal relationships. Some will struggle with personal problems, painful experiences, or hard decisions, feeling that here insight or help from God is most likely to come

Interior, Clear Creek Meetinghouse, McNabb, Ill. KEN & DONNA BISSET/COURTESY OF FRIENDS JOURNAL.

to them. Some see the meeting as the most appropriate place to give thanks. As one Friend sums it up: "Some have their mantras, their ways of tuning in and out. But most acknowledge that prayer doesn't come easily and what they call God is not often revealed to them."[12]

Most Friends come expecting, however, that someone present will feel moved to share some message with the meeting, what many Friends call "vocal ministry." As one Quaker scholar notes, "as much as Quakers love silence, we also seem to crave words; we want everyone to speak." While the physical setting may be similar to that of previous centuries, the nature of Quaker speaking in unprogrammed meetings, except in a few Conservative meetings, has changed dramatically in the last century. As noted above, most unprogrammed yearly meetings have ceased recording ministers. John Punshon describes the old view of ministry as the speaker being "sort of a flute for the Holy Spirit to play on." Ministers often recorded lengthy struggles before they first dared to speak in meeting, always fearing to "get ahead of the guide," to do something that was not clearly the will of God. Any sort of preparation, even bringing a Bible to meeting to refer to, was regarded as a mistrust of the Spirit. If God wanted the Bible quoted, God would put the appropriate verse in the minister's head. (One minister, reproached for quoting the scriptures incorrectly from memory, responded that that was evidently what God intended him to do.) Quaker sermons might go on for hours, filled with long quotations from the Bible.[13]

This sort of ministry has almost completely disappeared, but much of the underlying theology remains. Unprogrammed Friends still feel it inappropriate to arrive at meeting with the determination to speak. Instead, one must see oneself as simply an instrument of the divine. One Conservative Friend has written that the best ministry is when "one has the sense that the speaker has been spoken through or played through, rather than having spoken herself." Sometimes that may be embarrassing or even humiliating to the speaker, but, in obedience to the will of God, it must be borne. That does not preclude thinking about what one might say on a given occasion, should it present itself. Rufus Jones, who seldom attended a meeting for worship without speaking, was once asked if he ever prepared sermons in advance. He answered that he spent considerable time constructing them, but then waited to be told when and where to give them. Not a few suspect that many fellow Friends prepare for meeting by "stuffing their minds with quotations, newspaper clippings, poems, and even ideas."[14]

Friends readily acknowledge that there is no infallible method for testing whether a leading to speak is real or a delusion. They are usually patient with each other. Some see corporate worship as a kind of group seeking after truth, in which some attempts to name or frame it are bound to be unsuccessful. One Friend told how once, against all reason, he felt led to speak in French in meeting. Later he learned that there was a French visitor present who spoke no English and who benefited enormously. For many Friends, the leading to speak must still be powerful, almost overwhelming. Paul Lacey described it this way:

> The first time I ever felt moved to speak, I thought something was physically wrong with me. The meeting was very deep, by which I mean that I was aware simultaneously of both an intensity of attention in myself and a sense of being at rest. . . . After a time, the thoughts and images which had come into my mind, modified, clarified and intensified by what others had said and by the silence in which we met, began to take on new patterns. Phrases and images arranged themselves, first in clusters, then in a loose sequence. They began to take shape as a *message*, a brief set of words I felt I should share.

Lacey felt physically weak, his heart pounding and breath short, certain that he should break the silence only if "impelled and awed." Many other Friends report similar feelings before speaking.[15]

Howard Brinton argued that "no rules can be laid down for Quaker ministry. The spirit leads where it will." Friends agree that what happens when someone speaks is something unique. As one wrote in 1987, "a spoken message in a Quaker meeting is clearly not a sermon or homily but something more modest and yet more wonderful. It consists of opening one's soul to fellow worshipers and either humbly offering some insight that one finds helpful and hopes they also may value; or offering one's spiritual need in the hope that others may be led, by dwelling on their own Inner Light, to illumine some aspect of the matter." However, speaking in meeting proceeds according to myriad unwritten rules. What one Friend saw applying to another Quaker group is also true here—Friends "have their own kind of rhetoric, some of it stemming from our testimony of truth and from our 'folkway' of understatement." Most Friends agree that it is undesirable to speak simply to refute or take issue with another speaker. To speak in anger or hostility will often bring reproach afterward. Many criticize what Friends call "popcorn meetings," in which Friends rise rapidly to speak, one after another, leaving no time to consider what has been said. In the explanation of worship available at the San Francisco Friends Meeting, the ideal is clear: "This is not a discussion group." Brevity is treasured. Usually, the first fifteen or twenty minutes of the hour of worship will be silent. These constraints mean that seldom is Quaker ministry in this setting of the teaching variety; there is not enough time. Instead, it is concerned with "spiritual formation." Friends point out that George Fox once said that the goal of Quaker preaching was "to bring people . . . to the end of all preaching." It should direct them not to the minister but to God, manifested inwardly or outwardly.[16]

It is difficult to generalize about the substance of the messages that Friends hear during unprogrammed worship, since they vary from place to place. Often they refer to current events. Ministry may begin: "Lord, did you read in this morning's *New York Times* that? . . ." Humor, once virtually unknown, is now common. Ministry may refer to an everyday experience, for example, impressions of God while wheeling the trash can to the curb. A Friend probably described the experience of many in an account of his meeting:

> We approach experimentation gingerly, and while one does indeed hear Christian language, or biblical passages and portraits, in meetings for worship, it is most often offered lightly, almost with apology. As often, if not oftener, the language is that of social science, psychology, current

events, personal references. Prayer is offered rarely. The Bible is seldom read directly in meeting. We skirt around theological areas of interpretation and commitment and fall back on silence to pull us together.

Sometimes messages may build on each other; many Friends like such "clustering." And, as Paul Lacey notes, they may counter each other: a message of finding delight in one's children may bring a reminder of children's suffering around the world, or some expression of finding pleasure in everyday life will bring "a passionate assertion that, while any of our brothers and sisters anywhere around the world is suffering, the Friend speaking will never feel joy."[17]

One of the challenges that unprogrammed meetings face is their vulnerability. Virtually all Friends who have attended one for a significant period of time have favorite stories of bizarre behavior, of "a particularly inappropriate intimacy shared . . . or a lengthy harangue delivered." People will come to read long letters, or to exhort. During the Vietnam War, some meetings found themselves faced with members who wanted to devote worship to denunciations of U.S. policy. One meeting contained a small group that had determined to assume control, speaking rapidly in succession meeting after meeting. Germantown Meeting near Philadelphia was the object of the attentions of a nonmember who arrived weekly to proselytize for his newly formed organization, the Peoples of the World United for Peace, of which he was the only member, and to denounce the meeting for its lack of support.[18]

Meetings have mechanisms to deal with such problems: ministry and oversight or worship and ministry committees responsible for the spiritual health of the meeting. They often assume responsibility for "eldering" problem Friends. Speaking that members find especially offensive might be met by others rising in silent protest or bursting into song. Sometimes speakers who are clearly troubled emotionally or psychologically may be invited to meet privately with Friends or even escorted outside.[19]

Most problems in unprogrammed worship are more prosaic. Some Friends mourn the loss of what they see as a spiritually incisive Quaker "prophetic ministry" that regularly directed hearers to great spiritual truths and provided religious nourishment. As one Friend put it, "Some people confuse 'personal experience' with 'personal experience of God' and share stories rather than share ministry." Another has been even more critical: "There is no disciplined ministry in our Meetings; except that which is provided oftentimes by graduates of the Earlham School of Religion who actually know something about the Bible, about Quaker history, about theology, and can give some content. . . . So the spoken ministry is generally poor." Friends complain about too much "breast-beating" on social and political issues, about breaking out into songs that few present know, about poignant personal stories with unfathomable points, or "a rush of jumbled messages five minutes before the end." Sometimes silence is a relief. An old Quaker story tells of one Friend remarking to another after meeting: "I'm glad this morning that those who had nothing to say refrained from giving verbal evidence of the fact." Thomas Merton, the famous Trappist monk and contemplative writer, once attended a Friends meeting and was deeply moved by the silence, only to have the effect spoiled when it was broken by a woman sharing photographs of her latest trip. "How urgently we need men and women who can speak experientially, powerfully, and convincingly to the disillusionment and despair, the longing and seeking of our contemporaries," one Friend concluded.[20]

Still, disenchantment is not the dominant note in the experience of unprogrammed Friends worship today. Obviously those who participate find meaning in it. At its best, taking part in meeting brings, in the words of one Friend, "a filledness, or a brightness, or a rain of sweetness, or a breathing, or just a clear normality." Parker Palmer, the Quaker educational philosopher, described his first experience of unprogrammed worship in words that resonate for many Friends:

> But when I walked into the meeting for worship on oak floorboards that glowed with the patina of age; when I sat on one of the simple wooden benches arranged in a squared circle at the heart of a century-old stone barn; when I settled into the silence with thirty or forty people, a silence that flowed on for an hour or so, rippled only occasionally by soulful speech; and when as never before, I felt God's presence in the sunlight that came through the window and on the floor at my feet—then, what passed through me time and again was the peace that passes all understanding.

Unprogrammed Quaker worship at its best, in the minds of those committed to it, is a kind of conversation. Elton Trueblood summed up this view: "Is there anything queer or strange in listening together for God's voice? What would be really *strange* would be a conversation, in which one did all of the talking." For Friends in the unprogrammed tradition, *listening* to God, and to each other, is at the heart of worship.[21]

In the summer of 1997 a reporter for the *Los Angeles Times* investigated what she termed "one of southern California's fastest-growing evangelical churches." What she found surprised her. The surprise was not in "the squeal of electric guitars" or in "the ballplayer-turned-pastor" hugging "thousands of people streaming off shuttle buses from distant parking lots"; or in the model she found in the lobby of "a planned sanctuary as big as the Crystal Cathedral," a landmark of California evangelicalism; or in the "microphone-waving singer at the altar" swaying to "My Life in You, Lord." These were scenes that would be familiar to anyone attending any of the growing evangelical community churches across the United States. What surprised her was that this was the Yorba Linda Friends Church, and these noisy, enthusiastic worshipers were Quakers.[22]

Certainly not all pastoral Friends have followed the path that Yorba Linda Friends have chosen. But programmed Quaker worship, the method of about two thirds of all American Friends, provides striking contrasts with unprogrammed worship. Many American Friends, even lifelong Quakers, pass their lives knowing only the programmed version, and others find the alternative strange and uncomfortable when they do encounter it. Paradoxically, programmed worship, while based on certain common assumptions, probably manifests more diversity than unprogrammed. Some programmed Quaker worship is like that at Yorba Linda, filled with sound and music, intended to convert unbelievers and strengthen believers with every tool that modern psychology, technology, and communications offer. Other programmed meetings see their mission in holding closer to traditional Quaker methods, with significant periods of silent, or what they often call "open," worship. And other meetings are found at almost every point between these two extremes. The most common comparison many Friends make is to other Protestant denominations. One Friend from FGC, tongue in cheek, has labeled Friends United Meeting, which includes a majority of pastoral Friends, "Friends United Methodists." And many do find it easy to sort pastoral meetings according to their resemblance to mainline Protestant churches, such as the Methodists or Presbyterians; or charismatics influenced by the Pentecostal movement; or holiness denominations like the Nazarenes and Wesleyans.[23]

Virtually all pastoral Friends share certain assumptions about worship. Whatever they think of the document as a whole, they would endorse the vision of "public worship" found in the Richmond Declaration of Faith:

Worship is the adoring response of the heart and mind to the influence of the Spirit of God. It stands neither in forms nor in the formal disuse of forms; it may be without words as well as with them, but it must be in spirit and in truth. (John iv.24). . . . Having become His adopted children through faith in the Lord Jesus Christ, it is our privilege to meet together and unite in the worship of Almighty God, to wait upon Him for the renewal of our strength, for communion one with another, for the edification of believers in the exercise of various spiritual gifts, and for the declaration of the glad tidings of salvation to the unconverted who may gather with us.

This statement embodies several assumptions that one would not necessarily find in most unprogrammed meetings: that one's relationship with God should be the focus of worship, as opposed to one of several important spiritual matters; that Quakerism is explicitly Christian and looks to Christ as the heart of the faith; and that worship should have an evangelistic element, proclaiming salvation through Christ. As will be seen later, pastoral Friends often disagree as to how best to enact these ideas and what their implications are, but all embrace the basic concepts.[24]

Like unprogrammed Friends, pastoral Friends believe that for worship to have value, God must direct it. As one influential Quaker pastor put it: "Quaker worship is a response to the initiative of God in Jesus Christ through the workings of the Holy Spirit on the mind and heart, the will and the emotions of man." They argue that structure does not preclude Spirit-led worship, and may even enhance it. "Spontaneity in worship, real worship, is a myth," wrote one Oregon Friend. "Unplanned worship, poorly prepared worship can be a bumbling, embarrassing, miserable thing. Even unprogrammed meetings require guidelines." As Paul Anderson argues, "The Spirit may also lead in the planning of a service, and . . . the order of the service should be able to be laid down if the Spirit dictates."[25]

Programmed worship grew out of the revival movement of the late nineteenth century, when, as has been seen, many meetings employed pastors to preach regularly and care for converts. Today, pastoral Friends are relatively few along the Atlantic coast, save in North Carolina. Pastoral meetings in New York and New England yearly meetings, once numerous, have, for the most part, moved toward unprogrammed worship again. From the Appalachians to the West Coast, and in Alaska, programmed meetings embrace the overwhelming majority of American Quakers. As the label suggests, this is worship that proceeds according to a plan that usually varies little from week to week (although virtually all programmed Friends will insist that it can and does change when the Holy Spirit leads them), in forms that resemble those found in most other Protestant denominations.

Pastoral meeting houses or churches (programmed Friends are as likely to use "church" as "meeting" or "meeting house") vary considerably in architecture and design. In Ohio and Indiana especially, many were built when all Friends were unprogrammed and adapted when the pastoral system developed. A good example is the New Garden Friends Church near Fountain City, Indiana. From the outside, one can still see the traditional design, similar to Quaker meeting houses in the east. But later generations added a small steeple, and the interior has been completely remodeled so that no sign of its former function remains. Friends usually agree that there is no such thing as "sacred space" in Quakerism, that all places are equal in the eyes of God and that worship can happen anywhere. Thus they do not believe that God is more present in their meeting houses and churches than anywhere else. But they usually have clear views on what is appropriate in the decoration and furnishings of such places. Pews usually face the front, focused on the pulpit. Many buildings have, behind the pulpit or to one side, a space for a choir. Organs and pianos are standard features;

Pastoral congregation: New Garden Friends Church near Fountain City, Ind. FRIENDS COLLECTION, EARLHAM COLLEGE; PHOTO BY GREGORY P. HINSHAW.

Pastoral congregation: West River Friends Meetinghouse near Economy, Ind. FRIENDS
COLLECTION, EARLHAM COLLEGE; PHOTO BY GREGORY P. HINSHAW.

Pastoral congregation: Amboy, Ind., Friends Meetinghouse. FRIENDS COLLECTION, EARLHAM
COLLEGE; PHOTO BY GREGORY P. HINSHAW.

Pastoral congregation: First Friends Church, Marion, Ind. FRIENDS COLLECTION, EARLHAM COLLEGE; PHOTO BY GREGORY P. HINSHAW.

some large pastoral meetings have elaborate pipe organs. Stained glass is also common; the focus of the meeting house in Spiceland, Indiana, for example, is a stained-glass window of Christ in Gethsemane that was purchased from the chapel at a Presbyterian college. Some Friends churches may have banners or some art, a piece of sculpture or a painting, particularly a figure of Christ, but religious imagery has no particular place in worship, and one is just as likely to find a complete lack of decoration. There is no altar or baptismal font or any other equipment associated with physical observance of the sacraments. Flowers are usually displayed, and many congregations have committees for that purpose. The general layout is not much different from most Protestant churches, and pews and other furnishings are often purchased from the same ecclesiastical supply companies.[26]

The program's broad features are common to almost all pastoral meetings and churches. Almost always, there will be a musical prelude. A few congregations encourage those present to be silent as they enter the sanctuary (the term that pastoral Friends, like other denominations, tend to use for the room in which they worship). In most, however, the prelude is a time for visiting. Worship (most pastoral Friends are comfortable with calling it a service) will usually open with some sort of invocation and Bible reading, usually from the pastor, sometimes from a member of the congregation who serves as an associate. Some congregations also place early in the service a time for announcements or expressions of prayer concerns, such as deaths or illnesses among the congregation. Others, however, put these at the end, believing that announcements of committee meetings or youth gatherings, while necessary and proper, are not properly part of worship.[27]

A favorite Quaker joke asks why unprogrammed Friends sing so badly. Answer: because they are always reading ahead to make sure that they agree with the words. Herein lies one of the important differences between pastoral and unprogrammed Quakers. For virtually all programmed Friends, music is a vital part of worship, and sometimes a source of conflict. The pre-1860 strictures against music are utterly alien to them. Instead, they agree that "good congregational singing must be fervently sought after and prayed about." Most pastoral meetings have choirs—weekly choir practice is as much a part of the life of a Quaker congregation as any other—and special numbers by soloists and groups are common. Many larger Friends meetings and churches now employ ministers of music, at least part time.[28]

The choice of music tends to follow developments in the larger religious world and often reproduces conflicts there. A few pastoral meetings use the Friends General Conference hymnal, *Worship in Song*, which was designed specifically for Quakers. Most pastoral Friends, however, find its omission of standards that employ military imagery, like *Onward Christian Soldiers*, and its rewording of others to remove patriarchal language unacceptable. So they depend on a variety of hymnals from non-Quaker sources. A focus of considerable conflict in the last decade has been the importation of musical practices from charismatic churches. Some Friends churches, especially in Evangelical Friends International (formerly Evangelical Friends Alliance), have moved away from traditional hymns toward simple choruses, often projected on a screen at the front of the sanctuary, or even Christian rock. (One compromise, especially in growing congregations straining their physical capacity, has been to hold separate services with different kinds of music.) Some pastoral Friends, both liberal and Evangelical, worry that music, or at least the wrong kind of music, has become too central to Quaker worship. A California pastor was emphatic in 1994. "Many revivalist gospel songs call to mind music traditionally played at the merry-go-round or ferris wheel," he wrote. "Like these traditional entertainments, they go nowhere, either theologically or musically. . . . Further, the majority of contemporary Scripture songs and choruses being written nowadays are so cliché-filled and commercialized, they are not much more than advertising jingles." But such concerns have generally had little impact and have not nurtured a specifically Quaker philosophy of hymnody or ministry of music. Programmed Friends have been largely content to take their music from non-Quaker sources.[29]

The focus of a programmed meeting is the pastor's sermon. Expectations of what the sermon will embrace and the manner in which it will be delivered vary significantly among congregations, but there are certain common features. Virtually all pastoral Friends agree that preaching should have a clear application to the lives of the congregation, have a scriptural basis, and be relatively short. Elton Trueblood was fond of telling his seminary students: "If you've drilled for oil for twenty minutes and haven't hit, it's time to stop boring." Eastern Region Evangelical Friends lay down very specific guidelines: "Preaching, whether evangelistic or teaching in character, must always be aimed at a verdict: acceptance of salvation, obedience in discipleship, or taking steps toward maturity in Christlikeness." Some Quaker pastors believe so strongly that all preaching must be focused on directing hearers to Christ that they rarely take texts from the Old Testament. Some large Friends churches, like Yorba Linda or First Friends in Canton, Ohio, have moved toward multimedia presentations, in which texts and an outline are projected on a screen at the front of the sanctuary. The manner of delivery also varies according to both the individual inclinations of the pastor and the tastes of the congregation. Some Quaker pastors, like many television ministers today, insist on portable microphones so that they can move about freely. For some, it is carrying on Quaker tradition to speak extemporaneously, with few notes. The degree of emotion and nature of the language will vary. One pastor wrote that directness was vital: it might "shock cultured hearers, but some rhetorical features are needed to slam home the sin of sin." Some Friends ministers believe it entirely appropriate to preach what some would characterize as "fire and brimstone," to threaten sinners with divine judgment, and to be specific about naming their sins, ranging from lust to greed to homosexuality to liberal theology. Many of their hearers will greet such proclamations with visible and audible approval, ranging from exclamations of "Amen!" or "Hallelujah!" or will wave their arms or applaud, a practice imported from other evangelical churches. Many Quaker pastors will conclude a sermon with a call for those seeking the new birth, or a deeper experience, or desiring prayer or healing, to come forward and kneel with them. But in other pastoral meetings, anything that suggests the atmosphere of a revival meeting or the practices of Pentecostals or a television minister may initiate a conversation with the ministry and oversight committee about the pastor's very uncertain future.

Many pastoral Friends find such practices undignified and un-Quakerly, unsuitable for a Friends meeting.[30]

The one practice that programmed Friends have carried over from older days is what they variously label "silent worship," "contemplative worship," "communion after the manner of Friends," or "open worship." This is a period, sometimes preceding, sometimes following the regular sermon, in which the meeting settles into silence and all present are free to speak as they feel led by the Holy Spirit. Virtually all Friends pay at least lip service to this idea; Paul Anderson argues that it is potentially "the most sacramental of Christian experiences." Even Eastern Region Evangelical Friends, for example, while seeing the substance of worship in "prayer, praise, and preaching," also recommend "frequent times for reflection, meditation, and decision." Some pastoral meetings have sought to extend the period of open worship. New Garden Friends in Greensboro, North Carolina, for example, purposely keeps other parts of the service brief in order to devote almost half of the hour to silent waiting. For several years First Friends Meeting in New Castle, Indiana, has had an alternative service that consists only of a message from the pastor, with two thirds of the time given to open worship. In most pastoral meetings open worship runs a maximum of five minutes. Still, many report occasions when the Holy Spirit is obviously present, moving individuals to speak, to such an extent and with such evident power that the pastor puts away his or her prepared sermon and allows open worship to continue. And occasionally it can lead to unusual outbursts of emotion and enthusiasm. In 1978, for example, a young man in Northwest Yearly Meeting dragged a cross to the front of a church sanctuary, nailing a necktie and Bible to it "to dramatize the fact that Friends had crucified the Truth in much the same way as Christ had been crucified centuries before."[31]

Given the diversity of pastoral Friends, it is not surprising to find considerable disagreement over the proper conduct of a programmed meeting. Some see the charismatic practices of a Yorba Linda, for example, as completely unacceptable, while advocates of "contemporary" worship respond that more restrained methods are simply evidence of spiritual languor. Some Friends argue that attenders do not prepare themselves adequately, do not come seeking a truly spiritual experience, or spend too much time watching the clock, worried that an extension of a few minutes, no matter how powerful the Spirit, will make them late to their favorite restaurant for Sunday dinner. There is considerable worry over the quality of much of the preaching. An influential California pastor claimed in 1978 that "today's sermons, in their shallowness, frivolity, dullness, biblically unhinged moralisms, are but a reflection of the preacher who has lost his faith in preaching," a judgment that many share today. As with many unprogrammed Friends, there is fear among pastoral Friends that they have largely lost the gift of prophetic ministry. Many echo the judgment of Elton Trueblood about some pastoral meetings forty years ago: "All that we have left, in many neighborhoods, is a little congregation, dutifully droning through three gospel songs, listening patiently to a sermon and a benediction. This is not Quakerism; this is simply Protestantism at the end of the line."[32]

Some of this uncertainty and dissatisfaction centers on open worship. In the minds of some Friends, too many compromises have been made; pastoral meetings have become like Protestant churches where worshipers are content simply to sit back and watch the pastor. "The curtailment of open worship is a sign that worship is becoming entertainment and something is going seriously wrong," concludes John Punshon. Others sense that most pastoral Friends really do not understand the purpose of open worship and are so accustomed to constant diversion in their lives that they find it impossible to pass even a few minutes without such stimuli. "There is a fear of waiting upon the Spirit of the Lord in many of our churches and yearly meetings," one Friend concluded. He argued that distaste for open worship was heightened by pastors and other leaders who feared that "the practice is unproductive, that it alienates new believers, and that it ultimately can lead to a loss of control." Others point to the sometimes less than satisfactory speaking that can emerge from periods of open worship. But other Friends conclude that the combination is an example of trying to put new wine in old skins, certain to fail. "We have crossed open worship with programmed worship and have gotten confusion which follows a program," wrote one.[33]

To the extent that there is a problem, however, it reflects in large part the diversity of pastoral Quakerism. For some, vital Quakerism is a matter of effective evangelism. Thus the noise and crowds of such meetings as Yorba Linda are bearing fruit and should be encouraged to spread elsewhere. For other pastoral Friends, Quakers, as part of the Christian family, are called not so much to grow in numbers as to preserve certain Christian beliefs and testimonies. This conflict is seen not only in different versions of worship but also in how Friends of various persuasions approach the concept of ministry.

The Ministry of All Believers

A word game that mischievous Friends sometimes play involves the question of whether or not Friends have ministers. Those encountering unprogrammed worship for the first time may quickly conclude that, since there is no one designated as the priest or pastor, there is no minister for the congregation. And someone approaching a programmed meeting will decide that the pastor is *the* minister. Yet both would be incorrect. One point on which there is broad consensus among all persuasions of Friends is that *all* Quakers are called on to be ministers.

This Quaker belief has roots in the very beginning of the movement, when Friends repudiated the idea that ministers must be scholastically trained. God called those who were to preach, and that was the only qualification necessary or possible. Theoretically, anyone might be called. And since all true ministry must be at the direct instigation of God, through the Holy Spirit, it was presumptuous to state certain people would preach at certain times. Friends recognized that this put them at odds with virtually all other Christians. But they invested considerable energy in defending their position as scriptural. Robert Barclay provided the most succinct statement of the Quaker understanding: "We do believe and affirm, that some are more particularly called to the Work of the Ministry; and therefore are fitted of the Lord for that purpose: whose whole work is to instruct, exhort, admonish, oversee, and watch over their Brethren," he wrote in his *Apology*. But he qualified this in an important way. "That which we oppose, is, the distinction of *Laity* and *Clergy* (which in the Scripture is not to be found) whereby none are admitted unto the work of the *Ministry*, but such as are Educated at *Schools* on purpose."[34]

From this basis, Friends recognized that some people had a particular gift for speaking in meeting, or preaching, and by the early eighteenth century were formally recognizing that gift by making a record of it. The original purpose was a kind of credentialing, to decide who had the right to be admitted to the business meetings of acknowledged ministers. By the mid-eighteenth century, being recorded had become a kind of status in the social structure of the meeting, although it did not automatically confer leadership or power of the kind that ministers or priests in other denominations claimed. But, as has been seen, Quaker ministers, both men and women, often achieved great influence and were at the forefront of all of the major developments in American Quakerism in the eighteenth and nineteenth centuries, from the development of humanitarian movements like abolition (John Woolman) and women's rights (Lucretia Mott) to the separations (Elias Hicks, John Wilbur, Joseph John Gurney) and the revival movement among the Gurneyites after the Civil War.[35]

The Hicksite Separation of the 1820s did not, at first, produce any questioning of the status of ministers. That came only in the 1840s, with the rise of the Congregational or Progressive separatists from the larger Hicksite body. They opposed anything that hinted at special status or privilege, and so they ended the practice of recording ministers. It is difficult to see whether this had any influence on the larger Hicksite body, which continued to record ministers well into the twentieth century and in fact saw a preaching ministry as vital.[36]

Different conceptions of ministry and ministers eventually developed between unprogrammed and pastoral Friends in the twentieth century. Following the lead of London Yearly Meeting, which ended the recording of ministers in 1924, the Hicksite yearly meetings stopped the practice. They perceived it as elitist, distinguishing some Friends above others. The rising level of education and the willingness of more Friends to speak in meeting for worship may also have played a role. In contrast, the Conservative yearly meetings continued to record ministers and to look to them as leaders. Nor surprisingly, ministry there tended to run in the older patterns of most speaking coming from recorded ministers, at least until the mid-twentieth century. That began to change even in Conservative meetings, however, after 1950.[37]

Most Gurneyite Friends were moving in a very different direction, developing the pastoral system. In the eyes of Hicksites, Wilburites, and most Friends in the British Isles, this was the most radical innovation possible, one that was at odds with virtually every conception of ministry as Quakers had understood it. The pastoral system seemed to violate three cardinal principles of Quaker ministry: it limited preaching to one designated person; it embodied an assumption that that preaching would be done at regularly stated times; and it implied a "hireling ministry," preaching for pay. All had been anathema to Friends for two hundred years, and in the minds of many, meant that pastoral Friends had forfeited all claim to the Quaker label. Many unprogrammed Friends still hold these views.[38]

Today, while there is considerable disagreement over the idea of officially recognizing some Friends as ministers and not others, there is also consensus among all persuasions that all Quakers are called to be ministers in some way, that all people have gifts for some kind of ministry. Unprogrammed Friends, often suspicious of hierarchy of any kind, tend to resist conferring any sort of official status in recognition of these gifts, although this determination may be softening. This hesitancy, in their eyes, is a testimony to equality that they are reluctant to relinquish. Pastoral Friends, of course, are committed to recognition of the gift. Within these two broad groups, however, there is significant diversity of opinion about the implications of the idea of the ministry of all believers.

An examination of the regulations of unprogrammed yearly meetings reflects that diversity. Some yearly meetings, such as North Pacific, make no provision for recording ministers at all; significantly, the latest edition of North Pacific's *Faith and Practice* has no entry in its index for "minister" or "ministry." Philadelphia Yearly Meeting does not record ministers as a yearly meeting, but allows monthly meetings to do so. Baltimore Yearly Meeting, which is entirely unprogrammed, retains a provision for recording, carried over from the practice of the smaller FUM body that merged with the larger FGC-affiliated one in the 1960s. Some yearly meetings that are predominantly unprogrammed, namely New England and New York, still retain the provision. The three Conservative yearly meetings—Ohio, North Carolina, and Iowa—also retain provisions for recording.[39]

While Conservative Friends and FGC Friends may disagree on the desirability of formal recognition of gifts in ministry, they are united in their disapproval of Quaker pastors. One of the most vehement critics was Lewis Benson, a recorded minister in New York Yearly Meeting who won considerable influence among Friends after World War II for his scholarship on George Fox and for his prophetic preaching and writing. "George Fox's vision of the church reborn had absolutely no place in it for this kind of leadership," he wrote. "I believe that all dreams of the rebirth of lay Christianity are doomed as long as the layman is regarded as a Christian with a special calling, and as long as it is believed that some Christians are *not* called to be laymen." More liberal Friends see pastoral meetings as indistinguishable from other Protestant churches. For them, a pastoral meeting is one that, by definition, too often precludes the ministry of other Friends.[40]

What, then, does ministry mean for unprogrammed Friends today? For a minority, almost all in Conservative yearly meetings, it means carrying on the traditions of the past. In Ohio, the most conservative, recorded ministers are those with a gift for speaking in meeting, and only that. Other Conservative Friends take a more expansive view. As one wrote: "All Friends are called into a ministry sooner or later, whether public or private, in word or deed or silent prayer, of long duration or short." This Conservative Friend has argued for a revival of the old practice of extensive travel by ministers. He sees this as often beginning with a sense that one is called to do good in some place, even if it is impossible to name that good. Obedience to divine leading will show the way. He rejects the argument of many liberal Friends that recording singles out certain people to the exclusion of others. He says that it is no different from recognizing other gifts, such as the ability to serve as treasurer or as a First Day School teacher.[41]

In FGC and other liberal meetings, visions of ministry tend to be both more expansive and vague. Liberal Friends certainly endorse the ideas that all Friends are called on to be ministers, that all have certain gifts, and that it is the duty of the meeting to help discover and nurture those gifts. They see ministry as going far beyond simply speaking in meeting. An FGC

Fieldguide to Quaker Ministry
(unprogrammed)
by Signe Wilkinson

Common
(Heard Weekly)

EDITORIAL BORED
"The New York Times This Morning reminds us how REALLY Bad things are in..."

WEEK IN REVIEW
"...and after THAT meeting my niece visited and then my friend Isabel called which reminds me how..."

IN CLOSING
"While each of our speakers had a point, they could all be summed up by the Verse..."

Occasional
(Spontaneous Eruptions)

MS. MALAPROP
(OR- YOU GET THE MINISTRY YOU PAY FOR!)
"As Jesus said, 'To be or not To be!'"

ALL QUIET ON THE SPIRITUAL FRONT
"Isn't silence wonderful? Silence IS wonderful. I come for the wonderful silence..."

SHRINK RAP
"As I was saying to my therapist before he went to sleep..."

Random Sightings

DROP-IN
"This meeting means so much to me though I'll never join, contribute or show up on work days..."

OLD CHESTNUT
"Like the tree out front... (the roots) (the branches) (the leaves) remind us that..."

Your Favorite

Clip and send to the Journal

A satiric look at unprogrammed Friends ministry. SIGNE WILKINSON/COURTESY OF *FRIENDS JOURNAL*, APRIL 1997.

committee in 1998, for example, defined a minister as "someone whose deep intention is to move Godward, to listen and obey God and have one's life be changed because of this." Another good example is Ohio Valley Yearly Meeting's definition of ministry: "With the changes that are occurring in society today, a vital human ministry is performed outside Meeting for Worship—in the family, in the Meeting, and in the community—by spiritually motivated Friends. Friends today volunteer their services in work for social betterment of minorities, improvement of living conditions, public health, penal reform, peace, and other meeting and community concerns with a spiritual basis." Therefore, this and some other FGC yearly meetings make provision for recording ministers in certain circumstances; Philadelphia points to Friends providing pastoral care in prisons and hospitals as particularly suitable cases. For other Friends, ministry is a way of life that all Quakers should embrace. This was the point of the view of the late Sandra Cronk, an influential Quaker writer and spiritual leader: "In our world of degrees, exams, and training programs, it is easy to forget that ministry is not primarily a task; it is a way of being in the world," she wrote in 1991. "It is living in relationship with God and being a witness to God. Ministry is being able to listen to the Word of God and thereby have a word of life to share with others. Fundamentally, we do not *do* ministry. We *are* ministers." For many unprogrammed Friends, this is a vision of ministry, and spiritual life, to which all should aspire. Special recognition of those who have attained it seems inappropriate.[42]

Monthly meetings usually have committees on worship and ministry, whose responsibility is not only to ensure the quality of worship but also to help individual Friends develop their ministry gifts. Typical is the charge given by North Pacific Yearly Meeting, that the committee "should seek to deepen the spiritual lives of the individuals in the Meeting and to encourage their varied gifts for ministry and service, whether through vocal ministry, teaching, and counsel, or through aesthetic, social and practical ways of expression."[43]

All unprogrammed Friends recognize that individuals need pastoral care and that meetings must provide it. In the twentieth century, committees have assumed this duty. Philadelphia Yearly Meeting, for example, provides that each monthly meeting will have a committee of overseers. The original function of overseers had been to report violations of the Discipline, but now their job is "to assume leadership in maintaining a caring community, helping all members to find their right roles as nurturers of others." "Pastoral care and counseling" are the committee's special responsibility, although individual Friends should also be "conscious of their duty and privilege of caring for the members of the Meeting." North Pacific Yearly Meeting makes counseling skills a desideratum for the members of its Committee on Oversight, as well as gifts of compassion and discernment. The goal is "a fellowship in which all members find acceptance, loving care and opportunity for service." But even this has an end: "Then all may grow in grace and, liberated from preoccupation with self, be helped to serve humanity creatively."[44]

Ministry, then, for unprogrammed Friends, is something to which all can and should aspire. But, save in the Conservative yearly meetings and with occasional dissent, the drift of liberal Quaker thought seems against recognizing the gifts of some Friends more than those of others.

"To this day some Friends still consider the notion of a Quaker pastor to be an oxymoron," wrote one in Indiana in 1998. "To the rest of us it remains a theological mystery."[45]

The pastor wrote tongue in cheek, but her statement is accurate. Pastoral Friends comprise about two thirds of all American Quakers, and the overwhelming majority of Friends around the world. Most Quakers have made the decision to accept this innovation. Yet they wrestle with how to square it with Quaker tradition and how, if at all, the ministry of a Quaker pastor should differ from that of other Friends or of pastors in other denominations.

When pastoral Friends and yearly meetings describe the characteristics of the ideal pastor, they set several standards. Foremost, of course, is evidence of a divine call to ministry, which will manifest itself in corresponding gifts, talents, and virtues. One naturally is character. Eastern Region states that "the Pastor must give an example of zeal, godliness, transparent honesty, living above reproach, purity and temperance in all things, dignity, gentleness, and self-sacrifice." One Evangelical Friend focused on three roles of the pastor: 1) intercessor, battling against Satan for the congregation; 2) preacher, "effectively proclaiming the Word of God," recognizing that "good preaching comes from countless hours of study and devotion"; and 3) example of Godly love, living a life that testifies to the grace of God. An outgoing personality is often an unwritten requirement. One successful Quaker pastor wrote that she thought that she was "paid just to hang out with people."[46]

Pastoral yearly meetings usually set up educational or training requirements, to be met over a period of years, and provide for careful evaluation before taking the final step of recording. Before 1950, more liberal pastoral Friends tended to prefer graduates of one of the Quaker colleges who had attended Hartford Seminary, which had a significant Quaker presence on its faculty. Evangelical Friends looked to Quaker Bible colleges. Today most prefer college graduates with some kind of seminary training, although many Quaker pastors, especially those employed part time by small meetings or churches, lack this. Contemporary Quaker pastors range from alumni of mainline seminaries like Yale, Union, or Chicago; to graduates of newer Quaker seminaries at Earlham, Houston, and George Fox; to products of assorted Bible colleges; to alumni of influential Evangelical or fundamentalist seminaries like Fuller and Asbury. Although still accepting George Fox's dictum that formal education does not make a minister, most pastoral Friends argue that other duties, such as counseling and financial management, require professional training. Most yearly meetings encourage or require some form of continuing education, often through annual pastoral conferences. A few Friends can still be found, however, who hold that the only qualification necessary for pastoral service is a call from God to serve.[47]

The duties and roles of a Quaker pastor are, in most respects, not different from those required of other Protestant ministers; one yearly meeting superintendent thought that 90 percent were identical. Sacramental duties, except in a few EFI churches, are nonexistent, of course. Considerable energy goes into preparation for the Sunday service. Pastoral congregations usually look to their ministers to officiate at weddings and funerals; these events among pastoral Friends are usually not different from those of other denominations. Pastors provide counseling of various kinds for members. They also act as coordinators for meeting and church activities. Often congregations will encourage them to be active in the community, in activities such as jail ministries or youth or nursing home programs, sometimes purely as a form of service, sometimes as a kind of outreach. Individual congregations call pastors, rather than having them assigned by a higher authority, and each congregation will have a ministry and oversight or equivalent committee to work with the pastor.[48]

How do pastoral Friends reconcile the system that they have developed with the ancient Quaker testimony against "hireling ministry"? Two lines of argument have developed, one dating back to the origins of the pastoral system, the other a product of the second half of the twentieth century.

The older argument posits, with some accuracy, that the objection of the early Friends was to ministers, mainly of the Church of England, who accepted salaries and livings without any sense of call or responsibility for their parishioners. Friends distinguish between such "hirelings" and ministers with a divine call who accept pay in order to carry out that call. This "liberates" them to concentrate their gifts and talents where they will do the most good. Certainly no reasonable person could look at the salaries that the overwhelming majority of Quaker pastors receive and see any sign of a hankering for ill-gotten gain. Compared with salaries in other Protestant denominations, they are low. And few question the sincerity of virtually all Quaker pastors.[49]

In the last fifty years, a second argument has been more prominent. This was probably most forcefully articulated by Elton Trueblood, who argued that Friends had not abolished the clergy but instead abolished the laity. Friends, in contrast to other Christians, had a vision of "equipping ministry." Based on the assumption that all Christians were called to be ministers in some way and had the gifts to do so, it became the role of the pastor to facilitate and help develop those gifts. Trueblood once said, in one of his typical aphorisms, that "the pastor should never do anything that another can grow by doing." For Trueblood, this was conceivably the greatest gift that Friends could make to the larger Christian world: "There is no hope for a Christianity in which we do not expect every Christian to be a minister."[50]

This vision has found considerable support among pastoral Friends in both FUM and EFI. Jack Willcuts, for example, wrote in 1983 that "all of us, of course, are to have all the fruits of the Spirit, but not everyone, including a pastor, will have all the gifts needed in the church." Another saw dangers in the one-person pastoral model: "If the pastor does all the ministry, his weakness will become the weakness of the church. If many people serve, then Christ can use various gifts to give a balanced ministry." Northwest Yearly Meeting's *Faith and Practice* states that the pastor "should in no sense dominate the church but should serve it, helping members through individual encounter and organized endeavor to become more effective in Christian proclamation, fellowship, and service." As one Friend recently told a group surveying American Quakers: "The best Quaker pastors I've known . . . have been quite clear. . . . The title *pastor* doesn't give them any greater status than any other Friends, but they had a particular ministry to help other Friends be empowered to facilitate the spiritual life of their meeting."[51]

Virtually all pastoral Friends agree that most pastoral meetings and churches struggle to meet this standard. "There is an increasing gap between clergy and laity, when those terms should be anathema among evangelical Friends," wrote one in 1989. Too often, they find, members of pastoral meetings are content simply to sit back and observe, lacking any real zeal for ministry. They want to be served, rather than to serve. Relatively few have any real sense of being a minister. Other Friends worry, at least privately, that some pastors, especially those who have built large congregations, are fearful of anything that might diminish their power.[52]

At least two other explanations, absolutely irreconcilable, have been advanced for this situation. One is that Quaker congregations have not been willing to grant pastors the authority that they need to be real leaders, and thus they have been unable to meet the needs of their congregations. "The growing church will have a pastor with a great deal of authority," writes one Quaker pastor. "We must . . . intentionally empower our pastors with the authority to lead and affect the direction and pace of our meetings." Some leaders in EFI have been especially articulate about the need for greater pastoral authority and the duty of congregations to submit to that authority. And at least one Friend has argued that "enabling ministry," as Friends try to practice it, has brought too many compromises. "The minister's primary task is not social worker, psychotherapist, business manager, or morale officer. The minister's task is to faithfully proclaim the truth," he wrote. "A minister surrendering his authority in the name of enabling ministry is a pitiful thing to behold."[53]

Even those who have doubts about this call for greater pastoral authority admit that often Quakers are so ambivalent about the exercise of power by anyone that they make it difficult, if not impossible, for pastors to function effectively. One popular and effective Oregon pastor concluded in 1992 that many Quaker pastors "have been so beaten up by their local Meetings that they are afraid or just too tired to exercise visionary leadership." Another Friend, a counselor, concluded that Friends have a "love-hate dichotomy" between pastors and congregations, that Quakers may simply be too independent to be led. Some believe that entrenched families and leaders fear that effective pastors will displace them; "the priesthood of all believers" thus becomes a weapon to be keep pastors "in their place." Some congregations have been so riven by unresolved conflicts that they are effectively dysfunctional, "the perpetrators of generations of corporate pain. With each new pastor the congregation hopes that he or she will be the 'miracle worker' who will make the pain go away. Instead, it continues to be passed on . . . with the pastor, in many cases, becoming identified with the patient within the system." And, in some cases, Quaker pastors are gentle souls, even good preachers, who simply lack talent for leadership.[54]

Other Friends conclude, however, that the idea of a Quaker pastorate contains so many internal contradictions that it is bound to fail. Even sympathetic Friends worry that in many ways the system has hindered Quakerism's development by limiting leadership to a small group, and that calls for greater pastoral authority may mask arrogance and "a slick but corrupt professionalism." Another argues that "there is no future for pastoral Quakerism along its present course," because it fails to offer a clear alternative to other forms of pastoral religion, and what it offers other denominations do better. Even one New England Quaker pastor argued that the system has given rise to "the very practices [Quakerism] was founded to oppose: lack of participation by all members; slackness in commitment to social reform and revolutionary spirituality, loss of identity as set apart from the unbelieving world, and members driven into entrenched, reactionary conservatism."[55]

Thus worries about the future of pastoral Quaker ministry are easy to find. But pastoral Friends show every sign of continuing commitment to the system. The fastest-growing Quaker congregations in North America are pastoral. Their challenge will be to resolve the problems that they perceive.

Decision Making

If Friends have taken traditional ideas of worship and ministry in radically different directions in the last century, they have shown considerably more unity in holding to old ways of decision making. A Quaker business meeting, what previously would have been called a meeting for discipline, is much the same among pastoral and unprogrammed, Evangelical and liberal Friends, albeit again with some regional variations.

Although Friends generally consider themselves to have a democratic polity, they are clear that they do not vote. Instead, they make decisions by seeking a kind of spiritual consensus or unity. This practice goes back to the earliest days of the Quaker movement. Edward Burrough, one of the most influential first-generation Quaker leaders, described it this way in 1655:

Not in the way of the world, as a worldly assembly of men, by hot contests, by seeking to outspeak and overreach one another in discourse, as if it were controversy between party and party of men, or two sides violently striving for dominion, in the way of carrying on some worldly interests for self-advantage, not deciding affairs by the greater vote, or the number of men, as the world, who have not the wisdom and power of God.

Instead, Friends acted as led by "the wisdom, love and fellowship of God, in gravity, patience, meekness, in unity and concord, . . . and in the holy spirit of truth, . . . in love, coolness, . . . as one only party, . . . to determine of things by a general mutual concord, in assenting truths as one man in the spirit of truth and equity, and by the authority thereof."[56]

Friends of all persuasions still embrace this vision. Eastern Region Evangelical Friends, for example, describe their business practice thus: "Friends believe that business should be conducted as an exercise in corporate worshipful seeking of the Divine Will, which in general will be attested by waiting until the Meeting arrives at a high degree of unity." In principle, this is indistinguishable from the view of North Pacific Yearly Meeting, one of the most liberal of all American Quaker entities: "Friends conduct business together in the faith that there is one divine Spirit which is accessible to all persons; when Friends wait upon, heed and follow the Light of Truth within them, its Spirit will lead to unity." (Of course, Evangelical Friends see the divine will as emphatically Christian, an assumption that not all North Pacific Friends share.) Friends have held to this tradition, even as they have modified or discarded others. One scholar who studied Quaker decision-making processes was probably right when he concluded that one cannot underestimate the legitimizing power "which comes when a group believes that its decision is divinely guaranteed."[57]

Not surprisingly, given their different assumptions about other aspects of their faith, Friends advance different justifications and rationales for their dedication to this business method. Friends of evangelical views often point to scriptural precedents, arguing that it is essentially the practice found among the early Christians in the Book of Acts. They also argue that sometimes the will of God or the mind of Christ can best be "articulated by a few who have a special burden or sense of His will." They point to Friends in the past, such as John Woolman opposing slavery, who originally were in a minority but through persistent ministry brought Friends to see the rightness of their position. Although they usually admire democracy in secular settings, they argue that it is unsuitable to religious affairs; one Friend even has been willing to argue that Friends are closer to a theocracy than a democracy. As Northwest Yearly Meeting says in its *Faith and Practice*, in business, Friends aim "at determining the will of God rather than collecting majority opinions." Evangelical Quaker writer Richard J. Foster provides a convenient summary of this outlook: "The divine Yes or No settles all minority reports." Majorities may not always recognize the will of God and thus are not always right.[58]

As Wilmer Cooper has pointed out, however, many Friends, while agreeing that the end of Quaker business procedure is to find the will of God, argue another benefit: respect for the contributions and consciences of all. The Quaker commitment to seeking unity guarantees that all voices will be heard and respected. One Friend has argued that the method "assumes that God has provided abundantly for us, so that problems can be solved without doing violence to anyone." As a group struggles with a difficult question, with all sincerely trying to know the will of God, "a degree of wisdom comes into the deliberations which no individual could achieve alone."[59]

Friends are generally clear that what they seek is not really consensus or compromise, although their decisions may have elements of both, and they often use "consensus" as a convenient shorthand. Careful Friends shy away from the label, however, feeling that it denotes secular political compromise rather than spiritual discernment of truth. As one wrote: "Consensus is people-made; sense of the meeting is created by God." Many Friends also sense that consensus implies a kind of lowest common denominator, and, as Howard Brinton once noted, Friends strive to elevate, not lower, themselves. They seek what Patricia Loring calls the "deep, interior unity which is a sign the members are consciously gathered together in God and may therefore trust their corporate guidance."[60]

For this method of seeking the will of God to work, considerable self-discipline and group discipline are necessary. Discussions begin in various ways, often with a recommendation from a committee, or perhaps with an individual Friend expressing a concern, what Friends call a "leading." The clerk will then ask what Friends want to do with the matter, inviting all to speak as they are led. John Punshon argues that "one of the best guides to the divine will is to wait patiently until the meeting is enabled to go forward in unity." That may mean wrestling for long periods of time with especially difficult questions. Friends must be willing to listen carefully to one another, both to be sure that they understand one another and so that they do not continually restate points already made. They generally agree that appeals to emotion and prejudice have no place in such a setting; opinions should be "expressed humbly and tentatively," and with "an artless willingness to face the weaknesses in one's position, rather than to paper over with distracting allusions." Quakers tell wonderful stories about this kind of understatement—for example, responding to a recommendation from a nominating committee with the simple sentence: "That is not a name that would have occurred to me." Friends should also recognize that some will bring more knowledge to some subjects than others possess, and thus their statements should have more weight; one might give more attention to the views of a financial planner on investments, for example, or a teacher in the First Day School on religious education. Mutual respect and trust are absolute necessities. And, at times, Friends must be willing to stop, to wait in silence, in the hope that some new wisdom or insight will come among them. If all goes well, they will begin to sense a direction emerging. Friends recognize that direction in varied ways, including, in the words of one who has studied the process, "the general reputation of the leading speakers for each viewpoint, the extent of information and experience each brings to the topic, the apparent conviction beneath a remark, and other intangible factors."[61]

At the heart of this process is the person who presides over the business meeting, the clerk. (Some Friends argue that what the clerk does is emphatically not preside, but maintain order, an important distinction in their eyes.) In the past, clerks were often autocrats, quite capable of pronouncing what they felt to be the will of God in the face of vociferous opposition from the meeting, but those days are almost entirely gone. One experienced clerk argues that a clerk must be able to function at two levels, being sensitive to the group while simultaneously seeking divine guidance. That includes being sensitive to those who do not speak but may manifest their feelings in other ways. The clerk does have power to direct the discussion by asking Friends to focus on specific topics or trying to silence those who are incoherent, abusive, or just long-winded. Some Friends argue that a clerk should never express an opinion or speak at all except to attempt to draw the minute that summarizes and ends the discussion. Others argue that it is acceptable for clerks to ask questions that may clarify and guide a discussion. "Clerking" (only Quakers use it as a verb), requires considerable self-restraint; "the clerk is to be obedient to the considered will of the meeting even when his or her personal judgment may be different." When the clerk senses that unity is near, he or she may propose a minute embracing "the sense of the meeting." Occasionally it may be a "false minute," the rejection of which will confirm that it is not the direction that Friends wish to take. And sometimes a clerk will frame a minute that is somewhat different from any view that has been expressed but incorporates all of them so well that all present unite with it. Some meetings require that all minutes be framed and read back during the meeting, while others entrust final wording to the presiding clerk working with the recording clerk. The presiding clerk will then ask if the meeting approves of the conclusion proposed. Friends present will indicate that assent, sometimes simply by saying "approved" as a group, sometimes in more individual ways, such as "The Friend speaks my mind" or "I like the minute."[62]

Not all responsibility lies on the clerk. Individual Friends can help by suggesting points of agreement or possible directions or even eldering others gently in ways that the clerk cannot. Occasionally a Friend may do great good by suggesting a time has come to pause and wait, or offering vocal prayer. One of the most memorable such occasions for many Friends still living came during the Friends World Conference in Oxford, England in 1952, when it found itself at a particularly difficult impasse. Barrow Cadbury, an elderly English Friend of great presence, stood and prayed simply: "Oh Lord, help us. We're in a fix."[63]

One of the most difficult questions that Friends wrestle with is how much dissent can prevent them from taking action. All agree that a principled objection from a single Friend can be enough to require the meeting to stop and reconsider a proposed action; indeed, many see this as a virtue of the Quaker process. On the other hand, Friends recognize that clerks have the right and the duty to ignore frivolous or pointless objections. Sometimes, Friends who object to a proposed action but are unwilling to stop it because of time constraints or failure to see a moral principle involved will accept that it is done in good order and announce that they are standing aside, not joining in the unity but not blocking the rest of the meeting.[64]

Ultimately, this raises a question that all Friends confront: How does one determine, or "discern" (a favorite word among Quakers) the will of God in a particular situation, individually or corporately? Often meetings are called on to decide matters that began as individual ideas or leadings of Friends. A venerable part of Quaker practice has always been for Friends to submit these leadings to confirmation or modification by the larger group. The tests for individual and group discernment are much the same. Various Friends propose various standards. Many are drawn to those found in a study of early Friends: a true leading will embody moral purity; require patience; be consistent with past leadings of the spirit; and produce unity among Friends. Others pose various tests: Is the proposal consistent with reason and common sense? Is it consistent with Scripture? Does it serve others, rather than puff up self? Does it cross, rather than indulge, our will? Does it bring us closer to Christ?[65]

Friends acknowledge that the process does not always work, that many barriers arise. Howard Brinton concluded that the most common was simply the lack of "the right attitude of heart and mind." An Evangelical Friend reported once coming on a group of Friends conferring on how they would dominate a meeting for business by giving a prearranged series of speeches—all presumably led by the Spirit, of course. Sometimes new members will bring the assumption that in order for there to be unity, everything must be reconsidered and reinvented with their arrival. A prime example was at Pendle Hill, the Quaker study center outside Philadelphia, around 1970, where one student insisted that Quaker procedure meant that if those who were there only temporarily decided to disband the institution, that should be determinative. Attendance at business meetings is often poor; among both programmed and unprogrammed Friends, monthly meetings, the basic business unit, often draw less than 10 percent of their membership. Only controversial issues bring larger groups, and then unity becomes all the more difficult to find because many of those present are not seasoned in the process. Some Friends fear that relatively few members really understand or appreciate the decision-making method. Some see it as valuing endless discussion over action and paralyzing those with bold visions by giving undue weight to small groups of obstructionists.[66]

Still, despite the problems that they see, American Friends are unwilling to give up decision making by seeking unity in the will of God. Only Evangelical Friends have made even cautious provisions for voting as an aid to, not a substitute for, determining the sense of the meeting. Perhaps it is because so many Friends have experienced situations in which the process really did work as it should. Three yearly meetings in Friends United Meeting in the 1990s, for example, found themselves so bitterly divided that some Friends thought that separation might be imminent. In Indiana Yearly Meeting in 1992, the issue was appointment of members of the Earlham College board; in North Carolina in 1995, it was a series of questions relating to homosexuality; in Iowa in 1996, it was whether the yearly meeting should continue to be affiliated with FUM. In all three meetings, through a determination to try to seek the will of God on the part of weighty Friends and a willingness to submit to what seemed to be a divine leading in the clerk's action, division was averted. Friends in many other meetings tell similar stories. Even though they may be uncomfortable with the label, a kind of theocracy, rather than pure democracy, is likely to continue to be characteristic of Quakers for the foreseeable future.[67]

Simplicity

Dramatic change has happened in virtually all persuasions of Friends over the past century, and one of the most visible manifestations of that change has been the near disappearance of what was once one of the most distinctive characteristics of Quakers: a commitment to the plain life. In 1800, one could immediately distinguish a Friend by the way that she dressed or the way that he spoke. To be a Quaker meant being committed to a way of living that Friends described as "plain." Today, only a handful of Conservative Friends still hold to these outward requirements as vital to Quaker faith.

Most Friends insist, however, that they have preserved the spirit that once led them to set themselves off from the world. They point to the testimony of simplicity as one of the distinguishing aspects of Quakerism. The journey from plainness to simplicity was complicated, but some understanding of it is necessary to understand what simplicity means for Quakers today.

The first generation of Friends thought it necessary to set themselves off from the rest of the world for a variety of reasons. For them, "the world" was a corrupt place, and Christians were called to come out and be separate from it. At the heart of Quaker faith, moreover, was obedience to the Inward Light. Anything that distracted from that obedience was to be avoided. The Quaker commitment to equality played a role; Friends were skeptical about many of the practices that visibly distinguished some people from others, such as expensive or luxurious dress or costume, or that puffed up vanity, such as the use of "you" when addressing a single person. Finally, as Friends (and many other sects) understood Scripture, certain practices that the larger society embraced, such as wearing jewelry or elaborate hairstyles (for men and women), were dangerous. Friends saw great value in abstinence from such practices. Not only did they have the virtue of being true to Scripture, but, in many cases, by causing humiliation or a sense of peculiarity, they were a spiritual tonic, crossing the will, always a good thing in the minds of Quakers. The word "plain" is rare in early Quaker writings, and a testimony to "simplicity" is not found. Friends had no collective label for these beliefs and practices save "obedience."[68]

By the early eighteenth century, these broad understandings had begun to manifest themselves in a series of folkways, often not recorded in writing or yearly meeting books of discipline but nevertheless widely shared. The plain speech of "thee" and "thou" and "thy" was one manifestation. Another was dress. Increasingly, Quaker dress was of drab colors. Ruffles and lace and other forms of ornamentation, as well as unnecessary cuffs and collars and lapels and buttons, were forbidden. Other rules gradually developed over the course of the eighteenth century. Tombstones were removed from Quaker graveyards. Music and singing of any kind came under the ban; even to own a musical instrument was to court disownment. Friends looked on reading fiction of any kind with disfavor.[69]

Not all Friends accepted these developments. One of the most outspoken critics was old Margaret Fell Fox. In 1700, well into her eighties, she roused herself to protest. This most important of early Quaker women was quite certain that what she was witnessing was not in the spirit of Christ, as Friends said, "we must look at no colours, nor make anything that is changeable colours as the hills are, nor sell them nor wear them. But we must all be in one dress, and one colour. This is a silly poor Gospel." But hers was a lonely voice.[70]

By the early nineteenth century, Friends had developed new justifications for what they now called the plain life. Perhaps the most important was that it acted as both a light and a hedge. It was a light in that when others saw people in Quaker dress or heard their plain language, they would be reminded of the better way that Quakerism represented. It was a hedge because non-Friends encountering people in Quaker dress or using Quaker language would probably not be inclined to suggest sinful amusements or vain pastimes. The plain dress was a kind of outward armor against temptation.[71]

By the last years of the nineteenth century, the old, plain ways were losing their hold on most Friends. In the Gurneyite yearly meetings, revivalists directly attacked them as suggesting salvation by works. Hicksites, for the most part, were also gradually discarding them. Not surprisingly, Conservative Friends held to them longest, especially in their schools. As late as 1912 Olney, the boarding school under the control of Ohio Yearly Meeting (Conservative), was cautioning students against imitating the vain customs of the world in bidding each other "good morning" and "good night" and receiving packages at Christmas; music was banned there as late as the 1940s. But even Conservative Friends were fighting a losing battle. By the twentieth century, Friends in plain dress were few and usually elderly, and the plain language was largely confined to the Quaker family, when it survived at all.[72]

Friends, however, did not see themselves as setting aside the heart of the tradition that the plain life represented. Instead, they argued that they were adapting it to contemporary needs. Now they spoke in terms of sim-

Friends in plain dress. Ashley and Lydia Johnson, Monrovia,
Ind., about 1860. FRIENDS COLLECTION, EARLHAM COLLEGE.

plicity, which they saw as allowing themselves to live more fully in the
world, yet not be of it. Outside observers agreed that this had become one
of the great Quaker lessons for the rest of the world.[73]

Most Friends reject older understandings of plainness. A mark of how
far they have moved is the statement of North Carolina Yearly Meeting
(Conservative) in 1983: "Simplicity does not mean drabness or narrowness
but is essentially positive, being the capacity for selectivity in one who
holds attention on the goal." Many argue that simplicity is an inward state,
so focused and dependent on God that it has no tolerance for anything that
detracts from that focus and dependence. That leads, as one Friend concluded, to "an inner security that lessens . . . dependence on money and
reduces fears about future dangers and uncertainties."[74]

Friends see this inner state as manifested by certain ways of living that
set them apart from their neighbors. One writer in *Friends Journal* in 1994

saw it in "the creation of a sustainable life, a sustainable economy, a sustainable society, . . . vulnerability, openness, peace, equality, connectedness, love." Daniel Seeger, an influential Friend, views plainness as "respect for limits, skepticism about unending material progress, and a realization that everything has its price." Evangelical Friends tend to think in more traditional terms. Northwest Yearly Meeting, for example, asks its members: "Are you free from the burden of unnecessary possessions? Do you avoid waste? Do you refuse to let the prevailing culture and media dictate your needs and values?" Richard Foster argues that "the Lamb's People are to provide a genuine alternative to the prevailing lifestyle. Modern culture is sick. To be well-adjusted in a sick society is to be sick. A new lifestyle is needed."[75]

The manifestation of that alternative lifestyle, however, can reflect other theological and doctrinal divisions among Friends. A few, some in Conservative yearly meetings, some attending other unprogrammed meetings, feel called to wear plain dress and use the plain language. (Actually, old-style Quaker plain dress can no longer be found, so these Friends usually supply themselves from Amish stores.) They argue that this has several advantages: plain clothing simplifies choices; provides a witness to the world; and also impresses the wearer with the importance of being an example to the world. Plain language, they argue, is more affectionate and distinctive. But other Friends assert that these are, in Rufus Jones's words, "easy, short-cut methods." As one argues: "The conspicuous simplicity of plain clothes in the twentieth century draws more attention to the wearer and thus perverts the original intention of modesty."[76]

One point of agreement among Friends is that simplicity involves time management, being careful not to overcommit oneself, to avoid assuming so many responsibilities that there is no time for family or individual spiritual life. One Friend finds it ironic that Quakers constantly complain of busy lives: "True simplicity in its most basic form is putting God's will first in our lives, and letting the specifics fall into place around this ideal." Such simplicity brings healing of both mind and spirit, concludes Elizabeth Watson, long one of the most respected Friends in FGC.[77]

The relationship in the minds of Friends between wealth and simplicity is particularly complex. A good example is a story told by Sara Little, the wife of Arthur Little, for many years a professor at Earlham College and a convinced Friend who first encountered Quakers as a conscientious objector during World War II. After the war, the Littles went to visit Philadelphia. After a day of paying calls on affluent Quaker families in Main

The excesses of Quaker simplicity. SIGNE WILKINSON/COURTESY OF *Friends Journal*, Jan. 1/15, 1982.

Line suburbs, Sara finally told her husband, "Arthur, this is all very nice, but I doubt that you will ever earn enough for us to live this *simply*."[78]

Certainly, for three centuries now Quakers have had the reputation of generally being economically well-off. For some Quaker families, being indifferent to wealth while at the same possessing it was a mark of a life lived in the Light. "Money was as taboo a subject of discussion as sex in our family," remembers one Friend who grew up before World War II in Moorestown, New Jersey. "If any people I knew had a dream of acquiring riches and living a life of luxury, they sure didn't talk about it." But Friends did acquire wealth, often great wealth, as Philadelphia Quaker families like the Pembertons and Whartons and Strawbridges testified. Their mansions might not compare with the Gold Coast splendors of the Vanderbilts or the Astors, but they were mansions nonetheless. "Of the best sort, but plain," was their motto.[79]

Friends generally agree that materialism is the opposite of simplicity and is utterly incompatible with it. Materialism hinders spiritual development, puts ourselves before God, separates the rich from the poor, and disrupts human communities. Thus it is to be avoided. Philadelphia Yearly Meeting, for example, in 1970, echoing John Woolman, called for all Friends to examine whether in "their possessions, practices, and relationships" there were "seeds of exploitation and oppression."[80]

How does one separate oneself from a material world? Unprogrammed Friends have tended to be more imaginative, perhaps because, as will be seen, they are generally more critical of other values of the larger American society. Simplicity means reducing their possessions, giving up stressful jobs and careers for less demanding ones, and eschewing things that many Americans consider necessities but really are not, such as cable television. One Quaker family made it a rule that simplicity meant that each family member would receive only one gift on his or her birthday. For some Friends, a simple lifestyle means returning to the land—building one's own house, raising one's own food, and giving up things, even telephones and indoor plumbing. Some Friends have shown an interest in living in intentional communities or leaving cities for small towns, convinced that a simple lifestyle is easier there. There is general agreement, however, that simplicity does not necessarily mean poverty. As Patricia Loring notes, struggling to procure basic necessities of life hardly simplifies one's existence, while "a modest sufficiency is more apt than poverty to free the individual's time, energy, and attention."[81]

In the 1990s Friends had object lessons in the ravages that materialism and the consumerism of the larger society could bring. They had always made a close connection between simplicity and integrity. In the early days, Quaker merchants would not even haggle or bargain with customers, because selling the same goods for different prices suggested a compromise with honesty. The plain life's restraint of the pursuit of material goods also restrained temptations to cut ethical or legal corners. Friends consistently valued integrity as one of their distinguishing traits; many today make it a central testimony. By the late twentieth century, however, many, especially in the pastoral yearly meetings, were clearly caught up in larger currents in evangelical Christian circles that identified financial success with godliness. Certainly many Friends have prospered legitimately, but a few have brought disgrace to themselves and problems to other Friends with their unbridled pursuit of wealth. One example was Phil Harmon, a Seattle Evangelical Friend who built a company, Friends Insurance Trust, providing insurance and financial services to Quaker pastors and organizations. He acquired considerable wealth for himself in the process. In 1996 it was revealed that Harmon's company was a fraud; he had embezzled its assets to finance a luxurious lifestyle that included multimillion-dollar homes and a yacht. Individual Friends and yearly meetings were left to pay bills for which Harmon was supposedly responsible.[82]

An intensely debated question for some Friends is the relationship between technology and simplicity. Some Friends have definite Luddite tendencies; in fact, in 1996, what was billed as the "Second Luddite Conference" was held in the Stillwater Meetinghouse in Barnesville, Ohio with a number of Friends present. Some Friends agree with Howard Brinton that "most machines are just as Satanic as ever and continue . . . to be a diabolic substitute for life through their pollution of the world we live in." One argued that simplicity means eschewing all but the simplest forms of technology. Thus wooden plows are acceptable, but flush toilets are "obscene luxuries for one who aspires to responsible global citizenship." A recent novel by a Quaker author, David Morse's *The Iron Bridge*, involves a time traveler returning to eighteenth-century England to try to "correct" the course of the Industrial Revolution, a transformation in which Friends had a leading role. Computers come in for considerable criticism in some Quaker circles, as do automobiles. Other Friends disagree, arguing that "to Quakers, simplicity does not mean turning the clock back on progress or rejecting the benefits of modern science and conveniences of modern technology." Technology in itself is compatible with simplicity and can even advance it, if we use the time saved well.[83]

Closely related to simplicity, indeed a manifestation of it in the minds of many Friends, is a concern for the environment. This tends to be more prominent among unprogrammed Friends, some of whom have developed an interest in "deep ecology." They argue that simpler lifestyles, especially those that use less technology, will be good for the earth and are another benefit of simple living. Thus a number of unprogrammed yearly meetings have committees or working groups to forward environmental concerns, and an international Quaker group supported mainly by unprogrammed Friends, Friends Committee on Unity with Nature, has attracted considerable support. As one Friend wrote in 1990, "If the world, then, is a manifestation of God, then it and every creature in it must be treated with kindness." A simple lifestyle would do that. But programmed Friends show similar concerns. Several yearly meetings, such as Indiana, North Carolina, and Wilmington, include in their queries environmental matters, emphasizing stewardship of natural resources as a matter of simple living. Eastern Region says that "God in the beginning gave people dominion over the earth and expected them to be wise stewards. Wasteful and destructive use of the earth's resources is contrary to God's purposes."[84]

Other Friends advance other measures. A commitment to simplicity is connected in many Quaker minds with a commitment to using words that convey exactly what they mean, nothing more and nothing less. Again, Friends link simplicity and integrity. Richard J. Foster, for example, argues that a consistent Friend would not say, "I am starved," when he or she simply meant that he or she was hungry. Another insists that Friends should never introduce or recognize each other by secular titles or occupations; all should simply be brothers and sisters. Quaker enterprises face constant questions about whether they are too luxurious, copying too much the fashions of the world rather than holding to Quaker simplicity. And those who organize Quaker conferences and gatherings find themselves under constant pressures to balance finding facilities that can handle large groups, provide vegetarian and vegan menus, and accommodate people with disabilities against objections that such hotels and conference centers do not meet Quaker standards of moderation.[85]

All persuasions of Friends generally agree that Quakers today are not meeting the standards of simplicity that they profess. "In the affluent culture of American society, we have almost completely forgotten simplicity in our manner of living," complained one Evangelical Friends pastor. "Simplicity has become something we talk about for an hour while our [cars with] velour, air-conditioned interiors wait patiently outside," wrote another pastor. Thomas S. Brown, a leading Philadelphia Friend, agreed in 1982. "Friends have floated upward with the rest of middle-class America in their assumptions about the level of things (including status and security) we simply cannot do without." Another unprogrammed Friend worried that too often those who attend unprogrammed meetings "talk about simple living, but very often it turns out to be Volvo simple living."[86]

Failure to live up to the ideals that Friends set for themselves has never been reason to discard the ideals. American Quakers show no inclination to lessen their commitment to simplicity as a goal, even if they do not attain it.

Education

Quakers are no different from the overwhelming majority of other Americans in placing a high value on education, and they value it for most of the same reasons, ranging from the acquisition of vocational skills to the development of morality and ethics. The history of Quaker education is complex, however, and American Friends today are divided in their views of what it should embrace in the same ways that they are divided over questions of worship, ministry, and simplicity.

The first generation of Friends showed considerable ambivalence about education. Given their hostility to the scholastic training of the clergy, it is not surprising that they had little use for universities. They feared anything suggesting that a secular education was the equivalent of being "scholars in the school of Christ." But Quakers were not necessarily anti-intellectual. Since Friends came disproportionately from the middle class, involved in trade and business, basic literacy and numeracy were necessities. Even George Fox, who was vocal in his scorn of educated clerics, in 1668 urged Friends to establish schools to instruct both boys and girls "in whatever things were civil and useful in creation."[87]

In America, the founding of schools generally went hand in hand with the establishment of meetings. William Penn, for example, urged that learning be "liberal" but consist of "useful knowledge, such as is consistent with Truth and Godliness." Quaker schools did teach Latin and Greek, which were useful both for understanding the Bible and "for the management of Foreign Transactions and Correspondence." But they also tended to emphasize mathematics and the natural sciences more than their non-Quaker counterparts.[88]

By the late eighteenth century, Quaker education served a sectarian function: strengthening the separate identity of Friends by providing a "guarded education" for Quaker children, protecting them from influences that might draw them away from the Light. After the American Revolution, New England, Philadelphia, and New York yearly meetings established boarding schools for this purpose. Other Quaker schools under private management served the same end. All shared certain characteristics, perhaps most striking, an unbending insistence on observing and inculcating the peculiarities of Friends. In many cases, the goal was to be "select," open only to Quakers. The Hicksite Separation probably encouraged this tendency, as both sides saw the necessity to educate the rising generation to understand "true" Quakerism and to resist the other side. Some Friends were skeptical of these enterprises. They perceived them as serving mainly well-to-do Friends and as sources of "pride and Idleness and the nursery of that spirit that made such devastation among the flock and family of God in the primitive Church, and of latter times has got into the society of friends like a wolf in sheep clothing."[89]

Before the 1830s, there was little Quaker interest in higher education. While other denominations established colleges in the early nineteenth century, Quakers stood aloof. The reason was clear: colleges served largely to educate the clergy, and Friends saw that as striking at the roots of their faith. But in the 1830s, this began to change, reflecting in part the changing nature of American higher education, which became increasingly secularized, preparing students for careers as attorneys or teachers rather than as ministers. By the 1850s, at least a few Friends were enrolling in non-Quaker colleges, ranging from Harvard, Amherst, and Bowdoin in the east to Oberlin and Antioch in the Ohio Valley. Still concerned with providing a "guarded" education, Friends responded, after considerable debate, by establishing their own institutions. The Haverford School near Philadelphia, a Gurneyite stronghold, established a collegiate department in 1856, and in 1859 Indiana Yearly Meeting (Orthodox) renamed its boarding school near Richmond Earlham College. Discussions among Hicksite Friends began in 1860 that would culminate in the opening of Swarthmore College near Philadelphia in 1869.[90]

The years between 1870 and 1900 saw an explosion of Quaker schools. As the number of Friends in the east declined, Quaker schools adjusted by admitting non-Quaker students, whose parents were attracted by the schools' moral atmosphere and general reputation. In the Midwest, Friends responded to a growing interest in secondary education by establishing a series of academies. These often acquired reputations as being among the best schools in their states and received public funds to educate non-Quaker children, thus doubling as public high schools. Conservative Friends showed the same interest, albeit placing considerably more emphasis on preserving Quaker peculiarities. Gurneyite Friends also embarked on a campaign of founding colleges, establishing six between 1870 and 1900 that were associated with yearly meetings. The development of the pastoral system among them gave these colleges a new function in the eyes of many of their supporters: training ministers and religious workers. Out of a sense that Quaker colleges were not meeting this need, yet another form of education developed in the 1890s: the Quaker Bible college, as represented by Walter and Emma Malone's Friends Bible Institute in Cleveland.[91]

The twentieth century saw increasing diversity in Quaker education, reflecting the growing differences, regional and doctrinal, among American Friends. Quaker elementary and secondary schools had virtually disappeared west of the Appalachians by 1940, continuing only in a few strongholds of Wilburism. FGC and pastoral Friends there had acculturated to a degree that they were now comfortable with public education. The Quaker colleges survived, still drawing large numbers of Quaker students but increasingly depending on non-Quakers for support. The three Quaker colleges in the Philadelphia area, Haverford, Swarthmore, and Bryn Mawr, became elite national institutions even as the proportion of Quaker students and faculty declined. Colleges like Guilford, Earlham, William Penn, Whittier, and Pacific (renamed George Fox in 1947) endured battles over the teaching of the Bible and evolution similar to those that racked the Gurneyite yearly meetings. In most cases, liberals prevailed. Increasingly, the most evangelical Friends looked to the Cleveland Bible College or similar Quaker institutions, like those in Westfield, Indiana or Haviland, Kansas, for their leadership.[92]

In the east, however, Quaker day and boarding schools survived, reflecting a greater sense of Quaker distinctiveness and the greater popularity of private schools in the region. After World War II, Quaker education experienced something of a renaissance. Quaker elementary and secondary schools drew a number of convinced Friends as teachers, in many cases conscientious objectors and their wives, and were supported by meetings with new members of like minds. They saw Quaker schools as laboratories for experimentation and progressive education, combined with a strong spiritual element.[93]

Today, distinctively Quaker elementary and secondary education is almost entirely associated with unprogrammed Friends and is still largely found on the eastern seaboard, although a few pastoral meetings have schools affiliated with them and a growing number of unprogrammed meetings in other parts of the country have shown an interest. About 27,000 students are enrolled, the overwhelming majority not Quakers. (A recent survey found a range of from 1 percent to 20 percent Friends in Quaker schools.) Nor are most of their teachers Quakers. Some Quaker schools are elite institutions whose graduates compete with graduates of Philips Exeter or St. Paul's for admission to the nation's leading colleges and universities. The Sidwell Friends School in Washington, D.C. found itself the center of considerable attention when Chelsea Clinton enrolled there in 1993.[94]

What makes a school Quaker, if most of the students and teachers are not Friends? Over sixty years ago, Rufus Jones concluded that the difference between Quaker schools and other schools lay not in subjects or pedagogy but in their "atmosphere of sincerity," in the "subtle aura which pervades" them. Quaker schools focused on truth and spiritual influence. Most Quakers today agree. Without question, the most influential formulation of Quaker education of the past two generations has been that of Howard Brinton, who taught at Guilford, Haverford, and Earlham colleges and was for many years, with his wife Anna, the director of Pendle Hill, the Quaker study center near Philadelphia. He argued that four testimonies were common to almost every Quaker school: community, harmony (a manifestation of the Quaker commitment to peace and justice), equality, and simplicity. Paul Lacey concludes that most Quaker schools still see these principles as foundational.[95]

Those who have studied Quaker education see two experiences as expressing these principles and creating a distinctive ethos. One is the declaration, by most liberal and unprogrammed Friends, of the idea of "That of God in Everyone" as the foundation of Quakerism. As will be seen later, the centrality of this idea for Quakers is contested. But it informs much of what Quaker schools do. Studies have found that it usually translates into a sense that all people are good and that the role of education is to nurture that good, rather than to change or transform the student. The other distinctive experience is the meeting for worship, still part of the week at every Quaker school. Two alumni of Germantown Friends School, for example, remembered it as "our school's greatest classroom." Another Quaker studying Friends schools found that the meeting for worship was a place in which "all voices [were] equally valuable," that it served to "center the hive of activity that consumes active learning environments. This basis of harmony and equality builds community, where the foundations of a Friends school are laid."[96]

Quaker educators see Quaker education manifesting Quaker values in numerous ways. Lacey argues that a Quaker school shows "respect for each individual's uniqueness, creativity, and originality, appreciation of cultural and religious diversity, trust in others, openness to a wide range of sources for enlightenment, and an emphasis on cooperative and collaborative learning." Douglas Heath, who wrote extensively on Quaker education, discerned nine characteristics of a good Quaker school. It is talkative, open, expressive, giving, accepting, feeling for others, imaginative, fun, and deeply ethical. It is often characterized by innovative teaching methods, especially those that cut across disciplines and make teachers and students equal partners in collaborative learning. Some teachers want Quaker education to offer a radical alternative that will eschew any kind of practice that hints at competition, such as class ranks or grades. "We grade meat, not students," was the comment of one Quaker teacher; another scorned such practices as "authoritarian and demagogic." Discipline often aims at reformation through reflection rather than penalties. Naturally, the school will show a deep social consciousness, aiming to prepare students to solve social and political problems. At Pacific Oaks, a California Quaker school, for example, part of its mission is "education for world peace." Most Quaker schools emphasize a vision of wholeness, giving attention to both intellectual and spiritual formation. But they generally resist prescriptive outlooks. As one student of Quaker education has written: "The Quaker Way is not so much a system of beliefs as it is a framework for asking the right questions."[97]

Given their high aspirations, it is not surprising that often the students and teachers at Quaker schools, as well as observers, see failures. One researcher found that often Quaker schools so emphasized individualism and obedience to the Inner Light that they lost a sense of community. Students complained: "They say this is a Quaker community, but they have a disciplinary committee and all kinds of organizations to keep people in line. . . . I thought Quakers weren't supposed to impose their values on other people." Too often, Lacey argues, they focus on changing the community to meet individual needs rather than transforming individuals. Religion is a problem. Often meetings for worship become debating societies or places to vent resentments against school policies. Non-Quaker students, and even Quaker students, especially in the upper grades, resist anything that suggests religious teaching, often supported by parents who see it as a waste of time that might better go into "competitive academic training." The insistence of some Friends that Quaker schools should accept all students, regardless of ability, and avoid anything that might even slightly lower self-esteem seems to others to lead to a lowering of standards and a "dumbing down" of the curriculum. Others worry about anything suggesting elitism; one Friend even argued that to focus on college preparation was un-Quakerly. On the other hand, since, as Lacey notes, "many Quakers value education highly but are not eager to pay a lot for it," the need to attract students forces schools to emphasize academic preparation. There is a constant shortage of Quaker teachers. And Quaker schools share in the conflicts over questions like multiculturalism and Eurocentrism that are issues in other institutions.[98]

Most observers see the future of Quaker schools as uncertain. Financial pressures are constant, and the stagnant number of Friends in the regions where most are located is another source of apprehension. One observer noted that with 45 Quaker schools in the Philadelphia area requiring that a majority of board members be Friends, it was becoming increasingly difficult to find them. But given the tradition of the schools themselves, the desire of many Quakers for distinctive education, and the generally high academic reputation of Friends schools, it is likely that most will survive, while constantly challenged to retain their Quaker identity.[99]

As noted above, most Quaker students are not in Quaker schools. Among the pastoral majority, almost all children attend public schools, and pastoral Friends who are teachers are mostly in the public schools. Some EFI Friends have been drawn into the Christian school movement, which integrates evangelical faith with every aspect of education. Yorba Linda Friends in California, for example, have established a Christian school. But most evangelical Friends appear unwilling to give up on public education. Other Friends have been drawn to home schooling. They often come from opposite ends of the Quaker spectrum—intensely evangelical, if not fundamentalist Friends, unwilling to expose their children to what they see as the moral compromises of public education; and unprogrammed Friends who denounce "the inappropriate pressures and attacks on self-esteem" they see in the public schools. For both, the chance to meld faith and learning is important. Evangelical Friends can imbue their teaching with Christian beliefs, while unprogrammed Friends children will have, as one of them put it, a "time to listen to my inner voice."[100]

Generalization about Quaker higher education is almost impossible. Twelve colleges in the United States identify themselves as Quaker-affiliated in some way through their membership in the Friends Association for Higher Education: Haverford, Swarthmore, and Bryn Mawr in the Philadelphia area; Guilford in North Carolina; Malone and Wilmington in Ohio; Earlham in Indiana; William Penn in Iowa; Friends and Barclay in Kansas; George Fox in Oregon; and Whittier in California. The first three are among the most prestigious liberal arts colleges in the United States, while Guilford, Earlham, George Fox, and Whittier generally fare well in national rankings and surveys. A 1996 survey showed that the average percentage of Quaker students was about 6 percent, while Quakers usually made up between 15 percent and 20 percent of the faculties.[101]

Each college has taken on a somewhat different identity. Friends University has relatively few resident students and functions as a community college for Wichita. William Penn has developed a flourishing adult education program. Malone has increasingly emphasized an evangelical Christian identity, downplaying its Quaker roots as distractingly sectarian. Quaker identity is probably strongest at Guilford, Earlham, and George Fox, with the first two increasingly appealing to unprogrammed Friends and George Fox having a more evangelical vision. Only Earlham, Malone, Wilmington, George Fox, and William Penn are still formally affiliated with a yearly meeting.[102]

The schools differ dramatically on what it means to be a Quaker college, but all emphasize service. Barclay College, which until 1990 was Friends Bible College, points to the large number of alumni who serve as Friends pastors. Earlham and George Fox have seminaries to train Quaker pastors and other Quaker leaders. Guilford has inaugurated a highly successful Quaker leadership program for undergraduates. Wilmington has a center for John Woolman studies. Several have programs in peace studies and conflict resolution, which they see as peculiarly appropriate for Quaker schools. All have codes of student or community conduct that draw on the Quaker origins of the school. One such expression is Swarthmore's:

> Although it has been nonsectarian since 1908, and although Friends now compose a small minority of the student body, the College still values highly many of the principles of that Society. . . . As a way of life, Quakerism emphasizes hard work, simple living, and a generous giving as well as personal integrity, social justice, and the peaceful settlement of disputes. The College does not seek to impose on its students this Quaker view of life or any other specific set of convictions about the nature of things and the duties of human beings.

Earlham's "Community Principles and Practices" is phrased in Quaker testimonies and queries, focused on traditional Quaker principles like simplicity and nonviolence. Most, although not all, of these schools use the Quaker business method in their decision-making processes. Most point to non-Quaker students who become Friends as a result of their attendance.[103]

Faculty in Quaker colleges, and Quakers teaching in other institutions, vigorously debate whether there is such a thing as a distinctive Quaker pedagogy. Former U.S. Commissioner of Education Ernest Boyer, for example, saw Quaker higher education as a matter more of "climate" than content. Richard Felix of Friends University agreed in 1983: "I believe Quaker values are caught, not taught." On the other hand, some Friends believe that a Quaker professor will have a distinctive teaching style that might be based on "awakening the Inner Teacher" or "radical nonviolence" or be devoted to forwarding the causes of peace and justice.[104]

One of the continuing themes of the history of American higher education has been tension between church colleges and their sponsoring denominations. Quaker colleges have been no exception. They find themselves the center of constant worries that they are losing their Quaker or Christian identities and making too many compromises to attract students or appear more prestigious. The schools affiliated with Evangelical Friends in some way—Malone, George Fox, Friends, and Barclay—have probably had the fewest tensions, largely because of sensitivity to the concerns of the yearly meetings. Malone, for example, decided to permit dancing on campus in 2000 only after Eastern Region Friends changed their *Faith and Practice* to allow it. These schools emphasize their evangelical Christian identity. The president of Barclay presented it as a place where "rather than having a scoffer or an infidel as a professor and counselor, the student has the possibility of sharing his times of crisis with godly men and women," and where students would meet and marry fellow Christians. These colleges require faculty to subscribe to faith statements and generally consider an evangelical faith more important than Quaker ties.[105]

Other Quaker colleges have experienced tensions with their constituent bodies of Friends. William Penn has faced accusations from Iowa Yearly Meeting that its teaching of the Bible was insufficiently evangelical, that too few faculty were Quakers, and that student lifestyles were inconsistent with the yearly meeting's expectations. Earlham has been the center of tension with Indiana and Western yearly meetings for most of the twentieth century. In the last two decades, many of the problems have focused on the support of most of the college's faculty and students for gay and lesbian rights. But even unprogrammed Friends sometimes express unease with the direction of institutions like Haverford, Swarthmore, and Bryn Mawr. In 2000, Swarthmore historian J. William Frost pointed out that none of them had Quakers in their philosophy departments or Quaker theologians in their religion departments. No longer were their faculty central to Friends General Conference.[106]

For most of these colleges, then, maintaining a Quaker identity is a struggle. Quaker students of college age are relatively few, and Quaker faculty, while relatively more common, are often not available in the fields or at the times needed. Still, the leaders of the Quaker colleges agree that they need a critical mass of Quaker students and teachers. They have to maintain a balance, weighing a sectarian tradition and identity against the need to appeal to a larger constituency. Lee Nash of George Fox College could speak for virtually all when he wrote in 1984 of the "multiple pressures to go mainstream—to play down Quaker traditions so a maximum number of non-Friends will send in their checks and their children, to avoid the embarrassment of being perceived as sectarian or eccentric, to refrain from any words or ways that would disturb the comfort zone of the 700 Club or a Moral Majority rally." If one adds to the last sentence the comfort zones of the American Civil Liberties Union and the National Organization for Women, one has an even stronger sense of the competing pressures that Quaker colleges face. Some, like Whittier and Malone and Swarthmore, have quietly made the decision that the future lies in downplaying that traditional tie but not discarding it entirely. Others, like Guilford and Earlham, see their survival as dependent on preserving and strengthening their Quaker identity.[107]

Beyond the collegiate level, in the last generation Friends, especially pastoral Friends, have put considerable energy and resources into graduate education in religion. Quakers came slowly to seminary training. Until the late nineteenth century, of course, Quakers of all persuasions viewed the idea of formal training for ministry as anathema. With the rise of the pastoral system, they looked either to the Quaker colleges or to Bible colleges to supply the need. Incipient Quaker pastors of holiness or fundamentalist outlooks attended schools like Cleveland, Haviland, or Westfield, while those more liberal went to places such as the University of Chicago, Union, or Hartford, which became a special favorite after 1910 because of the Quaker faculty there. It was not until 1960 that the first graduate Quaker seminary, the Earlham School of Religion, opened, amid considerable skepticism from both ends of the Quaker spectrum. Friends of hard evangelical or fundamentalist outlooks were convinced that nothing good could come out of Earlham (and many are still of that opinion), while some unprogrammed Friends viewed anything that strengthened the pastoral system as a dubious enterprise. Although ESR was originally established to focus on pastoral education, today its students study in a variety of fields; many are FGC Friends preparing for careers with Quaker agencies or with unprogrammed meetings. Meanwhile, Evangelical Friends have established their own institutions, first in Houston and at Azusa Pacific University in California and then with George Fox's merger with Western Evangelical Seminary in 1996.[108]

What makes this struggle ultimately worthwhile for these colleges and

Quaker schools generally is a sense that they produce special students. One faculty member at Earlham found that often it was the non-Quakers who were most committed to the Quaker values and testimonies of the school and to challenging Friends to uphold them. Howard Brinton wrote how he had found in the Quaker colleges with which he had been associated "a subtle, indefinable quality, a kind of community life centered in the higher values, independent of classroom courses, yet not wholly unrelated to them." A 1974 study of Quaker school alumni found that they turned out "proportionately more productive adults than other, intellectually comparable schools. . . . It seems probable that a specific Quaker influence is at work."[109]

The other form of education to which Quakers have a common commitment is what other Christians refer to as "Sunday school," distinctively religious education. Once the function of monthly meeting schools, it is now one of the most important responsibilities of meetings and churches.

Here again the lines of demarcation between programmed and unprogrammed meeetings are clear. Gurneyite Friends began copying the Sunday schools of non-Quaker evangelicals as early as the 1830s, originally referring to them as "First Day Schools for Scriptural Instruction" and intending them for children. Their focus was the Bible, and often non-Quaker instructional literature was used. With the revival of the 1870s, they became virtually indistinguishable from non-Quaker Sunday schools, and programmed Friends quickly took up that label. Adult Sunday schools also developed in the twentieth century. Today what is usually referred to as "Christian Education" is seen as one of the most important functions of programmed meetings and churches and embraces programs ranging from vacation Bible schools to retreats to camps. Many larger meetings have staff for just this purpose. The focus is still distinctively Christian, although FUM strives valiantly to try to educate Friends about the distinctive bases of their faith as well. Like members of other denominations, programmed Friends struggle with declining attendance and look for ways to draw more adults.[110]

Unprogrammed Friends, in contrast, were slower to take up First Day Schools. Wilburites regarded them with considerable skepticism, and they did not become common among Hicksites until the 1860s. Today, unprogrammed Friends generally still have First Day Schools and see them as vital, but they are intended for children. The pattern in most unprogrammed meetings is for children to attend the first fifteen minutes or so of worship, then leave for their own First Day School programs. Religious education for adults is a concern of FGC, which, like FUM, has developed curricula for that purpose. It takes place sometimes in meetings for discussion before worship, sometimes on weekday evenings.[111]

Commonalities

The diversity of American Friends is striking. While they agree on certain foundations of their faith, such as worship in the Spirit and the ministry of all believers, unprogrammed and programmed Friends have taken these ideas in radically different directions. And even the distinction between unprogrammed and pastoral meetings is not always helpful. An unprogrammed meeting for worship under Ohio Yearly Meeting would probably be very different from one in Lake Erie. And individual pastoral meetings and churches often have very different personalities.

More commonality can be found in Quaker commitments to doing business through seeking spiritual unity and to simplicity. Friends of all persuasions still generally try to adhere to the traditional Quaker method of not voting or submitting to the decisions of a leader but instead seeking unity through discussion, prayer, and waiting. Similarly, nearly all Friends have made the transition from a plainness that once set them off from the rest of the world to a commitment to simplicity, a simplicity that they, to be sure, often understand differently.

Finally, the Quaker commitment to education once again takes Friends in different directions. Quaker elementary and secondary schools are almost entirely affiliated with unprogrammed meetings. Quaker colleges, in contrast, are tied mostly to Friends in the pastoral tradition. All of these institutions wrestle with common problems, particularly the question of what it means to be a Quaker school and maintain a Friendly ethos when most students and faculty are not Friends.

Given the diverse understandings of their common heritage, it is not surprising that Friends face challenges at the beginning of the twenty-first century. Those will be the focus of chapter 5.

CHAPTER FIVE

Contemporary Quaker Debates

Relations among Quakers often suggest a tempting comparison to the theater: the script does not change, only the actors. Certainly anyone who knows Quaker history, looking at the debates taking place among American Friends, will find many that are familiar. Some of them, such as the place of Christ in Quakerism, the sources of authority for Friends, or leadership, or unity, continue century-old discussions. Other disputes, such as those over sexuality, are relatively new. These debates, moreover, do not simply separate pastoral from unprogrammed Friends or pit Friends United Meeting (FUM) against Friends General Conference (FGC). Very often they are internal, with opinions that cross formal Quaker boundaries. Moreover, difference is not always debilitating or paralyzing. Many Friends see disagreement and difference as signs of healthy diversity.

Seven debated issues stand out today. One is the centrality of Christ in Quaker faith—whether Quakerism is indeed "primitive Christianity revived," or restricting Quakerism to Christian boundaries is unnecessarily narrow. Closely related is the nature of authority, both in the sense of where Friends find ultimate legitimation for their faith and in the sense of the relationship of local Friends meetings to their yearly meetings, to broader Quaker organizations, and to each other. A third issue, perhaps the most explosive of the past two decades, is sexuality, particularly gay and lesbian issues, which has bitterly divided some yearly meetings and led many to perceive a widening chasm between programmed and unprogrammed Friends. A fourth is stagnant membership. Many yearly meetings have seen steady declines over the twentieth century, and, overall, the number of American Friends today is probably fewer than what it was a hundred years ago in a country whose population has tripled. A fifth issue is leadership. Most Friends say that they desire it, but others are convinced that the Quaker persuasion is inherently antipathetic to leadership. Friends of all kinds claim to look to the Spirit for guidance, but that raises the question of unity. How do they find it in increasingly diverse Quaker bodies? Finally comes the question of identity. What does it mean to be a Quaker today, when Friends are so different from the founding generations and are in conflict on so many questions?

Such debates are not unique to Friends. Leadership is a constant concern for most churches, ranging from the shortage of priests and nuns that the Roman Catholic Church faces to empty pulpits in many rural Protestant churches. Most denominations have found themselves debating questions of sexuality in the last thirty years. Older understandings of the place and nature of Christ and the authority of the Bible have been challenged. Decline in numbers has been the experience of the "mainline" Protestant denominations for a generation now. And the results in other denominations have often been fractiousness and even division.[1]

Is Quakerism Christian?

This question would not have occurred to any Friend before 1900. To be sure, from the seventeenth to the nineteenth centuries Friends often faced charges that because of their views on worship, ministry, the sacraments, and the Bible, they could not be considered Christians. Such attacks became less common as Friends became less aggressive after 1689, but as late as 1833 a Presbyterian minister published a ponderous tome entitled *Quakerism Not Christianity*.[2]

In the separations that began in the 1820s, Friends themselves charged that their opponents were not Christians, but the response was always denial. Whatever their disagreements, Friends of all persuasions probably would have agreed with Joseph John Gurney when he wrote: "Were I required to define Quakerism, I should not describe it as the system so elaborately wrought out by a Barclay, or as the doctrines or maxims of a Penn, or as the deep and refined views of a Pennington. . . . I should call it the religion of the New Testament of Our Lord and Saviour Jesus Christ, without diminution, without addition and without compromise." Certainly today most outsiders still think of Quakers as Christians. As John Punshon said in 1985, "The Christianity of the Society of Friends passes everywhere unquestioned except by its own members."[3]

Virtually all pastoral Friends, and many unprogrammed Friends, continue to see Quakerism as a branch of the larger Christian church, and their official documents always include such a statement. But some of the unprogrammed yearly meetings no longer make such explicit declarations. And others, if in some way they still declare themselves Christian, have no inclination to force that identity on all members. This raises two questions: For Friends who identify themselves as Christians, what does that mean in their lives? And, given the historically Christian character of Quakerism, how have some Friends concluded that it is not necessarily Christian?[4]

Evangelical Friends, in both Evangelical Friends International and Friends United Meeting, and some in the unprogrammed yearly meetings as well, have a simple answer to the first question. They embrace the statement of Northwest Yearly Meeting:

> We believe that the word of God spoken into every heart was supremely manifest in Jesus Christ, who in His virgin birth and sinless life was true God and perfect man. Christ is the Word. He is the Light that exposes our sin and brings us into the righteousness of God. He is the Redeemer through whose atoning death and resurrection we receive the forgiveness of God.

For them, salvation is possible only through Jesus Christ. He came to earth to redeem humans, to save them from the eternal damnation that all human beings, through their sinful natures, deserve at the hands of a just God. But God, being merciful, provided a way of salvation through Jesus. His sufferings on the cross paid the penalty for the sins of all human beings. When humans accept that sacrifice, they are redeemed, born again, saved. This message, often referred to as the "Plan of Salvation," is at the heart of evangelical Quakerism, just as it is at the heart of all types of evangelical preaching and teaching.[5]

Other Friends, usually categorized as liberal, claim for themselves the label "Christian" as well, but take issue with parts of the above system. They argue that it overstates the sinful nature of human beings; humans do have sinful tendencies, but since they were created in the image of God and have within them the Light of God, it is not proper to see them as utterly depraved. These Friends accept Jesus as redeeming mankind, but they emphasize the model of His life and teachings rather than His death. Some reject the idea that divine justice required the sacrifice of the Son of God. They argue that Jesus' death on the cross was the ultimate act of love, a way of showing humans how God suffers for the evil humans do. Rufus Jones summed up this point of view very well. "The Word of God took on our human nature, and lived among us, and loved, and suffered, that we might see how human life can be raised to a divine level by a higher Spirit and how the most perfect love and consecration can be revealed through simple acts of humility and daily service." The emphasis instead is on leading a Christlike life.[6]

For liberal Friends, the way to do this is through obedience to the Inward Christ, the Light, or "That of God in Everyone." "I am with you, always," Jesus told His disciples, and liberal Christian Friends find that presence in the Light. "The genius of Quaker Christianity lies in its dual focus on the person of Jesus Christ as disclosed in Scripture and the experience of the Light as His continuing presence among us," writes one. They argue that there is ample grounding for the doctrine in the Bible. And to be sure, many Evangelical Friends accept these assertions. They see the idea of the Inward Light as scriptural and agree that Jesus is present with believers. But they shy away from emphasizing this because they associate it with other aspects of liberal Quakerism that they fear: its failures, in Evangelical Friends' eyes, to take seriously enough sin, the authority of Scripture, and the necessity for evangelism.[7]

As is the case with other matters, however, what is inconceivable for some Friends is quite acceptable to others. For a number of unprogrammed Friends, perhaps a minority but certainly an articulate one, Quakerism is not necessarily Christian. They acknowledge its Christian roots and heritage, but they deny that Quakers must be Christians. These Friends usually define themselves as universalists, because they see all faiths as containing elements of truth, and all as potentially valid.

These Friends usually begin by pointing to a famous admonition of George Fox, one often heard among liberal Friends as well, that Quakers should "walk cheerfully over the world, answering that of God in every one." One Friend calls this "the closest Quakers get to a creed." A writer in *Friends Journal* summed up this point of view well: "Quakers believe that there is that of God in every person. . . . We believe that each person has, within themselves, an innate goodness. It is difficult for me to describe Quakerism except in these terms. In fact, I cannot think of much else on which Friends would be in almost total agreement." Universalist Friends usually make "that of God" indistinguishable from the Inner Light or the Holy Spirit. While acknowledging that some people show more of that spirit than others, they do not see it as limited to Christians. Mohandas Gandhi, for example, has a place in the universalist Quaker catalog of saints next to Lucretia Mott, John Woolman, and Martin Luther King Jr.[8]

On this basis, universalist Friends argue that, as one said, "If there could be that of God in everyone, there could be that of God in every religious expression." Thus it is entirely proper to "respect the validity for others of their religious path." As another Friend wrote in 1989: "When you filter the Light through different cultures you have a human prism where the Light is broken into colors and expressed in different ways. But behind all the colors you still have the same light." For her, a consistent Quaker accepts that "it is up to each individual to discover what God is." And some Friends are entirely comfortable with multiple identities, for God and for Quakers. A member of New York Yearly Meeting, where universalism is strong, notes that its membership includes not only Christians but also "Jews, Buddhists, Sufis, New Age proponents, agnostics, atheists." Such Friends are comfortable with messages in worship that quote from the Hindu *Bhagavad Gita* or the Muslim Qur'an. This vision of religion makes missionary activity or attempts to convert others from their faiths superfluous, since truth is found in all religions. And universalist Friends glory in the diversity that such a vision produces. As a Philadelphia Friend put it, "Quakerism can be a beautiful multi-colored shawl. . . . The disparate threads contained are, in the cloth of a religious society, ready to revolutionize the world and bring the Kingdom of Heaven into its full reality on earth."[9]

While they acknowledge that the founders of Quakerism saw it as a form of Christianity, some universalists assert that that reflects merely "the naively literalist vocabulary of the age in which Fox emerged and therefore is the terminology in which he had to speak." By this standard, "the Society of Friends is Christian by accident." From that point, many Quaker universalists offer a critique that questions virtually all traditional Christian doctrines. One of the most radical expressions was that of a writer in *Friends Journal* in 1988. The New Testament, she wrote, was "no more accurate historically than Greek mythology. It is not at all certain that Jesus ever lived, and if so, the Gospel's account is highly questionable." She argued that it was time to "let go of [the] Jesus myth." Other universalist Friends characterize central Christian doctrines, such as the Virgin Birth, the Atonement, and the Resurrection of Christ, as myths "suitable only to an earlier

Ambiguity and certainty among unprogrammed Friends. SIGNE WILKINSON/COURTESY OF *Friends Journal*, July 1989.

age." For still others, Jesus simply holds little meaning. As one Friend wrote in 1980: "I am interested in Jesus as an historical figure who was the starting point of an immensely significant movement, but there are other people and other ideas that better speak to my condition."[10]

That "immensely significant movement" is the heart of the problem for other non-Christian Friends. They identify Christianity with oppression and evil. "The patriarchal Judeo-Christian tradition subjugated women, contributed to the imperialistic destruction of indigenous cultures, and fostered violence down to the present day," wrote one such critic. As another put it, "the expression 'Jesus Christ' carried so much theological baggage that it often became a wall between me and those I wanted to reach out to." For some universalist Friends, Christ is "the symbol of exclusion and domination. Christ is used to demarcate clear boundaries of an inside and outside group. . . . This either/or thinking delimits a superior and inferior, and endorses the right of the superior to dominate the inferior." Christianity is the source of pogroms, racism, sexism, slavery, colonialism, homophobia, oppression of the poor, and degradation of the environment. These Quakers ask, "How . . . can others claim to be Quaker and live a spiritual life devoted to such a Christ of constriction and oppression?" Thus some universalist Friends react with hostility to the use of explicitly Christian language.[11]

These Friends represent an extreme even among Quaker universalists. Others take a more moderate position, seeing the essence of Quakerism *and* Christianity in a way of life rather than a set of beliefs. "Fact is, some Quakers help define and 'practice' Christianity by rejecting the use of the Christian name and its baggage. . . . To fuss over the baggage is to fail to follow the Christ," said a New York Friend. Universalists sometimes claim that they are rescuing the real Jesus from the corruptions of centuries. North Pacific Yearly Meeting, where universalism is strong, states that it is healthy to have both "emphasis on the Gospel of Jesus Christ" and "a universal perspective emphasizing the Divine Light enlightening everyone." It concludes that "an excessive reliance on one or the other . . . neglecting the essential connectedness between the two, has been needlessly divisive." And many Quaker universalists condemn explicitly anti-Christian prejudice as being as narrow-minded and deadly as any other form of prejudice.[12]

Even so, Christian Friends feel beleaguered and isolated in some unprogrammed meetings. As one wrote in 1987: "Those of us who have experienced the Christ often feel we are in a vacuum among humanist Friends, some of whom are unconcerned about the Christ experience and some of whom are antichrist." A Philadelphia Friend worried openly in *Friends Journal* that he was being forced out "for adhering to the same beliefs held by George Fox, William Penn, and Mary Dyer." In some cases, Christ-centered Friends form support groups, meet privately for worship, or even leave to form their own worship groups. Ohio Yearly Meeting, which is both unprogrammed and unquestionably Christian, now sponsors such groups within some of the FGC yearly meetings. Other Friends, however, perceive that the anti-Christian rhetoric is diminishing and that universalists are becoming more open to explicitly Christian ideas and language.[13]

Certainly universalist Friends often find their own assumptions and readings of Quaker history challenged. Chuck Fager, himself universalist in sympathy, writes that too often Quaker universalism is "a highly contemporary mishmash of Joseph Campbell, Carl Jung and some New Age or feminist spirituality visionaries." A scholar studying Philadelphia Yearly Meeting was struck by "the number of universalist Friends who revealed little appreciation of recent developments in biblical research. . . . To such Friends, all Christocentrics tend to be lumped together as benighted fundamentalists." Universalist interpretations of Quaker history often come under sharp attack. A good example is the idea of "That of God in Every-one." Coming from universalists, it is a statement about the basic goodness of all human beings and faiths. But other Quakers argue that while it is not clear exactly what Fox meant when he used the phrase, it *is* clear that he was not making a statement about human nature or the innate goodness of human beings. And few Quaker historians accept the argument that early Friends used Christian language simply because they were prisoners of their culture. Its meaning was far deeper and more fundamental for them.[14]

Given the starkness of these differences, is any middle way possible? For many Christian Friends, the place of Christ in Quakerism is beyond discussion. "There is only one issue really dividing Friends," asserted Jack Willcuts. "It is the acceptance or rejection of the lordship of Christ. . . . All our various testimonies, concerns, differences, organizational, or cultural diversities could be bridged. But the faithful, obedient proclamation and service in the power and righteousness of Christ who leads His Church is nonnegotiable Truth." A Conservative Friend who served as an FGC official agreed: "Failure to name Jesus Christ as our Lord and the source of our spiritual (and worldly) gifts keeps us from naming the gifts we have been given. If we as a faith community acknowledge the gifts, we may have to acknowledge the Giver."[15]

Many Christian Friends acknowledge that elements of Quaker universalism have firm grounding in Quaker tradition. They agree that a just God would not condemn those who had never had the opportunity to learn about Christ or hear the gospel preached. Even as staunch an Evangelical Friend as Everett A. Cattell argued that only those who deliberately rejected Christ would not achieve salvation. Others argue that certain cultural barriers are just as powerful. For example, Francis B. Hall, who was active for many years in Friends United Meeting, asserted that observing the role of professed Christians in the Holocaust, or segregation, or apartheid, might lead people who were firm in the Light nevertheless to reject Christianity. "If there are Quakers who cannot believe that Jesus is the Christ and yet who show that they have faith in the Divine Light, have experienced, and have followed it as fully as they can in their lives, who is to say that they are not truly Quakers?" he asked. Just as Robert Barclay in the 1670s asserted that in "pagan" lands some were Christians without knowing it, so others might be today, even if they are unable to profess Christianity. John Punshon writes that Satan might well lead misguided Christians to engage in religious persecution as a way to repel others from Christianity. Yet there are limits to this view. Ultimately, Christian Friends insist that whatever good is found in all people is the Light of Christ. Such a position is unacceptably narrow to many universalist Friends. And Christian Friends like Punshon conclude that if the Light is Christ, then the Light would never lead anyone to reject Christ. For them, salvation always, even if sometimes unconsciously, comes through Christ.[16]

Douglas Gwyn has written that "there seems to be a nagging untidiness, an insistent open-endedness to the Quaker testimony to Christ as the light of the world." The different meanings that Friends, often citing the same works of early Quakers, find for Christ is ample evidence of the truth of this observation. And given the disagreements over the Christian nature of Quakerism, it is not surprising to find equally strong disagreements over the nature of leadership among Friends.[17]

Leadership

"Using 'Quaker' and 'leadership' together is an oxymoron," commented one Friend. The judgment may be overly pessimistic, but many Friends argue that it only slightly exaggerates a real problem. While they are convinced that American Quakerism faces a leadership crisis, that perception is entangled with the profound ambivalence of many Friends, pastoral and unprogrammed, about anything that suggests an unequal distribution of power in their meetings and churches..[18]

Leadership is an issue for Friends. For many, it is a given that some will have that gift and that Friends should nurture and encourage it. Early Quakers, writes Paul Lacey, "did not . . . treat gifts in leadership as dangers to be checked or restrained. Instead, they confirmed people in their skills; they encouraged them to develop; as new people came into the community of faith, they were encouraged and educated into appropriate use of their gifts." Now many Friends believe that leadership is lacking. For the past thirty years or so, leadership in Quaker organizations, schools, yearly meetings, meetings and churches, and other institutions has been supplied largely by the generation that came of age in the 1940s and 1950s. Now these Friends are in their seventies and eighties, and many fear that not enough Friends are ready to take their places. This fear is expressed in the worries over finding Quaker teachers for Friends schools, in the declining proportion of Quaker staff in Quaker activist and humanitarian organizations, in the constant laments of yearly meeting superintendents about the shortage of qualified pastors.[19]

Friends generally agree that there is a distinctive Quaker leadership style. A Quaker leader is one who leads a group to unity in the Spirit. A 1979 conference concluded that Quaker leadership "consists first and foremost in being led. This conception involves a curious but profound paradox. True leaders are not in any important sense initiators; rather they are chiefly responders to the Divine Will. . . . The only authentic leadership is divine followership."[20]

A vision that Friends have found especially compelling over the past three decades is "servant leadership." The concept is the work of Robert K. Greenleaf, a Friend who was for many years an executive with AT&T and became widely known as a teacher and management consultant. In Greenleaf's vision, real leaders are those whose foremost priority is to serve others, to improve their lives. Friends have seen in this vision an attractive series of paradoxes: "the leader shall be led, the greatest shall serve, . . . the teacher shall learn from the student." Thus, "service, not dominance (the pagan way of power) is the true motif for leadership." In the words of another Friend, Quaker leaders are people who "can help us see the reality of God's grace and who can help us to act on the extraordinary possibilities of making life better that open up for those who trust in God's providence." But as Lacey points out, that means accepting that "the servant-leader must *lead*, which means to set goals and directions, to channel energy, to persuade and organize: to wield power, in short." Servant leadership is not necessarily incompatible with Spirit-led models, of course. Many Friends would argue that all leadership that is of the Spirit will be in service to others.[21]

Douglas Steere once told the story of a Friend who became an Episcopalian because he wanted "to belong to a church where the bishops were *visible*." This points to a reality in virtually all Quaker entities. Power is sometimes held and exercised by those who do not use it to lead, but stand in the way of those who want to do so. The dynamics are different in certain respects in programmed and unprogrammed meetings, but similar in others, and the results are the same.[22]

Unprogrammed meetings tend to include many Friends who are skeptical of anyone exercising power; "the Quaker DNA precludes any docile submission to self-proclaimed authority" was the comment of one Friend. This may reflect the mindset of convinced Friends who have been drawn by Quaker emphasis on individual religious experience. As one Friend put it, "we are reluctant to promote leadership because we rely in great measure on our individual consciences to act as the priests for our spiritual community." Many have a "Sixties" distrust of authority and see the essence of Quakerism in individual obedience to "the Spirit." Some bring memories of autocratic pastors in former denominations. Paul Lacey argues that Friends have even developed a kind of "antileader," "one who despises all compromise, who blocks any group action until he gets his way, who makes the leading of his conscience the final arbiter for the rightness of the group's action." Many see the results as debilitating. "Quakers want leadership, but they don't want leaders. They want things to be managed, they want people to take responsibility, but they are frankly allergic to people exercising authority," was the conclusion of one worried Friend. Lacey is even more blunt: "An invitation to serve a Quaker school as head or clerk, to serve a Quaker college as president, or to serve a Quaker board as executive director or secretary seems increasingly like an invitation to waste one's substance and break one's heart in dedication to illusory Quaker ideas of participation and responsibility for decision-making."[23]

One hears many of the same worries among pastoral Friends. "We are speaking to a profound crisis of authority among Friends, which results in an incapacity to find or support leadership," wrote Jack Willcuts. "We cannot find enough effective leaders to meet our needs. Strong people are exhausted and broken by the demands of serving us. Vigorous, far-sighted people give up; so unseasoned, powerless ones try to carry on." Naturally, much of the concern among pastoral Friends focuses on a chronic shortage of pastors. Some believe low salaries and limited opportunities discourage even the most dedicated. Others worry that on the local level, pastors who want to exercise leadership run afoul of petty sensibilities and entrenched families, especially in smaller meetings and churches. But the result is the same as in unprogrammed meetings. "There is nothing that some Quakers want less than excellent leadership," wrote one pastor. "I could easily name a dozen highly gifted and dedicated leaders whom I have seen shattered by the mindless opposition they have faced."[24]

Pastoral Friends tend to be more articulate about ways to face this perceived problem, perhaps because pastoral leadership is more central to the lives of their communities than other forms of leadership are in unprogrammed meetings. Their solutions, however, are often at odds. Some focus on education and discernment, helping Quaker young people find gifts and callings. Others argue that especially in pastoral positions, Friends have placed too much emphasis on formal education and should become more "experiential." Some see the solution in becoming more open to men and women who want to make mid-life career changes. One Friends church in

Ohio, for example, now has as its pastor the town's long-time fire chief. Some argue that growth in small meetings will displace the entrenched powers that cause problems. And some, especially Friends in EFI, see the answer as more submission on the part of Friends. Eastern Region Evangelical Friends, for example, identify their superintendent as "in a position of authority," and enjoin their members by quoting Hebrews 13:17: "obey them that have the rule over you and submit yourselves." One Evangelical Friend argued that Christian humility should make Friends "willing to accept the recommendations of leaders—the pastors, the elders, the clerks, the outreach committees, the Sunday school superintendents. These are God's special persons, called to serve Him and the church." Many who hold these views call for more authority for those in such positions.[25]

It is inaccurate to conclude that *every* Quaker entity experiences these problems. Many Quaker organizations, ranging from schools to humanitarian groups to pastoral churches, have resolved these questions and are functioning effectively. They do so by matching talents with tasks and identifying "weighty" Friends with the gift to discern the appropriate course in certain situations. Often, Friends see their success not in embracing any one model of leadership but simply in being open to the Spirit, which for them is the ultimate authority. But exceptions are numerous enough to be the cause of worry for many.[26]

Authority

When the largely Quaker city of Richmond, Indiana was founded early in the nineteenth century, one of its first settlers was a Friend named Robert Morrisson. He prospered, eventually becoming the president of the town's first bank. A Hicksite, he resolutely refused to discuss theology. When asked a question about Quaker doctrine, he always replied, "Thee talk with Dr. Plummer. I think just like he does."[27]

An aversion to doctrinal discussion, however, does not remove the necessity in any religious organization for some understanding of authority. Given the diversity of American Friends today, it is not surprising that they have different views of religious authority. Such differences are theological, however. In polity, almost all Friends have moved away from centralized authority toward greater congregational autonomy.

One common starting point is agreement that Friends do not have formal creeds, statements of beliefs that all must accept. "I cherish the freedom to seek truth wherever it may lead me," was the statement of Elizabeth Watson, a well-known Quaker author and speaker. One FGC publication argues that creeds are inappropriate because they are static; they do not adjust to changing reality. Elton Trueblood condemned them because by their nature they are easy to repeat and become lifeless forms rather than statements of living faith.[28]

On the other hand, as one writer in *Friends Journal* noted in 1985, "avoidance of creeds is not the same as avoidance of any shared convictions." Even if one believes in the widest possible acceptance and the broadest possible tolerance of individual opinion, for a group to survive there must be some standard to indicate what is acceptable to the entire body, or at least a shared understanding that such standards are less important than other questions. Friends embody these shared understandings in volumes that in early days were called *Advices* or the *Discipline,* and which are now almost universally referred to as *Faith and Practice.* They often contain provisions that date back to the beginnings of Quakerism, but all yearly meetings have made substantial changes over the years. Doing so usually involves a committee that attempts to solicit broad comment and often draws on the work of other yearly meetings. Sometimes, when yearly meetings try to reach unity on controversial issues, the process can take years; it occasionally may move Friends to withdraw if they believe some fundamental truth is being weakened or discarded. Others, however, argue that the patience and forebearance needed in such discernment are healthy.[29]

For many Protestant denominations, the starting point for any declaration of belief is simple: the Bible. For Friends, it is not that simple. As chapter 2 showed, one of the charges that opponents hurled at the early Friends was that Quakers did not value the Bible. Friends always denied this, but they challenged the doctrines of most of their contemporaries. They argued, for example, that the Bible was not the "Word of God"; Christ was. Similarly, because of their belief in direct revelation, they asserted that the Spirit that had inspired the writers of the Bible still moved human beings, and so the written record of prior revelations should not be set above continuing revelation. Robert Barclay provided the classic Quaker statement of the authority of Scripture. The Bible was not primary authority; the Spirit that gave it was. But the Spirit would be consistent, and so Friends should condemn any "pretended revelation" that was at odds with the Bible. This remained the position of virtually all Friends until the nineteenth century. Of course, adherence to this position did not preclude debates over proper interpretation.[30]

Today, the strongest support for biblical authority comes from the pastoral yearly meetings. Typical is Northwest Yearly Meeting's pronouncement that the holy scriptures were "given by inspiration of God. They are the divinely authorized record of the doctrines that we as Christians are bound to accept, and of the moral principles that are to regulate our lives and actions." Many Friends of fundamentalist sympathies go further and give them the label that early Friends denied them, "the Word of God." Some even say that Barclay was wrong in making them subordinate to the Spirit. "We need to *believe* that the Bible is God's inspired word," wrote one pastor. "It is the blueprint for every program and the textbook for every member and group." Another Friend wrote that he joined an Evangelical Friends Church "because the Bible was foremost. 'Look in the Bible and see what God says,' the preacher told me."[31]

Other pastoral Friends, in both FUM and EFI, and many Conservative Friends hold a different position that they argue is consistent with early Quakerism. They give the Bible a place of honor, but allow critical study and give final authority to the Holy Spirit. Typical is the California Friend who wrote that "the Bible is a resource, but not the source itself. Christ is the Source, and He uses the Bible as a tool." Even as committed an Evangelical Friend as Everett Cattell wrote that it was wrong to exalt the Bible over the Holy Spirit. George Fox University Professor Carole Spencer notes that many Evangelical Friends now admit that "the biblical writers were fallible human beings writing within their social-cultural context" and thus had "misconceptions about some things, such as the nature of the universe, acceptance of patriarchy, and the institution of slavery." John Punshon argues that Friends must distinguish between inerrancy of Scripture, which sees every word of the Bible as literally inspired and unquestionable, and infallibility, which sees the Bible as an absolutely trustworthy guide to moral questions. The former is fundamentalist, he argues, the latter Quaker. Punshon, urging that revelation still continues, does not rule out someday adding other books to the canon of the Bible, or books other than the Bible also being inspired by God. In short, these Friends, whether they call themselves evangelical or liberal or moderate, want to honor both the past revelation found in the Bible and the revelation that continues.[32]

Among unprogrammed Friends, especially universalists, attitudes toward the Bible are diverse. "I don't know why anyone reads it anymore" is one extreme. Some see it as hopelessly outdated. Still others stress what they see as its limits. As one put it: "The Bible, because transmitted by fallible, essentially limited human beings, cannot contain all Divine truth

EVANGELICAL FRIENDS CHURCH - EASTERN REGION

Application For Membership

I, _____ , hereby make application for membership in
the_____ Friends Church of _____

Membership Information

1. Do you believe in the Triune God: God the Father, Jesus Christ the one true Saviour, and the Holy Spirit?
   _____

2. Do you know by personal experience, based on the Word of God and the assurance from the Holy Spirit,
   that you are a Christian?_____

3. Will you endeavor to seek further spiritual growth? _____

4. Are you willing to attend faithfully the services of your church and will you seek to bear witness at every
   opportunity to your Christian experience?_____

5. Are you willing to give cheerfully of your finances to support this church and its approved program as God
   prospers you? _____

6. Have you acquainted yourself with the book of Discipline and will you earnestly endeavor to practice its
   precepts? _____

Membership Covenant

To become a member of the Church of Jesus Christ and a church of the Eastern Region involves a covenant relationship. The following is a covenant you make upon becoming a member of the Evangelical Friends Church,
Eastern Region:

I,_____ covenant with the _____ Friends
Church to bear testimony to a real conversion experience, based on the Word of God and assurance from the Holy
Spirit of sins forgiven and commitment to Christian discipleship. I further covenant to acquaint myself more
fully with the Book of Discipline and to support the doctrinal position of the church and to seek personal conform-
ity to the testimonies of the church. I will continuously seek spiritual growth, according to the Scriptures, attend
faithfully the services of the church, accept responsibility in its work, and cheerfully give for the financial support
of the church and its approved programs.

Signed_____

Report of Administrative Council:

After having met with the applicant, we unite in presenting the name of

_____for Membership in our church.

Signed_____ , Chairman

_____ , Secretary

CHURCH COVENANT

Your name has been presented and accepted for Membership into our Church. The following is a covenant this
local body of believers, the _____
Friends Church makes with you.

We welcome you into our fellowship and wish to convey to you our covenant to you as long as you remain a part
of this local Friends Church. We covenant with you to provide an opportunity for, and assistance in worship,
and in spiritual growth. We further covenant to help you in discovering your talents and gifts and give you an
opportunity to express these in service. We covenant to counsel you if you in any way stray from being true
to your opportunities and will faithfully strive to bring you back to a commitment to Jesus Christ and to our local
meeting.

Signed_____ , Elder

Date_____   _____ , Pastor

The application for membership in Evangelical Friends Church, Eastern Region, shows their
emphasis on evangelical belief and commitment. COURTESY OF EVANGELICAL FRIENDS CHURCH,
EASTERN REGION.

nor adequate direction for faith and morality." Some universalist Friends are refugees from fundamentalist groups. They "remember Bible study as forums for authoritarian sermonizing that discouraged questions. For these people, time spent in Bible study is remembered as being not only fruitless for their spiritual lives, but also as violating the integrity of their own search for truth."[33]

Universalist or liberal Friends who completely dismiss the Bible, however, are relatively few. Elizabeth Watson, a confirmed universalist whose aversion to creeds was quoted above, also has written of her delight in Bible study and has made characters from the scriptures the center of many of her writings and speeches. A number of observers note growing interest in Bible study among Quaker universalists. North Pacific Yearly Meeting, for example, includes in its *Faith and Practice* quotations from George Fox and Margaret Fell on the Bible and admonishes potential members to keep in mind "the significant place of . . . the Bible in the spiritual life of many Friends." Similarly, Philadelphia Yearly Meeting has stated that because of "the Bible's importance in shaping the ways Friends have expressed their experience of the presence and leading of God and its power to illumine our worship and our vocal ministry, we are encouraged to know it well." But such exhortations have limits. Generally, liberal Friends agree that they believe the Bible is truth because they find truth in it, rather than things being truth because they are found in the Bible.[34]

If the Bible is not final authority, then where do Friends, whether evangelical or liberal or universalist, find it? For many universalists, authority, which implies finality, is unimportant. Accepting postmodernism, so popular in academic circles, which denies the existence of any universal or absolute truth, they see uncertainty as an inevitable part of life. The process of seeking is what matters. And in that search they trust "That of God in Everyone" to guide them.[35]

But for other Friends, that is not enough. They value seeking, but they must find as well. Friends must make decisions. They find the answer ultimately not in the letter of Scripture but in the sense of the gathered meeting. As a New York Friend who was often skeptical about some manifestations of Quaker universalism wrote in 1994: "It is the church community, not the individual or unchangeable interpretations of Biblical laws, that determines our boundaries." Their faith is in the Quaker meeting, whether gathered for worship or for business. Friends are confident, as shown in chapter 4, that if they are faithful, the Holy Spirit will come among them and help them discern God's will. What higher authority could they seek?[36]

This emphasis on the gathered meeting illustrates another element of the Quaker debate over authority. As noted earlier, the Quaker structure that emerged in the 1660s was essentially presbyterian, with monthly meetings subordinate to quarterly meetings and quarterly meetings in turn subordinate to the yearly meeting. Yearly meetings in the Orthodox tradition continue this structure. Their regulations usually contain some statement on subordination. Typical is Indiana Yearly Meeting's that "subordination . . . does not describe a hierarchy but rather a means, under divine leadership, of common protection between Indiana Yearly Meeting and its Quarterly Meetings and Monthly Meetings." Northwest Yearly Meeting describes Quaker polity as "connectional." Congregations are not autonomous, nor are they subject to unlimited higher authority. Nevertheless, local meetings must acknowledge the power of the yearly meeting, which, as a last resort, has the power to intervene in their affairs, or even to dissolve them.[37]

The occasions in the last few decades when yearly meetings have intervened have been few and have involved clear violations of yearly meeting rules. In the late 1970s, Indiana Yearly Meeting offered a meeting in Michigan the choice of being laid down or voluntarily removing itself from the yearly meeting when it refused to appoint women to its Ministry and Oversight Committee. It withdrew. Western Yearly Meeting in 1982 laid down Hinkle Creek Monthly Meeting when a pastor from a non-Quaker background began offering physical sacraments in worship and expelling opponents from committees. In 1989, Iowa Yearly Meeting intervened in West Branch Monthly Meeting's call of its pastor when she "came out" as a lesbian. But these cases attracted attention largely because they were unusual.[38]

On the other hand, many observers have concluded that pastoral Friends are moving toward congregational autonomy, within a few broad limits. One EFI superintendent perceived this as early as 1982, when he wrote of a "rising tide of independence—the autonomy of our member meetings that seems to discount or discredit the yearly meeting." Many Friends, with no interest in religious affairs beyond their own congregations, see yearly meetings as at best irrelevant, at worst as sources of constant irritation and demands for money. And while yearly meetings set standards for membership, in some that has also become largely a matter of congregational autonomy. Some local meetings simply accept anyone who applies for membership without asking for any kind of profession of faith in Christ. Others set standards that go far beyond anything demanded by the yearly meeting. One monthly meeting in Indiana, for example, requires all members to eschew dancing and membership in Masonic lodges, even though the yearly meeting dropped such requirements decades ago.[39]

One looks in vain for much discussion of such issues among unprogrammed Friends, save those in Ohio Yearly Meeting (Conservative). Their position was well stated by a writer in *Friends Journal* in 1986: "Any discussion of corporate testimonies among Friends needs to acknowledge the primacy and autonomy of the individual monthly meeting." That writer thought it "absurd" that Friends should have to convince the wider body of Quakers to accept new views before the local meeting could act on them. This position is a kind of orthodoxy in the yearly meetings affiliated with FGC and other independent meetings. Some unprogrammed Friends increasingly identify not with their local meetings or their yearly meetings but with groups of like-minded Friends with particular identities or interests, often tied together by e-mail communication. Nowhere are the fruits of these tendencies more evident than in the profoundly diverse Quaker understandings of sexual ethics and morality.[40]

Sexuality

For the first three hundred years of the Society of Friends, sexuality was not an issue. Whatever their doctrinal disagreements, Friends embraced the sexual ethics other Christians endorsed. Sex outside marriage, even between consenting adults, was fornication, a sin that, well into the twentieth century, was dealt with as such by the meeting. Homosexuality was simply not discussed; George Fox's voluminous writings, for example, refer to it only once, obliquely. A few cases of Friends who showed homosexual tendencies were dealt with quietly and privately.[41]

This began to change, at least among more liberal Friends, in the 1960s. A turning point was the publication in England of a little booklet, *Toward a Quaker View of Sex*, in 1963. It called for more open discussion, especially of homosexuality, by Friends. By the 1970s, both the loosening of restrictions on heterosexual relations and the emergence of gay liberation had begun to affect Friends. The impact was polarizing.

For many Quakers of evangelical views, there is little to discuss. They hold to the traditional position that sexual relations take place morally only within heterosexual marriage. Typical is the statement found in the Eastern Region *Faith and Practice*: "Sex is a beautiful gift of God when it joins a man and a woman together in self-giving love. . . . We hold that this depth of relationship is appropriate only in marriage and that sexual relations should be abstained from outside the marriage bond." But even fervently evangelical Friends have shown signs of give that would have been unlikely a generation ago. Thus a writer in the *Evangelical Friend* could state, for example, that "sex is God's gift to a married couple for procreation, bonding, and enjoyment." The latter two aspects would have been dubious to most pastoral Friends before 1960. And, confronted with out-of-wedlock pregnancies in their congregations today, pastoral Friends are far more likely to be supportive and celebrate the births, even if they disapprove of premarital sex.[42]

Among unprogrammed Friends, there is considerably greater openness to departures from traditional sexual morality. Many argue that the only important matters in a sexual relationship are honesty and commitment, whether or not within the bounds of marriage, and such things are so private that no meeting has any right to interfere with them. "I am appalled at the suggestion that Quakers should make a corporate testimony on such personal ethics," wrote one Friend from Chapel Hill, North Carolina. "These are surely personal and private matters unless concerns over the issues are such that a Friend asks for a clearness committee from the meeting." Other Friends argue that Quakers simply need to adjust to changing times. "I do not believe the understandings of either God or sexuality common in the late 1600s are to be normative for Quakers today," wrote one.[43]

Such changes came to unprogrammed Friends with debate and not a little acrimony. Friends General Conference first allowed unmarried heterosexual couples to room together at its Annual Gathering in 1972. About the same time Pendle Hill, the Quaker study center outside Philadelphia, adopted a similar policy. Some theologically liberal Friends were outraged, seeing "a 1960s version of Ranterism"—an unflattering reference to an early anti-Quaker movement that equated sexual license with sanctity. "When it comes to sexual ethics," wrote a New York Friend, "we now seem to act as if Jesus had said to the woman caught in adultery, 'Go and do your own thing.'" Such objections have been strong enough to prevent some FGC yearly meetings from adopting statements that seemed to endorse heterosexual sex outside of marriage. Similarly, in 1988, the Columbia, South Carolina Friends Meeting blasted what it saw as tolerance of sexual activity in its yearly meeting youth program. Friends, they said, should offer "a haven where young people can find a haven from pressure toward early sexual activity that is so prevalent in the larger society." For most Friends in unprogrammed yearly meetings, however, sexual activity becomes a matter for the meeting only when it is perceived as exploitative.[44]

Friends have paralleled other American denominations in their responses to gay and lesbian issues. The unprogrammed yearly meetings, with the exception of Ohio Conservative, have largely embraced the cause of gay rights. The EFI yearly meetings, closely tied to American evangelicalism, continue to believe that any kind of homosexual activity is unnatural and sinful. Their response to the political manifestations of gay and lesbian life, however, such as Proposition 2 in Colorado, which banned any kind of local gay rights legislation, has been more complex. The yearly meetings in FUM have seen the most protracted and bitter debates, sometimes threatening them with division.

Doubtless there have always been gay Friends. The first public discussion of homosexuality among Quakers came with *Toward a Quaker View of Sex*. Response among even liberal Friends in the United States was muted, however, and it was not until the early 1970s that the issue was addressed. By that time, "gay liberation" had become a cause in the larger American society, often bound up with the civil rights, feminist, and antiwar causes that Friends supported. Thus many were inclined to be sympathetic. About 1970, a group of gay Friends formed what they called a "Committee of Concern." In 1972, the committee on arrangements for the FGC Annual Gathering arranged for those who identified with this "Committee of Concern" to be housed together and to form a worship group. In 1978 they and like-minded Quakers officially formed the Friends Committee on Gay Concerns, which soon became Friends for Lesbian and Gay Concerns.[45]

By the 1980s, acceptance of gays and lesbians and affirmation of their rights had become a hallmark of most unprogrammed meetings. For some, identifying with this persecuted minority was a natural extension of the traditional Quaker sympathy for victims of misapplied power. Certainly gay Friends saw the question in those terms. "Friends must recognize that their judgment of us as sinful in nature, and inherently worth less than those who are heterosexually identified, is an inappropriate claiming and abuse of power and its expression an emotional and spiritual bullying," wrote one. For some, like Elizabeth Watson, condemnation of gays and lesbians was archaic: "To base one's attitude toward gay and lesbian people today on ancient codes in the Bible, set forth in a vastly different time, is to ignore continuing revelation," she wrote. Others argued that the biblical passages used to justify such condemnation had been misapplied or misunderstood. Some stated that Friends should honor any kind of committed relationship:

FLGC Dance, 1985. ROBERT W. SCHMITT/COURTESY OF *Friends Journal*, Feb. I, 1986.

"I do not believe that a loving sexual relationship with someone of the same sex *is* immoral behavior. I do not believe that love is *ever* a sin," one wrote to *Friends Journal* in 1996. Many gays and lesbians speak of the acceptance that they found in unprogrammed meetings. To be sure, some unprogrammed Friends held to older views, a few strongly enough that they resigned in protest, but they were apparently a minority.[46]

One mark of acceptance was the movement in many monthly meetings to conduct gay marriages or ceremonies of union or commitment. The first "union" under the care of a Friends meeting was at University Friends in Seattle in 1981; the first to use the label "marriage" took place at Morningside Meeting in New York City in 1987. Many other meetings have followed suit. Philadelphia Yearly Meeting, for example, has published a guide for same-sex couples using the Quaker marriage ceremony. Long, intense debates often characterized the process of reaching unity to embrace such marriages and unions. Friends offered various justifications for this new practice. For some, it was a matter of encouraging commitment. "To refuse to support *committed* relationships for gay and lesbian people is to encourage *broken* relationships between persons," one supporter wrote. For others, it was a matter of equality: "We had set as fundamental that all persons, regardless of sexual orientation, were equally children of God. Could we then agree to letting some have the full benefits of one of the most intimate human rituals, while others received only part?" a New England Friend asked. Some gay and lesbian Friends complained that "even when good order is used," the process of reaching unity was painful for them.[47]

Among pastoral Friends, the divisions have been deeper. Generally, it appears that a majority of pastoral Friends share the belief of most evangelicals that homosexual activity is sinful. Some are ferocious in their rhetoric. Homosexuality is "a horrendous crime against God, nature, and humanity," one claimed. "God's judgment against Sodom and Gomorrah leaves no doubt that God classifies homosexuality as exceedingly corrupt," wrote another. Yet another saw AIDS as God's punishment for such a lifestyle: "One can argue with Romans 1:26–27 until he eventually dies of AIDS and the fact still remains that God set certain laws in motion in this universe and when we go contrary to these laws, we do suffer the consequences." All of the EFI yearly meetings, and some in FUM, have adopted statements that condemn homosexual activity. On the other hand, some pastoral Friends have taken stands similar to those of unprogrammed Friends, arguing that opposition to gays is based on misunderstanding Scripture.[48]

These differences have proved disruptive of long-standing relationships. The first manifestation came in 1977, when Evangelical Friends threatened to pull out of a Friends conference in Wichita if gay Quakers were officially recognized. Tensions have run especially high in some yearly meetings where monthly meetings were dual-affiliated with two yearly meetings of different opinions. Western Yearly Meeting, for example, which is mainly pastoral but includes several unprogrammed meetings that are also affiliated with FGC yearly meetings, has nearly been torn apart by battles over meetings that have conducted same-sex unions. Ohio Yearly Meeting (Conservative), in an unprecedented action, "disowned" Cleveland Monthly Meeting in 1994 because it had "witnessed" a same-sex union. Two ministers in Mid-America Yearly Meeting, both well known and respected among Friends, were stripped of their recording as ministers because they were part of a group that questioned the yearly meeting's condemnation of homosexuality. Earlham College has been subjected to repeated demands from affiliated Friends that it ban gay groups from the campus. In 1994 and 1995 North Carolina Yearly Meeting (FUM) was threatened with splits because of demands from fundamentalist Friends that some ministers who had expressed sympathy for gay rights be silenced. Friends United Meeting, which embraces almost the entire range of American Quakerism, has been particularly subject to tensions. Its decision in 1988 that it would accept only staff and workers who confined sexual activity to heterosexual marriage brought angry condemnation and destroyed its volunteer program. On the other hand, when FUM allowed FLGC to sponsor an "interest group" meeting at its 1990 triennial, it found itself accused of "justifying sin."[49]

Some surprising common ground may be found on gay and lesbian issues. Many liberal and universalist Friends have called for legal recognition of same-sex unions, which remain anathema to most pastoral Friends. On the other hand, when Colorado and Oregon had antihomosexual ballot measures, Evangelical Friends there did not take an official position, in contrast to many other evangelical and fundamentalist groups that endorsed the proposals. FUM, while it would not condone homosexual acts, also condemned discrimination in secular employment and rights. Indiana Yearly Meeting, which had categorized homosexual acts as contrary to the will of God in 1982, in 1995 adopted a ministry statement that also condemned discrimination and left it to local meetings to determine the ministry roles of all members. While such compromises are still offensive to many gays and lesbians, they are evidence of some change in attitudes. What remains to be seen is whether such incremental change will continue, or whether pastoral Friends have reached the limits of their openness to change.[50]

Identity

"Where two or three Quakers are gathered together, one is liberal, one is conservative, and a third keeps asking the others to define their terms." This was the comment of Tom Mullen, the former dean of the Earlham School of Religion, a quarter century ago, and it still applies to Friends today. As has already become apparent, they do not agree on a common definition of Quakerism.[51]

Numerous Friends see Quaker identity as problematic. Chuck Fager, one of the most spirited advocates of Quaker universalism, sees "near universal ignorance of our heritage—Quaker, Christian, and biblical." An Indiana pastor similarly concluded that "many Friends try to be anything but Friends." "We are not sure whether we are primarily Christians or Quakers or a combination of the two," wrote another Friend. "We tend to ape other groups rather than to capitalize on our own uniqueness."[52]

The argument begins with disagreement over the relationship of Friends to the larger Christian world. Probably most Friends see the Society of Friends or Friends Church as a Protestant denomination. But not all agree. Douglas Steere noted that many Friends "feel themselves part of something that is . . . a third force, that is neither Roman Catholic nor Protestant but a part of a Christian mystical stream that has nurtured and over and over again renewed them all." That, in turn, raises a question about whether Quakerism "is a method for discerning truth and the will of God" or "a body of principles and testimonies which are normative for Friends." Unprogrammed Friends generally give more weight to the former description, pastoral Friends to the latter, but many argue that it should be both.[53]

Given their diversity, it is not surprising to find differences among unprogrammed Friends in understandings of the essential nature of Quakerism. Lewis Benson argued that Friends should present a "genuine alternative to institutional Christianity"—alternative, but still Christian. Others acknowledge that "we are of the Christian tradition but know the Divine as more than any single entity. . . . In our worship we seek this contact with the Divine Source." Still others celebrate the *negatives* of Quakerism: "no theology, no dogma, no sacred books, no creed, no clergy or liturgy, no images."[54]

Expansiveness is not always perceived as a virtue. Some Friends in unprogrammed meetings worry that "in our eagerness to be ecumenical in spirit, are we not in danger of becoming all things to all people?" "A long-term visitor to most of our meetings would likely come away certain only of our uncertainty," wrote another. Such Friends fear that they have become so focused on being tolerant and welcoming that they have lost all deep conviction. As one puts it: "If we accept a plurality of faith convictions within our Society as normative, then what we are also saying is that, as a Society, we have no unique message of faith to proclaim to the world."[55]

One hears similar statements from many pastoral Friends. "In our efforts to be all things to all people we have made ourselves unsatisfactory to everyone," mourned one Evangelical Friend in Oregon. Another worried that too many programmed meetings and churches hope to grow by deemphasizing any distinctive Quaker identity. A professor at Friends University noted how many Quaker students told him that they learned little about Quakerism in their home churches. "Some of our local meetings are hardly distinguishable from social clubs or sister churches of other denominations," complained an Indiana pastor. These people see "fuzziness" as the root problem. Because they lack a clear identity, pastoral Friends have not grown.[56]

What, then, should Friends do to clarify their identity? They offer different answers. "All the Society needs is to be more Quakerly," argued one North Carolina Friend. Others want the opposite. "We have to forget about 'being Quaker' and concentrate every ounce of our energy on reaching out to the hurting world around us," wrote a yearly meeting superintendent in 1993. Other Friends equally committed to a Christian vision, however, reject the idea that Quaker distinctiveness is a problem. "To survive is to differentiate and have confidence in oneself. . . . We need Friends distinctives now as we have never needed them before," argues John Punshon. Unprogrammed Friends wholeheartedly agree. But what are those "distinctives" and what bounds should there be to differentiation? Some argue that Friends should be outsiders, separate from the larger culture, but disagree on the manifestations of that separateness. A few Conservative Friends are drawn to resurrecting Quietism and the plain life, but they are a small minority. Other unprogrammed Friends see the spiritual diversity and eclecticism of Quaker universalism as a good thing in itself.[57]

One manifestation of this uncertainty is the ongoing debate over the meaning of membership. All yearly meetings make provision for formal membership; all have detailed procedures for determining the sincerity of applicants. As has been seen, however, many monthly meetings are not rigorous in applying them. Moreover, in the last half century, as one Friend concluded, "the formerly clear distinction between members and attenders has evaporated." Many unprogrammed Friends think this is good; some even argue for abolition of formal membership as a way of being more inclusive. Others, however, respond that requesting membership is a necessary sign of commitment. In the pastoral yearly meetings, where assessments paid to the yearly meeting office are based on membership, many suspect monthly meetings do not encourage attenders to become members. And many Friends perceive that standards for retention are lax. "One can remain a Friend even if one's participation in the community's life is limited to occasional inquiries into the state of one's grandfather's grave," was the conclusion of one observer. Other Friends respond that Quakers should be more demanding in both admitting new members and retaining old ones.[58]

It is possible to overstate the seriousness of this particular "problem." Worry about clear identity may be limited to a relatively small but articulate group of Friends. Others see it as largely irrelevant to the lives of most members. This is especially true of EFI. Officials there believe that if they are winning souls with a clear Christian message, marking out distinctions from fellow Christians is unimportant. Similarly, as seen above, many universalist Friends see lack of a commonly shared identity as healthy diversity.[59]

Uncertain Quaker identity thus reflects the disagreements of Friends about theology, about worship, and about their relationship with the larger society. It also reflects their very uncertain relations with each other.

Unity and Diversity

One looks in vain for any positive comment on diversity as a desirable characteristic in the writings of Friends before the mid-nineteenth century. Indeed, to find that Friends held diverse opinions was an occasion for concern that might well end with the disownment of those out of unity with the main group. Unity is still vital to Friends, the end that their business process seeks. As Howard Brinton summarized it: "Since there is but one Light and one Truth, if the Light of Truth be faithfully followed, unity will result." But Friends now acknowledge that they must find unity amid diversity. Some celebrate that; others mourn it. Most see their diversity as presenting both opportunities and challenges, particularly when programmed and unprogrammed, Christian and universalist Friends attempt to work together.[60]

At the local level, Friends of all persuasions speak of the centrality of *community*. Virtually all agree with the observation of an Australian Friend that "Quakerism is . . . not a belief system for individuals standing by themselves—it can only be practiced by individuals in community, hence the Quaker meeting." They also agree on the nature of that community. It should be a "group of like-minded persons to whom they can belong and receive a sense of place as well as personal support." Both pastoral and nonpastoral Friends agree that with the increasing mobility of American society, the meeting at its best, in the words of one Chicago Friend, "becomes the family that's better than the family we were born into."[61]

The question of what should be the nature of this community divides Friends, however. A few have felt called to live in small, intentional communities to serve as models for the larger society. A more fundamental difference is that between universalist and evangelical Friends. For the former, community is an end in itself, and thus anything, even Christianity, that interferes with its formation should be discarded. The needs of individuals should shape the community. In contrast, evangelicals see the goal as salvation and the community as a means to help individuals achieve that end. As Everett Cattell stated, to be a Christian is to submit oneself to a community for both encouragement and reproof. Thus the community should mold the individual. Both programmed and unprogrammed Friends often perceive that they are not meeting the high standards that they set for themselves. Thus, they put considerable energy into community building. Unprogrammed Friends have achieved much success in generating high rates of attendance at their yearly meetings and at the FGC Annual Gathering, which for many is a "must-be-there" event. Pastoral Friends struggle more with attracting members to quarterly and yearly meetings.[62]

"Quakers love everyone, except each other." So one Evangelical Friend lamented a generation ago, and many agree that this is still true. Friends of all persuasions speak of incredulity, even disorientation, when they encounter Quakers whose ways are different from those they have known, whether they be unprogrammed Friends experiencing Evangelical Friends

Friends General Conference Annual Gathering, 1987. BARBARA BENTON/COURTESY OF *Friends Journal*, Sept. 1/15, 1987.

worship or pastoral Friends being introduced to an unprogrammed meeting. Some Friends will deny the bona fides of any Quaker who disagrees with them on matters that they perceive as fundamental.[63]

Many find this deplorable. They assert that Friends should model peace-making among themselves. "The distrust among Friends makes blasphemy of our Quaker faith and witness," writes one New England Friend. "In our diverse and fragmented condition, contemporary Quakerism hardly makes a credible witness to the testimonies, and thus their power and influence both within the Quaker family and in society is largely dissipated," comments another.[64]

Some Friends argue that the differences are exaggerated and the commonalities are greater. Too often, they assert, differences are based on stereotypes and caricatures. Certainly many Friends speak of a conviction that, among all types of Quakers, there is a common spirit. This was the experience of Jack Willcuts, the long-time editor of the *Evangelical Friend*. He found Friends who were "Christian *and* Quakerly, even though I have found individuals in each grouping that are neither. . . . I fear we dishonor the Lord in limiting Him to just one way or the other. God is bigger than all our Quaker boundaries in faith and practice."[65]

This is the note that many Friends strike, arguing that diversity can be a strength. Not surprisingly, most liberal Friends celebrate diversity; as one said, "we fairly wallow in it." Another wrote: "I am very glad that we do not always agree with one another. Think how dull that would be!" Some see diversity as inherent in Quakerism; because it "emphasizes the inner light of each person and disavows any human absolute authority, we must of necessity always be a community rich in diversity of opinion." But many pastoral Friends are just as willing to embrace diversity of views within the body. "In the past we have been guilty of trying to legislate uniformity within the Society of Friends," wrote one pastor in 1988. "This resulted in dispersions and divisions that seriously weakened the church." An Evangelical Friend wrote that just as God made flowers "with many colors and shapes, species of unimaginable varieties," so "the church is not to be a monolithic mold with only one style, mode, or name."[66]

Still, the differences are real. In the 1960s, Lewis Benson wrote that "in our Quaker conferences and discussions in recent years there is the outward appearance of a process of communication. But this is largely illusory because each different group of participants lives in its own universe of discourse. Very little that is said is heard by others in the frame of reference in which it is intended to be understood." Many observers still believe this:

Friends simply do not speak the same language. As one commented: "Liberal Friends want to sit around and talk; evangelicals want to proselytize and evangelize the world." The question whether Quakerism is Christian is for many simply beyond compromise, as is the issue of sexuality, especially homosexuality. "Why covenant with my oppressors?" was the angry question of one gay Friend who saw nothing to be gained from ties with pastoral Quakers. Active Friends have myriad stories to tell of unkindness and uncivil behavior on the part of "the other."[67]

The body that feels these conflicts most directly is Friends United Meeting, which embraces both programmed and unprogrammed meetings (al-

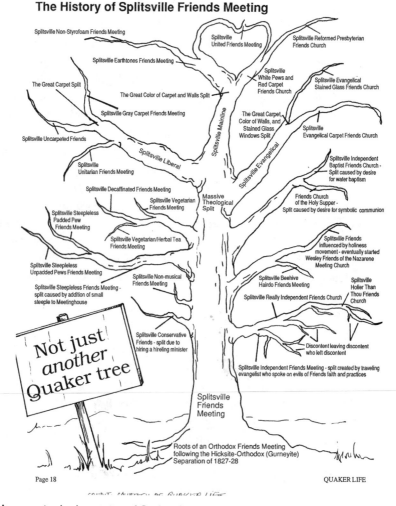

The History of Splitsville Friends Meeting

Splitsville Non-Styrofoam Friends Meeting

Splitsville United Friends Meeting

Splitsville Reformed Presbyterian Friends Church

Splitsville Earthtones Friends Meeting

Splitsville White Pews and Red Carpet Friends Church

Splitsville Evangelical Stained Glass Friends Church

The Great Carpet Split

The Great Color of Carpet and Walls Split

Splitsville Gray Carpet Friends Meeting

The Great Carpet, Color of Walls, and Stained Glass Windows Split

Splitsville Evangelical Carpet Friends Church

Splitsville Uncarpeted Friends

Splitsville Mainline

Splitsville Liberal

Splitsville Evangelical

Splitsville Unitarian Friends Meeting

Splitsville Independent Baptist Friends Church - Split caused by desire for water baptism

Splitsville Decaffinated Friends Meeting

Splitsville Vegetarian Friends Meeting

Massive Theological Split

Friends Church of the Holy Supper - Split caused by desire for symbolic communion

Splitsville Steepleless Padded Pew Friends Meeting

Splitsville Vegetarian/Herbal Tea Friends Meeting

Splitsville Friends influenced by holiness movement - eventually started Wesley Friends of the Nazarene Meeting Church

Splitsville Steepleless Unpadded Pews Friends Meeting

Splitsville Non-musical Friends Meeting

Splitsville Beehive Hairdo Friends Meeting

Splitsville Holier Than Thou Friends Church

Splitsville Steepleless Friends Meeting - split caused by addition of small steeple to Meetinghouse

Splitsville Really Independent Friends Church

Not just another Quaker tree

Splitsville Conservative Friends - split due to hiring a hireling minister

Discontent leaving discontent who left discontent

Splitsville Independent Friends Meeting - split created by traveling evangelist who spoke on evils of Friends faith and practices

Splitsville Friends Meeting

Roots of an Orthodox Friends Meeting following the Hicksite-Orthodox (Gurneyite) Separation of 1827-28

Page 18   QUAKER LIFE

A tongue-in-cheek overview of Quaker diversity. COURTESY OF QUAKER LIFE.

though the former are a majority) and which, as one Friend notes, "represents all of the colors of the Quaker rainbow." Ever since its foundation as the Five Years Meeting in 1902, it has experienced tensions. The more fundamentalist members of the pastoral yearly meetings fear that ties with universalist Friends compromise vital points of faith. As one observer stated, "They get scared and anguished about what will happen if folks are eternally separated from the presence of God because someone was too scared to make the claims clear. They worry that they would actually have blood on their hands if they were to stand silent and complacent." Convinced that FUM is a good thing, they feel that it is thus a target for assaults by Satan, and that his weapons are weakening its Christian identity, promoting acceptance of homosexuality, etc. On the other hand, unprogrammed Friends, who like the idea of FUM as a centrist organization, see it as insufficiently committed to social activism and are often appalled by its "excessively fundamentalist, evangelical frame of reference." They say they have been abused by Friends who claimed divine sanction for hurtful speeches and sermons.[68]

These tensions have produced demands for change in FUM, what early in the 1990s came to be called "realignment." The idea dated back to the 1970s, when Everett Cattell proposed a reordering of Quaker organizations that would join pastoral yearly meetings in one group and unprogrammed in another, "with such good will and deep understandings that new freedom would come to all." In 1990 and 1991, Stephen Main, the executive secretary of FUM, also proposed such a realignment. His argument was that differences between EFI and most FUM pastoral Friends were minimal, while the ongoing debates between universalists and evangelicals within FUM were draining it of energy. Support was most evident in Southwest and Iowa yearly meetings, but the idea found little favor in FUM's governing board or among other leaders. They argued that the realignment Main envisioned would not be as easy as he claimed because FUM Friends were to be found at all points on a broad spectrum and an "either/or" choice would divide both local and yearly meetings. A conference in Des Moines to promote the idea drew official delegates from only two yearly meetings, and so the realignment proposal lapsed. It did lead, however, to considerable soul-searching within FUM, and the adoption of a mission statement in 1992: "Friends United Meeting commits itself to energize and equip Friends through the power of the Holy Spirit to gather people into fellowships where Jesus Christ is known, loved and obeyed as Teacher and Lord." This was definitely Christian, but, as critics pointed out, hardly distinctive to Friends.[69]

The impact of these events is unclear. Dissatisfied, Southwest Yearly

Meeting withdrew from FUM in 1993 and joined EFI, but later was accused of reneging on promises to allow monthly meetings to retain FUM ties; at least one withdrew from the yearly meeting and affiliated with FUM. In 1996, Iowa Yearly Meeting came close to leaving, finally deciding to allow each monthly meeting to determine whether or not it was affiliated with FUM. However, many Friends believe that FUM is more united now, with both the departure of Southwest and the recognition by the unprogrammed yearly meetings that FUM is different from FGC, and that they need to appoint board members who are sympathetic to the FUM mission statement.[70]

Given these differences, what are the prospects for amicable ties, let alone unity, among Friends? Unification of all Friends in a common organization is almost certainly chimerical. Some see hope in respecting differences but finding ways that Quakers of different views can work together in common projects. The oldest organization with this goal is the Friends World Committee for Consultation, which was formed in 1937. Its name describes its function: to encourage consultation among the different bodies of Friends. It supports a range of projects, largely relief or community building, around the world. The Earlham School of Religion is another such organization. It was founded with the goal of bringing together Friends of all persuasions, and its alumni can be found in positions of leadership in EFI, FUM, and FGC, although it has faced charges in recent years of excessive liberalism. There are other such enterprises. One is YouthQuake, a biennial event that brings together Quaker teenagers from a wide range of yearly meetings. Its gatherings are invariably characterized by conflict, but also by heightened understanding of the different varieties of Quakerism. For almost three decades, there have been periodic gatherings of Friends from North Pacific Yearly Meeting, widely regarded as one of the most liberal in North America, and its EFI neighbor, Northwest Yearly Meeting. They have succeeded in overcoming some deep-seated hostility and suspicion. Such attempts at dialogue have their limits. They usually consist disproportionately of liberal Friends. Often Evangelical Friends regard such events with suspicion—knowing what they believe, they sometimes fear that discussion will only weaken their faith. And when Friends of different views do meet, observers often report participants "walking on eggshells, trying not to cause offense or create a conflict."[71]

Thus the outlook for relations among American Friends is uncertain. Attempts to create unity through organizations, such as the Five Years Meeting, have fallen victim to unforeseen new issues. Personal contact tends to lessen differences, but not always. But organizations like the FWCC and events like YouthQuake do promote dialogue that was lacking in previous generations. As one Friend in Northwest Yearly Meeting has proposed, if they are willing to make the effort, Quakers can identify "things we can work on together and learn from each other," while acknowledging that "there are some areas of disagreement that cannot be set aside."[72]

Growth and Decline

As noted earlier, American Friends are a small group, about 1/30 of 1 percent of the whole population of the United States. For some Quakers, this is a natural state of affairs. They subscribe to the philosophy that in religion, as in other matters, "small is beautiful." Others, however, believe that it is their duty to grow and try to gain adherents. But they disagree on how best to do that.

Certainly numbers are not encouraging. The membership of yearly meetings of all persuasions in the United States today is between about 90,000 and 110,000. (Statistics are somewhat uncertain, depending on whether one counts both adult and junior members or attenders.) This is roughly the same as in 1902, although the proportions have shifted. Most of the pastoral yearly meetings in FUM have seen dramatic declines. Indiana, for example, had a membership of about 20,000 in 1902. Today it is less than 5,000. Western and Iowa have had similar declines. Some of the EFI yearly meetings are in similar condition. Mid-America (formerly Kansas) went from about 11,000 to roughly half that a century later. But other meetings have seen growth: Eastern Region, about 5,000 in 1902, is now about 8,800. Change has been less dramatic in the unprogrammed yearly meetings. Baltimore and New England, for example, are somewhat larger than they were a century ago. Others, like Philadelphia, have shown small declines, in Philadelphia's case from about 15,000 to about 12,000. These have been balanced by the founding of many new meetings, embraced in a dozen new yearly meetings formed since 1945. The overall steadiness reflects a kind of thinning—Friends have kept their numbers relatively constant but are much more widely dispersed than in 1900.[73]

Pastoral Friends offer a variety of explanations for their decline. A study done for FUM a decade ago showed that 72 percent of all pastoral Friends lived in rural areas that were steadily losing population. One hears a common refrain. Rural communities offer few opportunities for young people,

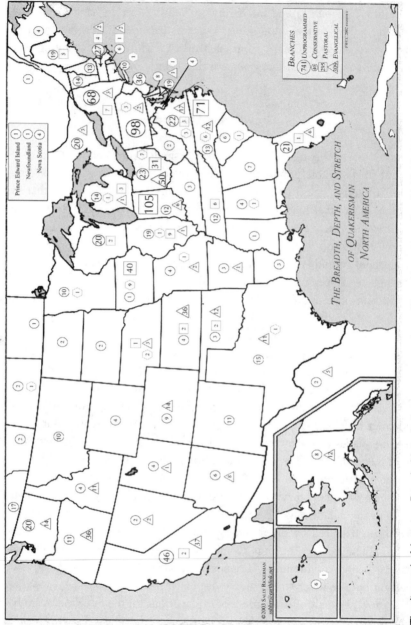

The dispersal of American Friends. Note the heavy concentrations still on the coasts and in the Middle West, but the existence of Quaker congregations in every state. SALLY RICKERMAN, PYM AND GAIL PIETRZYK, BYM.

so they leave, often moving to places where no Friends meeting can be found. As a result, membership in Quaker congregations is often disproportionately made up of people over age 65. One Friend offered his own meeting as a case study in this sort of decline. In 1965 it had 336 members. In 1988 membership was 150. In 1999 it was down to 65, of whom only 22 could be considered active. This experience is often profoundly demoralizing. A *Quaker Life* editor wrote of driving through the Midwest, viewing Friends meetings and churches: "All of them displayed on their front signboards (most of which were in need of repair) the same dull-sounding sermon titles. . . . All 'welcomed' passersby to worship on Sunday morning, and all looked as if they had not had a visitor traverse the intimidating front steps in a *long* time. You could almost smell the 'mustiness' emanating from the basement as you drove by."[74]

Social change does not entirely explain this trend. Some FUM Friends see Quakerism as a kind of "mainline" Christian denomination, sharing in the general decline of such churches, like the United Methodists and Presbyterians. Friends in FGC perceive that they do not do a good job of holding their children; one estimate is that three quarters of them do not remain Friends. A Philadelphia Friend speculated that the yearly meeting lost membership because it was "faithful to its heritage, a heritage that more and more of its members are incapable of sharing." And many Friends, pastoral and unprogrammed, resist growth, preferring to keep their meetings small, which in their minds is the foundation for friendliness and closeness.[75]

Such fears reflect ambivalence about seeking new members. Observers, Quaker and non-Quaker alike, have long remarked on this. A generation ago, Henry J. Cadbury, one of the most influential Friends of the twentieth century, commented, "Ever since its earliest days Quakerism has been something appreciated by the adherent rather than deliberately advertised." Friends today agree; as two put it: "The Quaker Light is often well-hidden under a stack of bushel baskets." One unprogrammed Friend, for example, reports that some in her meeting think it wrong even to advertise when and where it is held. Many Americans confuse Quakers with the Amish or Shakers, or are surprised to learn that they still exist.[76]

For many Friends, both programmed and unprogrammed, this is intolerable. "There is a segment of society that no one but the Friends can reach, and we ought to be doing it!" was the comment of one pastoral Friend. They argue that Quakers need to seek out "hidden Friends," people who are Quakers in spirit but do not know that they are. More liberal Friends agree. One posited that refusing to share the Light with a suffering world was like refusing food to the starving. They condemn "patterns of invisibility and hesitation to speak about our faith."[77]

Friends differ on how to carry out this vision. For most pastoral Friends, the response to this need is simple: obey the command to evangelize, to share the good news of salvation through Christ. For some, that means change. "We need to eliminate, alter, change, replace, or rebuild, whatever stands in the way of accomplishing our 'Mission Statement,'" was the conclusion of one pastor. A yearly meeting superintendent argued that meetings and churches simply have to grow, since it takes a minimum attendance of 150 to offer the programming that most families expect. Pastoral meetings try to reach out in a variety of ways that would be familiar to most evangelicals: radio ministries, bus ministries, telephone campaigns, youth programs, Bible study groups. In EFI, "sports ministry," using athletic programs to try to make contacts and draw attenders, has become a growing field. Most unprogrammed Friends, and some in pastoral meetings, see such actions as not keeping with Quaker distinctiveness, although at least one writer in *Friends Journal* asserted that "George Fox would have used television." These Friends look more to personal contacts to try to draw new members. Others point to convinced Friends who came to Quakerism through connections with Quaker schools or work with Quaker organizations like the AFSC.[78]

The effectiveness of such efforts is unclear. One liberal Friend was willing to state outright that "our efforts at organized evangelism, which we euphemize as 'outreach,' are laughable." Still, he concluded, they were more effective than those of EFI, which spent thousands of dollars per new member recruited. And leaders in pastoral yearly meetings mourn how frequently attempts at planting new churches fail and how hard it is to keep up financial support for them.[79]

On the other hand, Friends are drawing converts. Although hard statistics are lacking, most observers agree that a majority of American Quakers today are "convinced Friends." One study estimated that 87 percent of unprogrammed Friends were converts. The routes to Quakerism are diverse. Unprogrammed meetings are filled with "refugees from evangelical Christianity," which often gives their relations with evangelical Friends an edge. Many, perhaps a majority of these Friends, had their first Quaker contacts through political or social activism, often through the AFSC. Moderate pastoral meetings often draw those who see Quakerism as a kind of middle ground between fundamentalism and Unitarianism. And still others are drawn to Friends churches much as other evangelicals join churches. "We wanted a no-frills, Bible-preaching and believing church," was the explanation of a couple who joined an Indiana congregation. Optimists point to some large and growing churches, such as in southern California and parts of the Midwest.[80]

Given the survival of older meetings, the determined church planting of evangelical Friends, and the proliferation of small, unprogrammed worship groups, Quakerism is not likely to disappear anytime soon from the United States. But it will probably not grow significantly.

Conclusion

At the beginning of the twenty-first century, American Friends find themselves dealing with the heritage of the separations of the past two hundred years. In some cases, old divisions have been healed. In others, new issues have led to new splits. Certainly the differences among Friends are significant and show no signs of disappearing.

Fundamental are questions of theology. Are Friends a Christian denomination, or do they transcend Christianity? For a majority of American Friends, a Christian identity is vital and cannot be compromised. But others, drawing on ancient Quaker teachings of universal Light and "That of God in Everyone," argue that Quakerism should expand to encompass diverse visions of faith. Friends differ in their understanding of authority. Those in EFI give primacy to the Bible. More liberal Friends try to balance the authority of Scripture with continuing revelation through the guidance of the Holy Spirit. Universalist Friends tend to focus on "That of God in Everyone." All, however, accept the authority of seeking truth in a gathered meeting. In part, their variations are in emphasis, but varying degrees of emphasis often become unbridgeable differences.

Other issues are not unique to Quakerism. Friends of all kinds worry about leadership, yet disagree about what it means to be an effective Quaker leader. Sexuality is a deeply divisive issue. Unprogrammed Friends largely accept the "sexual revolution," especially the liberation of gays and lesbians, but for most pastoral Friends these are unacceptable challenges to basic morality. Friends must cope with their stagnant numbers, about the same as a century ago. And, given their diversity on other matters, they have fundamentally different visions of identity, of what it means to be a Quaker. With these divisions, unity seems likely to be elusive in the future.

CHAPTER SIX

Quakers and the World

Early in 2002, two groups of American Quakers found different ways to witness to the world. In February, a "team" from the Riverside Friends Church in Iowa traveled to New Orleans for Mardi Gras. They were not there for pageantry or parties. They went to "minister to the lost." The pastor took his banjo to draw a crowd and was aided by a baton-twirling Friend from another Iowa church. They stationed themselves near a line of portable toilets, singing and "proclaiming the Gospel," under banners proclaiming Know God, Know Peace. They spoke to anyone who would listen, from self-identified drug dealers to a "Viking rune reader" to abandoned wives and girlfriends. These Friends shared the same message repeatedly—repent and know salvation through Jesus Christ. This was their way of sharing their Quaker faith with the world, making it a better place.[1]

Two months later, on April 20, a number of Friends were in Washington, D.C. They also believed they were witnessing to their faith, but their message and methods were very different from those of the Quakers in New Orleans. They were there to protest against U.S. policies on issues that "ranged from Afghanistan to Colombia to Iraq, from the World Court to the World Bank." They joined thousands of other activists who shared these concerns but were especially critical of U.S. support for Israel in its conflict with Palestinians. These Friends were there to advance peace and justice in the world, and in doing so they were living out Quaker testimonies.[2]

For much of their existence, Quakers were a self-conscious sect, a group that shared certain fundamental beliefs with other Christians, yet consciously set itself apart. After 1700, the duty of the consistent Quaker was separation from "the world" and its manifold temptations away from plain living and the guidance of the Inward Light. Yet, by the nineteenth century, Friends had become largely known for trying to change the world: opposing slavery, advocating equal rights for women, reforming schools and prisons. Today, when the larger world is not confusing Friends with very different sectarian groups like the Amish or the Shakers, it associates them with pacifism and humanitarianism.

Quakers have conflicting feelings about this perception. The sectarian image bothers some, especially pastoral Friends, who see themselves as simply brothers and sisters in the larger Christian community. For others, the activist image embodies the essence of Quaker life. This chapter will examine Friends and the larger world. It will begin with an analysis of Quaker attitudes about "the world" and what their relationship with it should be, then look at two long-standing Quaker commitments, to peace and to racial justice, and how Friends try to achieve them today. It will conclude with a discussion of the two Quaker organizations that are most visible in trying to apply Quaker visions to that wider world: the American Friends Service Committee (AFSC) and the Friends Committee on National Legislation (FCNL).

Quaker Worldviews

"True godliness don't turn men out of the world, but enables them to live better in it and excites their endeavours to mend it." So wrote William Penn more than three centuries ago. Most Friends today still embrace his outlook. They believe it the duty of Friends to live their faith and in so doing make the world a better place. Compare, for example, two Friends, a leading Evangelical and a member of a liberal unprogrammed meeting. "If we are to follow Jesus Christ, we must stand in opposition to the prevailing mood of modern society and challenge and confront its idolatry," wrote Richard J. Foster in 1986. "In obedience to Christ, we must say 'no' to the greed and avarice that guarantee the poverty of others. In obedience to Christ we must say 'no' to the little tin gods of our modern nation-states that call us into their blasphemous intertribal wars. In obedience to Christ we must say 'no' to the racism and sexism that dehumanizes those for whom Christ died." This sense of separateness, of being called to be different, was shared by an Atlanta unprogrammed Friend, Janet Minshall, in 1987. "I believe if I live by those old Quaker testimonies as best I can, and if I honor our history as Friends, then I cannot in truth be part of the majority culture in my time," she wrote. "I can pass as a member of that culture, but when it comes to important issues, I find that I must exclude myself from the majority." Such Friends share what one has called the Quaker "passion for making the world over."[3]

Friends ground this concern in different ways. Many unprogrammed Friends came to Quakerism in the 1960s and 1970s because of Quaker commitments to peace and equality. As one observed, they see their meeting "as the place in which we can find personal spiritual growth, and confirmation and support for our social action." For such Friends, "right living is more important than right belief"; they conclude, as one wrote, that "it is impossible to experience a rich spiritual life if we stand apart from the fight for social justice." Another activist painted a vivid picture of the United States as she wanted it to be in a letter to *Friends Journal* in 1993. It would be a nation

that has protested—in peace marches, civil rights and environmental demonstrations, voter registration drives, and prayer. This is the nation of wilderness and historic and species preservation, of organic farming, of minority and woman's rights, of simplicity and human-scale technology, of peace with justice. This is the country that has listened to Gandhi, gone to jail with Daniel Berrigan, and given sanctuary to refugees along with Jim Corbett.

In most respects, this is the vision of the Left in American politics over the past thirty years. But it would be wrong to conclude that such a Quaker view is simply secular. This activism springs from spiritual roots.[4]

Not all Friends share this vision, and even when they do, they ground their commitment differently. Everett Cattell summed up their understanding succinctly: "No theology of service is adequate unless it is profoundly rooted in the Cross and thereby in the Atonement," he wrote. "Service must be regarded as an act of proclamation in itself—it proclaims the love of Christ." For such Friends, their duty is proclaiming the gospel as "the answer to the ills of society." Thus their diagnosis of social problems is likely to be much closer to that of the Christian Right and evangelical politicians.[5]

Quakers live out these visions in different ways. Pastoral Friends believe

Quaker demonstration near the SOA (School of the Americas) in November 2002.
COURTESY OF PEG MORTON.

they have a responsibility to improve the world, but they do it through proclaiming the gospel, winning souls to Christ. "We have got to be clearly driven, . . . by mission, by calling, by Christ's call to touch life, to be transformed, to be courageous, and to be biblically faithful," preached the superintendent of Eastern Region, John Williams Jr., in 2000. Thus much of their energy goes into missions, both in the United States and abroad. EFI Friends can claim credit for much of the growth of Quakerism in Latin America and Asia in the last century. Currently Evangelical Friends Mission supports outreach in Rwanda, India, Nepal, the Philippines, and Mexico, as well as among Navajos in the United States. Evangelical Friends have now begun evangelism in Ireland, arguing that even though it is a Catholic country, relatively few people there meet evangelical standards of Christian faith. Similarly, pastoral Friends in FUM support missionary work in Africa, Central America, and the Caribbean; it consumes by far the largest single part of the organization's budget.[6]

These Friends, however, do not limit themselves to evangelism. They argue that missions can and should take the form of service, whether in schools or hospitals or homeless shelters or day-care centers or "crisis pregnancy" centers that provide alternatives to abortion. They also see a role for government in upholding basic standards of morality and guaranteeing equal rights and justice. But many see limits to such service. Many pastoral Friends have the sense that they are living in the "Last Days" before the Second Coming of Christ; they are, for example, enthusiastic readers of the *Left Behind* series of novels, whose premise is the unfolding of the events foretold in the Book of Revelation in the contemporary world. Some Evangelical Friends fear that such premillennialism stymies the impulse to improve the world, but others perceive it as giving both their evangelism and their work to achieve justice greater urgency and energy.[7]

Generally, unprogrammed Friends do not accept the necessity of linking service to a specifically Christian message. For them, doing good is an end in itself, because it makes the world a better place and thus helps work God's will. Some applaud the involvement of Friends in radical protest movements, ranging from environmental to antiwar to racial justice causes. They do not fear being thought strange; for them that is part of being a Quaker. They are often paradoxical: they usually favor strong government regulation of economic activity but admire nongovernmental organizations and see governments as innately oppressive and to be distrusted.[8]

Such commitments inevitably have political implications. American Quakers today span the political spectrum. Relatively few have held high political office in the past century, although they have included two presidents, Herbert Hoover from 1929 to 1933 and Richard Nixon from 1969 to 1974. The last Quaker U.S. Senator was Paul Douglas of Illinois (1949–1967). Today only one member of Congress, Democratic Rep. Rush Holt of New Jersey, is a Friend. Quakers are more active at lower levels of government, such as state legislatures and city councils.[9]

We lack hard data on the political attitudes of contemporary American Quakers, but most observers agree that unprogrammed Friends, with the exception of a few rural pockets and a few old families, tend to be Democrats, when they are not farther left as Greens or Democratic Socialists. We do have statistics from a recent sample of members of Philadelphia Yearly Meeting. It showed that 77 percent identified themselves as "liberal, extremely liberal, or leaning liberal," in contrast to only 28 percent of the general U.S. population. A Republican Friend in upstate New York wrote that she felt an outcast at times, and some Friends avow their incredulity that one can be a Quaker *and* a Republican. Among programmed Friends, there is greater diversity, with patterns of political identification tending to reflect those of surrounding communities. Thus in pastoral meetings in rural Indiana, one is not surprised to find farm families voting Republican as they have for generations, or UAW members tending to be Democrats. The rise of issues like abortion, homosexuality, and school prayer has moved many Evangelical Friends to identify more closely with the corresponding wing of the Republican party. Typical is one EFI Friend who described the Republicans as the party of "Christian ideals" while the Democrats are the party of "humanism," which is "satanic." In 1988 the EFI Rocky Mountain Yearly Meeting listed as a "prayer concern" to "ask the Lord to raise up a man who is committed to traditional moral standards" as the next president.[10]

Still, to these generalizations there are significant exceptions. Some Evangelical Friends have been openly critical of the Christian Right. For example, it was the judgment of a George Fox University professor in 1986 that "the platform of the Religious Right deserves the indictment that it is, at best, a sub-biblical, secular, humanistic movement, masquerading as a Christian campaign." On the other hand, some theologically liberal Friends criticize Quakers whom they perceive as caring "nothing for God and who joined the Society simply because they were peace activists, or saw it as a platform for launching political protests." An example is Jack Powelson, a retired University of Colorado economist who has launched an online journal to combat what he sees as dogmatic anticapitalism among unprogrammed Friends. Early in 2002 Powelson resigned membership in his meeting from a conviction it no longer had room for those who did not hew to a narrow political agenda.[11]

Many Friends are uneasy with the political divisions they see among Quakers. They worry that activism crowds out spiritual growth among some liberal Friends and that too many evangelical Friends have lost all but a narrow sense of social concern. They argue that ideally, Friends would meld both.[12] But given the diversity of American Quakers, it seems likely that their views of the larger world, and their relationship to it, will continue to diverge. Nowhere is that divergence more clearly apparent than in their attitudes toward peace and war.

The Peace Testimony

If outsiders know nothing else about Quaker faith, they usually know that historically Quakers have been pacifists who believe that all wars and fighting are wrong. Virtually all Friends remain officially committed to such a vision today. The Richmond Declaration of Faith's statement on peace is perhaps the one section of that document that even the most committed universalist Friend finds acceptable. But official statements are often not normative for members. While most Quaker leaders remain committed to what Friends call the "Peace Testimony," and it remains in some form in nearly every yearly meeting's *Faith and Practice*, pacifism and peace activism are contested issues among American Friends. On one hand, probably a majority of American Quakers still see themselves as seeking peace but no longer consider themselves pacifists. On the other hand, many Friends still put tremendous energy into peacemaking work and are central to numerous efforts to try to create a more peaceful world.[13]

The movement of many American Friends away from uncompromising pacifism has been long and complex, and historians have yet to explore it fully. Some young Friends in time of war always deviated and enlisted in the armed forces. Between 1700 and the Civil War, however, such military service invariably caused disownment. The fervent commitment of virtually all Friends to the Union cause between 1861 and 1865 brought the first compromises. Many monthly meetings enforced the Discipline, but others took no action when members enlisted. As disciplinary rigor broke down after 1870, military service came to be regarded as a matter of individual conscience. Thus large numbers of Friends served in both world wars. In Indiana Yearly Meeting during World War I, for example, enlistees in the armed forces outnumbered conscientious objectors by at least three to one. All estimates suggest that the proportion was even greater during World War II. Those who have dealt with this question see it largely as a matter of acculturation. Pastoral Friends, including many converts who had no pacifist heritage, gave up the Peace Testimony along with other peculiarities. We know less about unprogrammed Friends, but what evidence we have suggests that they followed a similar path.[14]

A vital core of Friends, however, always remained committed to pacifism. A few went to prison rather than serve in the armed forces in the 1910s and 1940s. More found ways of rendering alternative, nonmilitary service. The experience of Civilian Public Service during World War II in particular was critical, producing a generation of Quakers who are only now, in their eighties, relinquishing leadership. They, in turn, inspired succeeding generations of Quaker pacifists.[15]

Today, Friends who are committed to the Peace Testimony view it as God's will. Christian Friends see it as simple obedience to Christ. The Richmond Declaration speaks for them: "all war is utterly incompatible with the plain precepts of our divine Lord and Law-giver, and the whole spirit of His Gospel, and . . . no plea of necessity or policy, however urgent or peculiar, can avail to release either individuals or nations from the paramount allegiance which they owe to Him who hath said: 'Love your enemies.'" Yearly meetings with strong universalist tendencies use similar language; Philadelphia Yearly Meeting, for example, urges members to "be faithful in maintaining our testimony against war as contrary to the spirit and teaching of Christ. Every human being is a child of God with a measure of God's Light. War and other instruments or violence and oppression ignore this reality and violate our relation with God."[16]

Individual Friends restate and expand these ideas. One, arguing that pacifism is "the core of Quakerism," put it thus: "Pacifism is the gospel of love translated into everyday life, and it is on this cutting edge that Quakerism will rise or fall." "We who call ourselves Quakers . . . make a commitment when we become Friends to live in such unity with God's spirit, that all occasions for bitterness, recrimination, and individual or group self-seeking become meaningless and vain," wrote a New York Friend. In such a life, there would be no occasion for violence. "War is always wrong, since it violates Jesus' command to love everyone," wrote Samuel Levering, an influential Virginia Friend. "How can we love a person and at the same time kill him or her?"[17]

Since their earliest days, Friends have debated the implications of the Peace Testimony. Abstaining from bearing arms and serving in the military were clear consequences, but other questions were myriad. Could one pay taxes for military purposes? Could one sail in an armed ship? Was law enforcement that used deadly force different from warfare? Did the Peace Testimony forbid capital punishment? Those debates continue.

Any consideration of individuals and groups working for peaceful settlement of conflicts and to create a "culture of peace" today will find a disproportionate Quaker presence. Individual Friends like C. H. Mike Yarrow, George Lakey, Landrum Bolling, and Kenneth and Elise Boulding have international reputations for mediating disputes or theoretical work on peacemaking. As will be seen, peace work is central for the AFSC and FCNL. Over the past three decades, Friends have also formed partnerships with the other historic peace churches, the Mennonites and the Brethren, to try to advance their common commitments. The first of these was New Call to Peacemaking in the 1970s. It has been joined by two other projects, Alternatives to Violence and Christian Peacemaker Teams. The former attempts to offer conflict resolution in varied situations, ranging from American prisons to Rwanda, the African nation that horrified the world with its massacres in 1994. Christian Peacemakers have traveled to the Middle East to try to encourage peace-minded Palestinians and Israelis and to keep their hopes for peace before the larger world. Yet another example of the organized Quaker peace impulse is the Compassionate Listening Project. It has tried since 1996 to listen "to thousands of Israelis and Palestianians with the intention of discovering the human being behind the stereotype" and "build[ing] the international contituency for Mideast peace while offering a practical tool for conflict resolution on the ground." Other Friends are enthusiastic internationalists, continuing a tradition that goes back to William Penn, who suggested a plan for a European union more than three hundred years ago. They look to the United Nations as an international law enforcement body, or even advocate the abolition of nation-states and their replacement with a world government. Samuel and Miriam Levering, Virginia Friends long active in Friends United Meeting, played leading roles in the international Law of the Sea treaty negotiations in the 1970s. These Friends admit that they have not prevented war or brought universal peace, but, as one puts it, "I don't think any of us knows the ripple effects of relatively small Quaker actions undertaken by a minority of Friends."[18]

The personal manifestations of pacifism among contemporary Friends are varied. A number of Friends feel called to "conscientious objection to the payment of war taxes." Some purposely keep their incomes below the threshold for taxation. Others withhold the portion that they calculate goes for military purposes; others refuse to pay any federal taxes. Still others advocate changes in federal law so that those who have conscientious objections to war may direct that their tax payments be used for only non-military purposes in a "Peace Tax Fund." Some are committed to direct action, like a few Friends who have tried to damage missiles or submarines or block the transport of weapons. Some argue that even to register with Selective Service with a declaration of conscientious objection is wrong. "If Friends truly value peace, the very least we can do is treat our fellow citizens to the spectacle of God's people being dragged off to prison for obeying his commandments," wrote one Philadelphia Friend. Many see the abolition of capital punishment as a natural implication of the Peace Testimony. A few argue that all governments are violent by nature and so should be abolished in a kind of Christian anarchy. Some, as a witness to nonviolence (and for ecological reasons), are vegetarians or vegans. "Quaker words for peace and justice are hollow if they do not renounce all exploitation of animals," asserted one Friend.[19]

Sometimes Friends are, as Arthur Roberts put it, "personally pacifist and publicly bellicose," ferocious in their denunciations of U.S. policies that they see as the cause of most of the war and misery in the world. For them, refraining from violence personally is not enough. They feel it their duty to remove "the occasions for war" by dismantling institutions and structures that, in their eyes, encourage war. Such an outlook informs the foreign policy views of a number of Friends. Thus many peace-activist Quakers are outspokenly supportive of Palestinian causes. Typical was one who condemned "the Zionist government of Israel" for behaving "as if the Jews were the only ones experiencing hatred or the only ones with a holocaust to remember." Such Friends over the past two decades have been equally outspoken in condemning U.S. policies toward Iraq, Cuba, and Nicaragua, and the use of military force in the Balkans in the 1990s.[20]

Many pacifist Friends see peace as inextricably intertwined with justice. They embrace the slogan, "No justice, no peace," not because they think that injustice justifies war or violence, but from a conviction that most violence grows out of injustice. Thus they see the roots of violent crime not primarily in personal moral failure but in systemic inequities in the U.S. legal and economic systems. "We must move away from a system based on retaliation, punishment, and disablement toward a nonviolent, non-repressive system of justice based on reconciliation—correcting wrongs through persuasion, mediation, conflict resolution, restoration, and restitution," is a sentiment that these Friends embrace. In the past decade, many pacifist Friends have come to see multinational corporations as sources of violence. Quakers have been involved in the widely publicized protests against the World Trade Organization in Seattle, Genoa, and elsewhere.[21]

Not all pacifist unprogrammed Friends accept such views. In the 1980s, some were disturbed by what they saw as Quaker toleration of leftist violence concurrent with vigorous condemnation of American use of force. "Quakers seem to feel that plain speaking about communist states . . . will put them in league with the John Birch Society," complained one critic. Others conclude that some forms of activism are misguided or even, as one Friend described war tax resistance, "stupid," since the government almost always prevails. One Quaker historian argues that Quakers should decouple the Peace Testimony from social activism. The best that any church can do, he argues, is "to pray for peace and leave the issue in God's hands. It cannot prevent war, because it has neither theology, mission, nor the leverage in society to do so." Enormous expenditures of Quaker energy in peace activism, he concludes, have had little impact and have never stopped a war. Therefore, while Friends, in obedience to God, should refrain from bearing arms, they should recognize the futility of activist efforts.[22]

Radical activism underlies popular views of contemporary Quakers, but it is the exception, practiced almost exclusively among unprogrammed Friends. Even some unprogrammed Friends who consider themselves equally committed to the Peace Testimony look askance at such activities. Among pastoral Friends, there is less commitment to pacifism and considerable hostility toward what many see as overly politicized Quakerism. These views are not polar opposites; the range of Quaker ideas about peace and pacifism is a continuum.

Certainly many pastoral Friends are committed pacifists. They embrace the statement of Northwest Yearly Meeting: "The teachings of Jesus, the whole spirit of His Gospel, and the provisions of His grace call us to live at peace with all men. We believe that war and violence are not consistent with the Christian holiness to which we are summoned in Christ." The end—abstaining from violence—is the same as what more liberal Friends seek. But for these Friends, a Christian basis is critical. War and violence, even in self-defense, are wrong because they violate commands of Christ and are incompatible with the holiness of life to which all Christians are called. Indeed, they argue that this belief is the only sound basis for peacemaking. "If we would be peacemakers, we will need to be in the process of becoming God's children," wrote one such Friend. "If we enter into peacemaking because the church ought to be doing it, or because we need to make the church relevant to this modern day, or because it is so satisfying to help others, we won't last beyond the committee stage." Such Friends concede that to most non-Quaker evangelicals, such ideas are strange, and they respond by citing the Apostle Paul that sometimes Christians are called to be "fools for Christ." Indeed, to "resist not evil," i.e., refuse to counter violence with violence, may bring suffering and even death. But those who trust in God can do nothing else. Jack Willcuts, for example, argued that Friends who could not accept pacifism should find other churches.[23]

Both evangelical and pastoral Friends have acted on their pacifist beliefs. Oregon (now Northwest) Yearly Meeting, strongly evangelical, had the highest rate of conscientious objection of any yearly meeting during the Korean and Vietnam wars. A recent poll of its young people showed that pacifism was still strong there. In the 1980s, Evangelical Friends leaders like Willcuts and Norval Hadley braved considerable criticism to oppose the Reagan arms buildup and to support the nuclear freeze movement. "One wonders what a national policy of giving food to the hungry, medical care to the ill, agricultural aid and business capital to the poor would do in making for peace as compared to exporting munitions and armaments to the small and larger countries?" Willcuts asked. "The only defense is to prevent a nuclear war," Hadley argued in 1982. "The only way we do that is to settle differences peaceably." Still, such Quakers are clearly uncomfortable with radicalism. When Friends in EFI joined in New Call to Peacemaking in the 1970s, leaders assured skeptics that "there is absolutely no thought of marches, boycotts, or any type of demonstration that brings more violence than peace. Actions will be really successful as they spring from hearts and minds cleansed by the blood of Christ and motivated by the kind of love that led Him to the cross." Today, some pastoral Friends support the Christian Peacemaker Teams. Some pastoral meetings try to counsel all young members as they approach the age for military service or make peace part of Christian education curricula.[24]

Many Friends are not pacifists. We lack statistical data, but it appears safe to say that the proportion of pacifists is higher in unprogrammed meetings, since they contain many convinced Friends drawn to Quakerism by what they perceived as Quaker emphasis on peacemaking. Skepticism about or outright opposition to pacifism is more common among pastoral Friends. That skepticism has numerous sources. Sometimes it is based on the Bible. "There is no place in Christendom for the conscientious objector!" wrote one Evangelical Friend. "The Word of God is rather clear on the subject." Many cite history, especially World War II, as proof that nonresistance leads to the triumph of evil. One Iowa pastor argued that "pacifism is not an essential of the faith as evidenced by the fact that the vast majority of Christians do not hold that view. One need not be a pacifist in order to be a follower of Jesus Christ." Many pastoral Friends see national loyalty as inseparable from their faith in God; they often embrace the view of non-Quaker fundamentalists that God has destined the United States for world leadership and that military might is an essential element. Still others fear that peace activism detracts from evangelism. Pastors who emphasize the Peace Testimony often report uneasiness and even hostility among their members. Others flatly refuse to preach on it because they do not want to offend members with family in the armed forces.[25]

Given these variations, some Friends see the solution in leaving decisions to individual conscience. Eastern Region Evangelical Friends officially endorse this position, implicitly making the Peace Testimony a nonessential matter of faith. Elton Trueblood made freedom of conscience on bearing arms a matter of Quaker witness against "moral dogma." But Friends with impeccable liberal credentials have embraced this position as well. "If a man feels that his conscience urges him to fight, he must be faithful to the measure of Light he has, however small this may be," wrote Howard Brinton. Some argue that Friends should distinguish between wars and limited use of force for police purposes, whether within societies or to separate warring groups under the auspices of the United Nations, as in the Balkans in the 1990s.[26]

All of these conflicting currents can be seen in the responses of Friends to the terrorist attack of September 11, 2001. Quaker organizations, such as FGC, FUM, and the AFSC, as well as many meetings, issued statements deploring the terrorism but also calling for the United States to refrain from a military response. Typical was that from Friends in New York City: "Although all people of good will condemn these attacks and seek to have the perpetrators identified, brought to justice, and punished, this attack is best answered by rejecting the violence of the perpetrators." The challenge for Friends was "to clearly articulate a realistic, pragmatic, nonviolent methodology of achieving that end." When the U.S. attack in Afghanistan began, many individual Friends expressed disapproval; the general secretary of FUM publicly criticized President Bush's "inflammatory rhetoric." Others went farther. "Our rich nation has done little to answer the cries of the hungry, the victims of exploitation, the fearful," wrote a Friend from Chapel Hill, North Carolina. Another argued that the offensive in Afghanistan was a "blatant war of conquest" driven by oil companies. But other Quaker voices were heard. Some used the police analogy to justify the use of force. Scott Simon, the National Public Radio correspondent and a Quaker, argued that September 11 had convinced him that sometimes force was necessary as a last resort. A Quaker seminary professor sadly concluded that sometimes "the state may have to use force in this broken world." Some pastoral Friends responded even more enthusiastically; one EFI church had a military honor guard carry a flag into its sanctuary. A pastor saw God's hand in George W. Bush being in the White House to lead the nation.[27]

The Peace Testimony, like other beliefs that once defined Friends, is contested territory at the beginning of the twenty-first century. For some Friends, particularly in unprogrammed meetings, it is foundational, and peacemaking and conflict resolution movements in the United States still have a disproportionate Quaker presence. For probably a majority of American Friends, especially in pastoral meetings and churches, the place of the Peace Testimony is not as clear. Thus the testimony and its implications have become yet another source of conflict for a diverse and often fractious American Quakerism.

American Friends and People of Color

Probably no aspect of their history is a source of more pride for Quakers than their central role in the crusade against slavery. Abolitionist Friends such as John Woolman, Lucretia Mott, and John Greenleaf Whittier are among the chief heroes in the Quaker pantheon. Closely related is the relatively enlightened Quaker treatment of American Indians. Quaker insistence on nonviolence and fair dealing was usually in marked contrast with the attitudes of non-Quaker neighbors.

Reality, however, is more complex. Certainly, for most of American history, Friends have been more enlightened than their neighbors. But they have attracted relatively few people of color to their meetings. As one Quaker has noted, today American Friends are "overwhelmingly white, suburban, and well-heeled." The racial homogeneity of American Quakerism is all the more striking compared with the growth of Quakerism in Africa, Asia, and Latin America. Today, a majority of the world's Quakers are people of color. Indeed, if one were to envision the "typical" Quaker, he would be a poor, black, rural Kenyan.[28]

As was noted in chapter 2, Friends in Pennsylvania worked hard to try to keep the peace with their Native American neighbors. After the American Revolution, Quakers continued this interest. By current standards, their record was mixed. While they condemned U.S. policies of conquest and removal and tried to hold the federal government to the terms of treaties, the Quaker vision for the Indian future involved assimilation and adoption of Christianity. In some cases, Friends could claim success, as among the Seneca in upstate New York. In others, they failed.[29]

A turning point came in the 1870s, when the federal government adopted a "peace policy" of entrusting the "civilization" of Native Americans to various religious groups. Both Gurneyite and Hicksite Friends joined the effort. Hicksites phased it out after roughly a decade, but Gurneyite Friends, even after they lost their government agencies, continued to run Indian schools. By the 1890s, they had also established several churches among Indians in what is now Oklahoma, congregations that continue down to the present day as part of Mid-America and Great Plains yearly meetings. The entity established to oversee the work also continues, as the Associated Committee of Friends on Indian Affairs. Largely evangelical in orientation, it sees itself as both a missionary and a service organization to Native Americans. Later missionary work also established a number of Friends churches among Alaskan Eskimos. Today, one finds other theological splits reflected in Quaker attitudes toward Native Americans. Liberal Friends emphasize the need to respect the "timeless quality of Native American beliefs and worship." Evangelical Friends, while respectful of American Indian traditions and culture, still resist anything that suggests a melding of "paganism" with Christianity.[30]

The relationship of Quakerism and African Americans is even more complex. Even as Friends concluded that slavery was wrong, they were slow to embrace black people as full members of the Society of Friends. Only after considerable discussion was the first African American member, Abigail Franks, received into Philadelphia Yearly Meeting in 1784. A few others followed over the next eighty years. Probably the best known was Paul Cuffe, a New Bedford, Massachusetts sea captain, who sometimes spoke in meetings for worship.[31]

Quaker racial attitudes are a matter of debate among historians. Jean Soderlund has concluded that even as Friends condemned slavery, their "gradualist, segregationist, and paternalistic policies" presaged the later attitudes of white America. Certainly, in some eastern Quaker communities, meeting houses and graveyards were segregated. Similarly, in the Phila-

Kickapoo Friends Church, a Native American congregation in Oklahoma. FRIENDS COLLECTION, EARLHAM COLLEGE.

delphia area, while many Friends were supportive of and taught in black schools, they usually did not admit blacks to their schools for white children. The situation was somewhat different among Friends west of the Appalachians, where there is no evidence of such segregation and where black children often did attend schools with white Quaker children. On the positive side, Quakers were often in advance of their neighbors in condemning racial prejudice and calling for equal legal rights for people of color, both east and west of the Appalachians. During and after the Civil War, hundreds of Friends went south as teachers among the freed people. Indiana Yearly Meeting (Orthodox) was responsible for the establishment of Southland College in Arkansas, the first black college west of the Mississippi. Yet, despite calls by some of these workers for establishing black meetings, only one, at Southland, was set up. In the first three decades of the twentieth century, Quaker interest in racial justice reached a nadir. Quaker schools and other institutions in the east were segregated. In Indiana in the 1920s, hundreds of Friends became members of the Ku Klux Klan.[32]

Some Friends, however, maintained an interest in racial justice, which abhorrence of Nazi racist ideology heightened in the 1930s and 1940s. One of the founders of the NAACP in 1910 was the long-time clerk of the Orthodox New York Yearly Meeting, Levi Hollingsworth Wood. Black students were admitted to Earlham College and the Cleveland Bible Institute before 1900, and by the 1940s Earlham students were openly challenging local segregationist practices. In the 1920s, the American Friends Service Committee developed an interest in race relations as an obvious field for Quaker work. By the 1950s, Quaker schools in the east had ceased to exclude black students. These commitments climaxed in the civil rights movement of the 1950s and 1960s. The AFSC was consistently supportive of civil rights work. The Friends Committee on National Legislation likewise played an important role, promoting civil rights bills in Congress between 1957 and 1968. And many individual Friends were actively involved in the movement in the 1960s. The first integrated kindergarten in Augusta, Georgia, for example, was a Quaker project, and the director of education for the 1964 "Freedom Summer" in Mississippi was a Friend, Staughton Lynd. Quaker periodicals gave the movement consistent support, and yearly meetings of all theological persuasions strengthened statements against racial prejudice.[33]

This activism had two results. First, it drew at least a few black attenders to Quaker worship, some of whom eventually became members. Second, it caused a number of Friends to cast a critical eye on themselves, asking why they attracted so few blacks.

We have no statistics on how many African Americans belong to or attend Quaker meetings. Impressions are that they are less than 1 percent of all American Friends. Black members report that it is common to find themselves the only people of color in their meetings. Yet some are drawn to Friends, both programmed and unprogrammed. Bayard Rustin, one of the central figures of the civil rights movement, was a lifelong Quaker, and credited that background for his own commitment to nonviolence. Some black Friends see in Quakerism a welcome contrast with the often autocratic pastors of black churches. Some are drawn by what draws other Friends, an attraction to Quaker testimonies.[34]

Still, such converts are few, and some Friends worry about what this says about American Quakerism. "The lack of black members and attenders in our Religious Society causes us untold problems. Our lack of racial

Bayard Rustin. COURTESY OF WALTER NAEGLE.

representativeness is an embarrassment and an anachronism," one wrote in 1983. "Unless our meetings and churches become more welcoming and inclusive and deal with issues of racism, the future of the Religious Society of Friends is in danger," was the conclusion of a conference in 1999. Not a few see white Quakers as infected, often unknowingly, by the racism of the larger American society. That racism manifests itself, they argue, in varied ways: the Quaker "culture" of disapproval of bright colors or gold jewelry or open displays of emotion; the often-glacial Quaker business process; the historic Quaker imagery of equating light with goodness and darkness with evil. Even the historic Quaker office of "overseer" carries unhappy connotations for African Americans. Some Friends see their meetings as characterized by "white privilege." In 1996, the Friends General Conference summer gathering included an "Underground Railroad Game" for youth. Its organizers saw it as a way of teaching about a bright spot in Quaker history. Some African Americans present, however, saw it as trivializing part of their heritage. These concerns come almost entirely from unprogrammed meetings, which, as some Friends point out, have seldom shown much interest in trying to recruit anyone. Friends face a conundrum: with so few black members and attenders, they have few ways of knowing what attracts or repels African Americans.[35]

Generally, pastoral Friends, while equally committed by their official statements to racial equality, worry less about their racial homogeneity. They acknowledge that they are not free from lingering racism, and some have shown an interest in trying to organize meetings and churches in urban black neighborhoods. EFI, for example, has started churches among Haitians in Brooklyn and Florida. Probably the best-known example among Quakers is the Chicago Fellowship of Friends. Located in the Cabrini-Green public housing projects in an especially violence-plagued neighborhood, it was founded by Steve and Marlene Pedigo, two Iowa Friends ministers. Its membership is almost entirely African American and constitutes a monthly meeting of Western Yearly Meeting. Other meetings have tried to form ties or partnerships with black congregations of other denominations.[36]

In their racial homogeneity, Quakers are similar to most American denominations. As sociologists of religion have noted, Sunday morning worship is still probably the most segregated time in American society. Friends, however, generally see themselves as aspiring to higher standards than the rest of American society. It is likely that for the foreseeable future their lack of racial diversity will be a cause of concern, if not grief, for many.

Realizing Quaker Aspirations: The American Friends Service Committee and the Friends Committee on National Legislation

Two Quaker organizations, the American Friends Service Committee (AFSC) and the Friends Committee on National Legislation (FCNL), embody the Quaker urge to do good in the world. Not all American Friends embrace them; both, especially the AFSC, have become controversial, and some Friends see them as insensitive to or even subversive of vital Quaker beliefs.

The AFSC is the older of the two. It came into being in 1917 as a way for Friends who would not serve in the armed forces to render service during World War I, and, in the minds of some of its founders, as a means of healing Quaker divisions. Hundreds of young Quaker men, and some women, went to Europe to aid in rebuilding war-torn areas between 1917 and 1919. After the war ended, Friends made the decision to continue the organization to try to meet other needs. The first was feeding hundreds of thousands of German children. Similar work in the Soviet Union followed. The 1920s also saw the first AFSC projects in the United States, and during the Great Depression of the 1930s the organization became involved in major relief projects, such as trying to resettle unemployed Appalachian coal miners on subsistence homesteads. Close relations between AFSC Ex-

AFSC unit in training, 1917. COURTESY OF AFSC.

ecutive Secretary Clarence Pickett and First Lady Eleanor Roosevelt in the 1930s gave the organization positive publicity. It also continued its relief work in war zones, first in Spain in the 1930s, then in Europe and Asia after the outbreak of World War II. These efforts won considerable acclaim, culminating in the awarding of the Nobel Peace Prize to the AFSC and its British equivalent, the Friends Service Council, in 1947, on behalf of all Quakers. Such work usually involved individual Friends, both pastoral and unprogrammed, giving up time to lend hands or expertise abroad. Gathering clothes and other items for relief became and remains a regular activity in many meetings. Another popular AFSC activity was weekend and summer work camps, which took Friends into impoverished areas for building and other aid projects.[37]

In the postwar period, the AFSC changed in two fundamental ways. In its early days, it drew funds and workers from both programmed and unprogrammed Friends; the first four executive secretaries came from pastoral yearly meetings. Increasingly, however, the AFSC depended less on volunteer Quakers offering service and more on professional staff. By 1960, a majority of AFSC staff were not Friends, and most of the organization's donations and money came from non-Quakers impressed by its idealism and accomplishments. Moreover, most of the Friends on the AFSC staff

Eleanor Roosevelt visits an AFSC subsistence homestead in 1934. FRIENDS COLLECTION, EARLHAM COLLEGE.

were connected with unprogrammed meetings. Many of them believed that many American Quakers had made dangerous compromises with the larger society and no longer maintained a strong peace witness. They wanted to use the AFSC to return Quakerism to what they saw as radical first principles.[38]

This led the AFSC in new directions. One was a growing emphasis on domestic affairs in the United States. In 1950, most AFSC funds were spent outside the United States. In 1960, most were dispersed within the country. Much of the new domestic emphasis supported the civil rights movement. The AFSC, for example, was responsible for the first mass distribution of Martin Luther King Jr.'s *Letter from the Birmingham Jail*. There was also more focus on war prevention. The turning point was the publication in 1955 of *Speak Truth to Power*, an articulate pacifist analysis of American military and foreign policy. It argued for unilateral U.S. disarmament, asserting that the Cold War national security state was undermining democracy and it was better to "give up our military security and accept the risks that this involves, than keep our guns and lose our democracy." This pacifist vision not only resisted participation in war but also sought fundamental social, political, and economic changes in order to remove the sources of all kinds of violence. In the late 1950s and early 1960s, the AFSC became increasingly visible in public protests against U.S. military and foreign policy.[39]

Thus it was not surprising that the AFSC threw itself into the anti-Vietnam War movement in the 1960s and early 1970s, participating in the earliest protests and teach-ins. By 1967, it was arousing fierce criticism over a decision to make medical supplies available to the North Vietnamese enemies of the United States as well as its allies in South Vietnam. By 1970, it was clear that some AFSC staff saw in New Left movements such as the Students for a Democratic Society, the Black Panthers, and women's liberation the forces that they thought would transform a racist, imperialist, and inherently violent American society.[40]

This vision of the ills of American society and the need for nonviolent revolution to transform it, as well as a sense of commonality with many groups on the Left, underpinned many AFSC policies in the 1970s and 1980s. It early endorsed abortion rights. In the 1980s, it was a vociferous opponent of Reagan administration foreign policy, from aid to the Nicaraguan Contras to the anti-Soviet arms buildup. The AFSC never condoned violence, but did not always see foes involved in violent struggles as moral equals. For example, while it called for peace in the Middle East and affirmed

Clarence Pickett. FRIENDS COLLECTION, EARLHAM COLLEGE.

the right of the state of Israel to exist, most of its criticism was aimed at Israeli policies. Citing pragmatic coincerns, some AFSC staff argued that they had the right as American citizens to criticize U.S. policies, but should remain circumspect about conditions in communist countries or risk the end of contacts and programs that were doing good. Increasingly the AFSC saw itself as an organization that not merely provided relief but also empowered victims of social injustice. It denounced state and federal policies that it perceived as burdensome on the poor, women, and racial and ethnic minorities. In order to serve oppressed groups and avoid the appearance of white middle-class paternalism, AFSC staff argued, it needed to hire more blacks, Latinos, and gays, who often were not represented among Quakers. In 1979, the AFSC made homosexuals an affirmative action group in hiring, thus embracing gay liberation in its early days. Quaker staff shrank to about 15 percent. The work camps that had been so important to so many Friends were abandoned.[41]

These changes did not come without criticism. Many pastoral Friends, not pacifist themselves, saw aiding the North Vietnamese in the 1960s as nothing short of treason. Some pacifist Friends, some even on the AFSC staff, were increasingly uncomfortable with what they perceived as an AFSC peace impulse that was grounded not so much in Quaker testimonies as leftist politics, with the AFSC allied with groups that were not pacifist by any stretch of the imagination. After the end of the Vietnam War, some Friends protested what they saw as a double standard, as the AFSC seemed uninterested in criticizing human rights abuses (or outright massacres) by leftist regimes. The seeming tilt toward Palestinians in the ongoing Middle East conflict brought charges of a double standard that ignored Palestinian terrorism. Others questioned the AFSC refusal to link its work in any way to a Christian vision, to act "in the name of Jesus." Vocal protests were evoked by AFSC support of gay and abortion rights. For many pastoral Friends, this was simply an embrace of sin. For other Friends, the changes in focus that brought about the end of the work camps and the extremely limited opportunities for Quakers to give short-term service were sources of irritation.[42]

AFSC Gulf War protest. COURTESY OF AFSC.

Today the AFSC has more than 400 employees working around the world. Its Quaker ties are largely with unprogrammed yearly meetings. Its projects are myriad, with a budget of between $35 million and $38 million a year; supporters argue that few groups accomplish so much with relatively limited resources. Over 50 percent of its funds still go to relief work, such as dispatching first aid and supplies to war zones in Afghanistan, the Balkans, and Africa. Much of its work is peace-related, as is evident in the Fall 2001 issue of the AFSC *Quaker Service Bulletin*. It highlights AFSC support for peace movements in Colombia and the Middle East and, not surprisingly, calls for a nonviolent U.S. response to the September 11 terrorist attacks. Resistance to U.S. Navy use of the Puerto Rican island of Vieques is applauded. Solidarity with Palestinians is clear. The AFSC is also concerned for justice. It has given particular attention to undocumented immigrants, or, as they are often termed, illegal aliens, calling for legalization of their residence. It refuses to abide by federal regulations requiring employees to document their immigration status. Still other AFSC programs seek to fight racism, homophobia, sexism, and discrimination against people with disabilities, challenging structures that it views as oppressive and empowering those who are oppressed. At times the rhetoric in some AFSC publications is indistinguishable from that of journals of the political Left like *The Nation* or the *Progressive*.[43]

Certainly many Friends are uncomfortable with the AFSC's direction. Critics, many of them unprogrammed Friends liberal in politics and theology, see the organization as hopelessly committed to what one called "fashionable liberalism." Another critic charged that the AFSC was fixated on a "victim theology" that had degenerated into "divisive debates" resulting in much of Quakerism disavowing any connection to it. In 1998, one staffer left, publicly claiming that "the wolves of political correctness . . . have bled me of what vitality I have to dedicate." Particularly upsetting to many are proposals to allow non-Quakers to become part of AFSC governance.[44]

Other Friends, however, respond with spirited defenses of the AFSC. As Mary Ellen McNish, the AFSC executive secretary, observes, "Even if they don't know what it's doing, they trust what it's doing." They see in it "a multicultural organization based on the principles of Friends," even if most of its staff are no longer Quakers. That religious diversity reflects the diversity of American society, which the AFSC should reflect if it is to help achieve a more just and peaceful world. They point out, moreover, that involvement with the AFSC has drawn many employees to join Friends.

And AFSC policy is still ultimately determined by a board whose members are all Friends. Supporters respond to charges of overpoliticization by arguing that Friends have long joined with non-Friends to advance Quaker testimonies and that Quaker involvement serves to moderate impulses that might otherwise turn to violence. At times the AFSC may be ahead of most Friends, but, as two supporters put it, "there is a benefit to Friends to have a Quaker organization testing new waters without all Friends having to find unity among quite diverse elements as a preliminary step." Indeed, as Ohio Yearly Meeting (Conservative) noted, it was "at a loss as to how the Service Committee might satisfy all who call themselves Friends." Given the diversity of American Quakerism, any organization as ambitious as the AFSC is unlikely to please everyone.[45]

The other Quaker organization with an impact on American society is the Friends Committee on National Legislation (FCNL). It is the offspring of the AFSC. During World War II, AFSC staff and supporters were deeply concerned about proposals for a continuing draft and universal military training, but the organization could not engage in lobbying or political activity. So the FCNL was founded in 1943 to try to translate Quaker political concerns into action in Washington; it was the country's first religious lobbying organization. In its early years, the FCNL focused almost entirely on matters of war and peace. Not surprisingly, its efforts for disarmament and reducing military budgets yielded few victories during the Cold War, save defeat of proposals for universal military training. In the 1960s and 1970s it also worked to end U.S. involvement in the Vietnam War and to support the civil rights movement.[46]

Today, the FCNL is highly respected as a small but effective religious lobby. In 1980, for example, the House of Representatives Republican Research Committee praised it for providing "no misleading or misdirecting figures or rubrics. Only objective information is included [in FCNL information packets]." Its leaders early recognized that Quakers could not lobby as a pressure group—their numbers were too few to threaten legislators with political retribution in the way that the National Rifle Association or the American Association of Retired Persons can. Instead, it tries to find issues, often not "hot" topics, where a small group, working with a few interested members of Congress, can affect policy.[47]

The governing group for the FCNL is a committee of about 250 members, made up of representatives appointed by 26 yearly meetings (mostly part of FGC, FUM, or independent) and 7 Quaker organizations. It in turn appoints standing committees, which work with staff to accomplish the FCNL's goals. All decisions are made through the Quaker business method of seeking unity by waiting for the guidance of the Holy Spirit. Every few years the FCNL drafts a "Statement of Legislative Policy." It incorporates both areas in which Friends have found unity and "challenges," where unity is not present. In turn, every two years the organization identifies legislative priorities for Congress, based on comments from monthly meetings and individual Friends.[48]

The most recent statement was revised in 2001. Its preamble sketches its overall goals: "We seek a world free of war and the threat of war. We seek a society with equity and justice for all. We seek a community where every person's potential may be fulfilled. We seek an earth restored." To realize this vision, it goes on to recommend dozens of specific policies. In the area of peace and war, they include increased support for the United Nations, reductions in armaments, and strategies for peaceful prevention of deadly conflict. It advocates "equity and justice" through changes such as abolition of the death penalty, criminal justice reforms, and honoring treaty commitments to Native Americans. It seeks to fulfill individual potential by advocating policies to aid the poor and others it perceives as vulnerable in society. A relatively new FCNL focus is "an earth restored" through work on environmental issues.[49]

Certainly many organizations, including other religious lobbies, take political stands that not all of their members embrace. The FCNL is careful never to claim to speak for all Friends, although it does see its constituent yearly meetings as "broadly representative." It does not take positions when the representatives do not find unity. As a former staff member observed, "Friends have not reached the clarity on economic issues that we have on questions of peace, overt violence, religious freedom, and racial injustice." This is even more true about abortion, an issue on which the FCNL has always acknowledged disagreement among Friends. Certainly the organization at times receives criticism from Friends whose positions differ from its own. Here is a paradox. Doubtless a number of Friends do not embrace the FCNL's calls for disarmament and opposition to the use of force, most recently in response to September 11, and in fact find them weak and unrealistic. Generally, the Democratic party, or even the Green party, is closer to the FCNL than the Republican party, which receives the votes of many American Friends, especially pastoral ones. But because FCNL positions on peace and other issues are grounded so firmly in traditional Quaker testimonies that their yearly meetings still at least theoretically endorse, and because the FCNL avoids hot-button issues like abortion, criticism is largely muted. And for many Friends the FCNL's accomplishments are a source of considerable pride. As former Republican U.S. Senator Mark Hatfield of Oregon wrote in 1993: "The agenda of FCNL has been nearly as broad as that facing the Congress itself. I know of numerous instances in which your voice has been heard, but the benefits of your work extend beyond its direct impact on legislation." Hatfield concluded that through its analyses and educational efforts, the FCNL had succeeded "in producing a clear-thinking, well-informed body of people across the country." Virtually all Friends see that as praiseworthy.[50]

Conclusions

American Quakers today do not face the world with a common set of attitudes. They agree that Quaker faith is expressed in commitments to justice and equality, but they understand and manifest those commitments in different ways. In politics, their faith is probably not always the critical factor. Like other Americans, many Friends probably vote their pocketbooks as often as they base their political thinking on their religion. In many respects, Quaker political attitudes mirror the larger American society: evangelical commitment usually translates into conservative politics, while theological liberalism usually coincides with political sympathies to the left of center. Similarly, Friends share a commitment to making the world a better place, but try to do that in different ways. Unprogrammed Friends use myriad forms of activism to transform societal structures and achieve peace, justice, and equality. Pastoral Friends, while often sympathetic to such causes, put more energy and resources into missions, preaching the gospel as the cure for the ills of the world, often defining "mission" broadly to include numerous types of service.

Quaker history qualifies this picture in important ways. Quaker tradition argues for pacifism, a worldview few other political and social conservatives embrace. As American Friends have become closely tied to the larger American society, however, many have lost that commitment. Other Friends, trying to translate the Peace Testimony into contemporary action, have become leaders in a variety of movements for peace and justice.

Quaker tradition, moreover, does not always draw into Quakerism those one might expect. Given their traditional commitment to opposing slavery and to the spiritual equality of all people, one would expect Friends to attract Native Americans and African Americans to their meetings and churches. Outside the United States, people of color now constitute a majority of the world's Quakers. But for complex reasons, in the United States, American Friends remain almost entirely white and middle class, a situation that many find troubling.

The diversity of American Quakerism is also clear in the work of, and the reactions of Friends to, the two leading organizations that try to translate Quaker concerns and testimonies into action, the American Friends Service Committee and the Friends Committee on National Legislation. Both have won praise from Friends and the larger society for their accomplishments, but neither has been able to unite all American Friends in a common vision of working Quaker testimonies in the world.

CHAPTER SEVEN

"A quarterly meeting in herself": Quaker Women, Marriage, and the Family

Delphina Mendenhall was, by all accounts, a formidable force among North Carolina Friends from the 1840s until her death in 1881—perhaps the wealthiest single member of the yearly meeting and a weighty elder. Her opinions had considerable weight among her fellow members. The Quaker poet John Greenleaf Whittier was once heard to exclaim: "Delphina? She is a quarterly meeting in herself."[1]

One of the distinctive features of Quakerism that invariably drew the attention, and sometimes the ire, of observers before 1900 was the standing of women. Almost unique among Protestant denominations, Quaker women spoke in worship and served as ministers. They also had a considerable role in leadership, although, as will be seen, not complete equality.

Today, all Friends take pride in this heritage. For most unprogrammed Friends, the role of Quaker women as "mothers of feminism" is something to celebrate. Evangelical Friends too remain committed to spiritual equality, to the belief that male and female are one in Christ. But trends in the larger society have had considerable impact on Friends over the last half century. Today Quaker women who describe themselves as feminists are as likely to draw on non-Quaker feminist theory and theology as on Quaker tradition. And many Evangelical Friends are deeply influenced by discourse about women in the larger American evangelical and fundamentalist movements.

These debates about the roles of women, in turn, have had considerable impact on Quaker families. All persuasions of Friends show conviction that in certain ways Quaker marriages and Quaker families will be different from those of "the world." But again, the impact of ideas drawn from that larger, non-Quaker world is clear. Outwardly, at least, most Quaker families are not significantly different from other American families.

Quaker Women: History

As chapter 2 showed, women were important figures in early Quaker history. Elizabeth Hooten was George Fox's first convert, and Margaret Fell not only became George Fox's wife but probably ranked second only to him as a leader among Friends after 1660. The Quaker acceptance of public ministry by women was one of the most distinctive features of the early movement. Quaker women traveled widely, not only in the British Isles but also in Europe, North America, and the Caribbean. Often, Friends described God, and their spiritual experiences, in language that was overtly feminine.[2]

Equality was not complete. Especially after 1660, Quakers shared the assumptions of the larger world that men would have more power than women. Thus men handled matters of finance and property. Bodies like the Meeting for Sufferings that operated as yearly meeting executive committees were exclusively male. By 1701, the London Morning Meeting of Ministers, another all-male body, was complaining about women ministers who took up all of the time in worship "when several public and serviceable men friends" were present.[3]

On the other hand, Quaker women did have more power within their denomination than any other group of Christian women. In the 1660s, Friends began to establish a parallel system of business meetings at the monthly and quarterly meeting level, with each gender dealing with disciplinary matters of members of its own sex. In North America, women's yearly meetings were early established, but there was no equivalent body in England until 1784. For Friends to act on any matter of business or doctrine, the unity of both men's and women's meetings was required. And, perhaps most important, Quaker women continued to be recognized as ministers and to travel widely.[4]

After the separations of the nineteenth century, Quaker women moved in divergent directions. Generally, Hicksite women were more attracted to radical feminism and the early women's rights movement than were Orthodox, although there were some exceptions. Lucretia Mott (1793–1880)

Lucretia Mott. COURTESY OF FRIENDS HISTORICAL LIBRARY, SWARTHMORE COLLEGE.

of Philadelphia was a central figure in the first women's rights convention in the United States, held at Seneca Falls, New York in 1848; three of the five organizers were Hicksite women. Similarly, Hicksite women were founders of the women's rights movement in Pennsylvania, Ohio, and Indiana. Congregational Friends were especially committed to legal equality for women. Susan B. Anthony (1820–1906), another Hicksite Friend, was central to the movement from the 1860s until her death, second perhaps only to Elizabeth Cady Stanton in influence. Hicksite Friends helped establish the Female Medical College of Philadelphia in 1850. Hicksite women were also vital to the founding of Swarthmore College in 1864 and in making the school, in contrast to most other eastern colleges, coeducational.[5]

The paths of Orthodox Quaker women tended to be different. Wilburites continued to recognize women as ministers, but showed little interest in women's rights before the late nineteenth century. Gurneyite Quaker women tended to be less aggressive than Hicksites in pressing for legal equality, instead focusing on humanitarian reforms in the ways that other evangelical Protestant women had been doing. Prohibition of the manufacture and sale of alcoholic beverages was a favorite cause. Rhoda M. Coffin (1826–1909) of Richmond, Indiana was a central figure in the prison reform movement after the Civil War, while another Gurneyite minister, Elizabeth L. Comstock (1815–1891) of Michigan, was known both as a prison reformer and for her relief work among the freed slaves. One of the American Quaker woman best known in the larger world after the Civil War was Hannah Whitall Smith (1832–1911), whose *The Christian's Secret of a Happy Life* is still considered an evangelical devotional classic. The Gurneyite Quaker colleges were all coeducational, except for Haverford, which after 1885 had Bryn Mawr as its female counterpart.[6]

Alice Paul. COURTESY OF FRIENDS HISTORICAL LIBRARY, SWARTHMORE COLLEGE.

In the early twentieth century, Quaker women continued to play a disproportionate role in feminist causes. A central figure in the campaign for the women's suffrage Nineteenth Amendment was Alice Paul (1885–1977), a Hicksite Friend from New Jersey who was also the author of the original Equal Rights Amendment. Emily Greene Balch (1867–1961), a convinced Friend from Boston, was one of the founders of the Women's International League for Peace and Freedom; she received the Nobel Prize for Peace in 1946 in recognition of her work for international disarmament and arbitration. Many other Quaker women worked for peace and social change through groups like the American Friends Service Committee (AFSC) and the Fellowship of Reconciliation. In contrast, most pastoral Quaker women were relatively subdued. They tended to support women's suffrage, and many were active in peace movements, most notably Hannah J. Bailey (1839–1923), a Maine Friend who for many years headed the peace division of the Woman's Christian Temperance Union. Often they were full partners in their husbands' work, like Emma Brown Malone (1859–1924), the wife of Walter Malone of Cleveland and cofounder of the Cleveland Bible Institute.[7]

There is much that we do not know about the experiences of Quaker women within their meetings and churches in the first half of the twentieth century, but the records we have suggest that Friends were becoming more like the larger American society. By 1920, virtually all had united men's and women's business meetings. That almost always meant that men became clerks and women took subordinate roles. Similarly, as Friends created organizations like the AFSC or the Five Years Meeting or FGC, men served as their leaders. The Hicksite abolition of recording ministers meant that women lost that distinction. In pastoral yearly meetings, women continued to be recorded as ministers and to serve as pastors. But the number steadily declined between 1900 and 1960. Many pastoral Friends accepted the views of other denominations that only a man could be an effective pastor. Increasingly, pastoral Quaker women carried out their activities in women's circles and missionary societies, as was the case in other churches. Still, many continued to feel that Quakerism offered them spiritual opportunities that they would not find in other denominations. As one elderly Quaker woman put it in 1975: "There has been the Quaker tradition of equality, and I've never felt the need to push for jobs or anything. I've never felt unliberated."[8]

Quaker women's response to the rise of feminism and women's liberation in the late 1960s was mixed. Some, especially in FGC and unprogrammed meetings, almost immediately embraced these movements as consistent with traditional Quaker testimonies of equality. The AFSC formed numerous programs to work for equality and fight the exploitation of women. With the FCNL and many other Quaker organizations, it endorsed the new campaign for the ERA. Even the Evangelical Friends Alliance, which tended to look askance at "women's libbers," formed a task force on women. These movements had significant impact. Over the next three decades, major Quaker organizations like AFSC, FGC, and FUM would have female heads. But other Quakers, both men and women mainly in pastoral yearly meetings, saw the demands of feminists as too strident, as threatening the family and traditional moral values, or even as communist inspired. These divisions, along much the same lines, still characterize contemporary American Friends.[9]

Quaker Women Today

There is no such person as a "typical Quaker woman." Most Quaker women today are outwardly indistinguishable from their neighbors. Some put considerable energy into translating the accomplishments of past generations of Quaker women into contemporary terms. For others, being a Quaker woman is less important than being a Christian and involves little distinctiveness.

Among unprogrammed Friends, probably a majority of women are comfortable describing themselves as feminists. As is true of the larger American society, each person understands that label differently. For some, it means being commited to equality: legal, political, economic, spiritual. Others argue that to be a Quaker feminist means seeking what one called "a path to a radically changed, more peaceful, more cooperative world." Some Friends suspect that numerous women in unprogrammed meetings have doubts about radical expressions of feminism but simply do not voice them, and that young Quaker women are not attracted by the feminist issues of the 1960s and 1970s.[10]

For many Quaker feminists, a starting point is freeing Quakerism from what they see as remnants of patriarchy, the social, legal, and religious conventions that have traditionally subordinated women to men. Thus in many unprogrammed meetings it is a given that all will use inclusive or gender-neutral language in speaking. For example, one would not speak of God as "he" or of "mankind." A Friend in Washington, D.C. told another that to hear God referred to as "he" was as offensive to her as hearing "nigger." "When I hear or read about 'he' or 'Our Father,' I, as a woman, feel devalued and disempowered," wrote another Quaker woman. One argued that the test should simply be whether a particular use of language is likely to hurt others and to act accordingly. "When I hear sexist language, I hurt. Isn't that enough?" she asked. Thus today FGC and other liberal Quaker publications strive to avoid offending in such ways. When FGC published a new hymnal a few years ago, it rewrote older hymns to use gender-inclusive language and excluded any written after 1960 that did not meet such standards. Some Friends criticize such sensitivity as excessive, but they appear to be a minority.[11]

Many Quaker women also incorporate feminism in their faith by exploring what they see as its female aspects, often drawing on the work of non-Quaker feminist theologians. Some focus on a perceived neglect of feminism in the Christian tradition. Elizabeth Watson is convinced that Jesus wanted to make women "equal partners in his new movement" and admires Mary as "the inner-directed woman who does not take her passive identity from men, but is an autonomous human being." She argues that the "subtle, all-pervading hierarchical structure in our society and religious tradition is . . . contrary to the mind of Christ." Other Quaker women focus on what they see as feminine aspects of God. Thus one writes that "Mother Nature is God, can be God, would be a better God than the male sky-God so many accept." Another argues that when God was understood as feminine or having feminine qualities, societies were "family-centered, artistic, and peaceful," while male gods produced competitive and violent cultures. This has drawn some Quaker feminists toward experimentation with Goddess imagery or even with Wicca, a contemporary faith that blends feminism with older, pre-Christian spiritualities. Others see lesbianism as a conscious and desirable antidote to patriarchy.[12]

Some Quaker feminists think that even unprogrammed Friends do not measure up to the commitment to full gender equality that Quakerism demands. "Sexism was alive and well in Quakerism" one survey of Quaker women concluded. Too often, they argue, men still hold leadership positions while women deal with child care and food preparation for meeting functions. Some worry that the Quaker emphasis on reconciliation has the byproduct of "short-circuiting and internalization of anger" and thus prevents "breaking new ground" that would make Friends confront the survival of sexism among them. Another has called for a revival of separate men's and women's business meetings as a way of encouraging more honest discussion and "celebrating gender differences."[13]

One finds more debate among pastoral Friends on feminism and the appropriate roles of women. Some pastoral Quakers embrace the label "feminist." Others shun it. Many endorse legal and economic equality but express doubts about the more radical aspects of feminism, such as its reconceptualization of the nature of God. Certainly many pastoral Friends, both liberal and evangelical, embrace the principle of equality for women. "It's not enough for the contemporary Christian male simply to tolerate female equality," wrote one EFI pastor in 1986. "It's essential that he promote it." Male superiority, another Evangelical Friend wrote, was "unscriptural and unquakerly." "I don't want my three daughters to live in a tiny *woman's world*," wrote Jack Willcuts. "I hope they will grow to understand that God's Spirit desires to cut through the tangled maze of tradition and misconceptions." Sexism, such Friends argue, is a sin from which Christ redeems believers.[14]

To understand pastoral Quaker attitudes about appropriate roles for women, it is essential to look at women Quaker pastors. As noted above, since the beginning of the pastoral system, there have always been some, although the number fell considerably between 1920 and 1970. Today it is increasing, albeit not without controversy.[15]

Certainly pastoral Friends remain committed, at least in theory, to the idea that women have just as much right to hold any position among Friends, including the pastorate, as men. One male pastor of evangelical views, for example, argued as early as 1982 that half of all Friends pastors should be women. "There is no question for Quakers as to whether or not God uses women in ministry," wrote Jack Willcuts. "Unless we remain clear on this truth, confirmed again and again by the Spirit's approval, we may be caught up in . . . myopic religious legalism." Overt opposition is seldom visible. And the number of women pastors has increased over the past twenty years, partly because of the determined support of some key yearly meeting superintendents.[16]

Yet virtually all pastoral Friends agree that there is resistance to women in positions of leadership among them. "We have a great image—but frankly, we've slipped," one Quaker woman wrote in 1987. "We have had a real leadership crisis and we aren't exactly bending over backwards to invite women to share in our pastoral, clerking, and superintendent positions of ministry." Yearly meeting superintendents supportive of women's ministry admit that there are pastorates that they do not encourage women to seek because of the rejection they would inevitably face. Resistance is generally greater in EFI than in FUM, doubtless reflecting the influence of non-Quaker fundamentalists who condemn women pastors as unbiblical.

Eastern Region, for example, had only one woman senior pastor in 2002, and she shared the position with her husband.[17]

Some pastoral Friends express doubts about aspects of the larger women's movement. One woman pastor remembered struggling with her call to ministry out of a fear that she would be labeled a "women's libber." Many pastoral Friends insist that there is nothing wrong with understanding God as male or as "The Father." To suggest otherwise, in their minds, is to tamper with inspired Scripture. "A distinction needs to be clear between the long-held belief and practices of Friends regarding scriptural teaching of the equality of women, and the political and sometimes strident demands of the Equal Rights for Women movement," one evangelical Friend urged. Many, both men and women, see contemporary feminists as "misdirected and frustrated women out of a sin-infused culture, women who have no concept of the power of submission within the ordained scheme of authority and order set in place by God."[18]

Perhaps nowhere are these tensions clearer than on the issue of abortion. Generally, pastoral Friends, especially those in EFI, are pro-life, while among unprogrammed Friends (except some Conservatives), pro-choice Friends are more visible and articulate. Neither group is monolithic, and both include many shades of opinion. At the extremes, the two sides begin from different vantage points. Pro-choice Friends see abortion as an issue of women's rights, while pro-life Friends, when they do not understand it as a matter of applying the Peace Testimony to unborn life, view it as one of basic morality.

Evangelical Friends are virtually one in opposing abortion. "If there were ever an issue that all churches and all Christians should unite on, it is opposition to abortion," wrote one. The Supreme Court's *Roe v. Wade* decision, said another, was based on "lies from the master of all lies, Satan." Most of the pastoral yearly meetings have taken stands against abortion, at least to some degree. Typical is Northwest Yearly Meeting's statement that it should not be used for "personal convenience or population control." Some Friends link opposition to abortion with opposition to war—both are wrong because God forbids taking the life of another human being. Others see abortion as simply immorality compounded, a way out for women who have engaged in extramarital sex. "If anyone should have to make a choice about abortion they have already made one mistake," wrote one Friend. Thus many pastoral Friends have been active in the pro-life movement. Others, however, especially those who think of themselves as relatively liberal on doctrinal matters, are more flexible, seeing abortion as unfortunate, but sometimes the least objectionable choice.[19]

Among unprogrammed Friends, a majority probably take a pro-choice stance. Even some who believe that life begins at conception believe that abortion should ultimately be an individual decision. A few FGC Friends are outspokenly pro-life, like one in New York who argued that nothing— rape, incest, danger to the life of the mother—justified abortion: "any of these situations can be transformed and healed by God." Rachel MacNair, a Missouri Friend, has served as president of Feminists for Life. Such Friends have prevented some yearly meetings from reaching unity on statements on abortion. But probably most unprogrammed Friends, even some who are personally opposed, see abortion as an individual matter and any attempt at legal restriction as another example of patriarchal oppression of women or a violation of individual conscience. Thus when the Supreme Court's 1989 *Webster* decision, which sanctioned limits on abortion rights, coincided with FGC's Annual Gathering, protests were vociferous. When a group of pro-life Friends tried to meet during the gathering, pro-choice activists disrupted them. Others began to talk of resurrecting the Underground Railroad to assist women seeking soon-to-be-illegal abortions. Such rhetoric has faded in the last few years, but support for abortion rights remains strong among unprogrammed Friends.[20]

Perhaps more than Quaker men, Quaker women have found ways to reach across barriers. A good example is the United Society of Friends Women International, or USFWI. Its roots go back to 1881, when women in the Gurneyite Western Yearly Meeting formed a group to support Quaker missionaries. Similar groups formed in other yearly meetings, including Philadelphia, and they came together to hold their first national conference in 1888. After several name changes, the organization became the USFWI in 1948. Its anchor is yearly meetings in FUM, but it includes members in both EFI and FGC. The structure parallels the traditional Quaker one, with local societies in meetings and churches coming together at the yearly meeting level and in turn uniting in the international organization, which includes women not only in North America but the Caribbean and Africa as well. Its main work is the support of Quaker missions and service projects by raising money and collecting materials for everything from scholarships to salary support to library books to purchases of medical supplies and baby scales. It has avoided the theological tensions that other such broad-ranging Quaker groups have experienced. And while probably most of its members question whether it is a feminist group, it does, as one leader put it, try to "encourage women's participation and leadership in ministry and in the world."[21]

Women are also responsible for perhaps the most remarkable recent attempt by Friends to meet, worship, and work across doctrinal lines. In 1985 two Oregon Friends, one a member of the EFI Northwest Yearly Meeting and the other a member of the unprogrammed North Pacific Yearly Meeting, formed a friendship while traveling on behalf of the Friends World Committee. They invited women from the unprogrammed Multnomah Monthly Meeting and the EFI Reedwood Friends Church to join them in a group "to discuss readings and provide spiritual support to each other." It called itself Multwood. Joined by members of two other EFI churches, it has continued to meet down to the present day, "seeking a fresh voice within the Society of Friends and learning new ways to act out our faith." In 1995 it gave rise to a new group, the Pacific Northwest Quaker Women's Theology Conference. Participants on both sides report that the groups have helped promote mutual understanding and break down barriers between Evangelical and unprogrammed Friends.[22]

Quaker women today thus reflect the diversity of both Quakers and the larger American society. There are differences, to be sure. For some, especially in FGC and other unprogrammed yearly meetings, to be a Quaker is by definition to be a feminist, committed to freeing society from patriarchal oppression. Other unprogrammed Friends are uneasy with what they see as excess. Among pastoral Friends, some embrace feminism. Others support equality, but have doubts about feminism when they see it linked with causes they think sinful, such as lesbianism or abortion rights. But all of these Friends see women as having a special role to play in maintaining and carrying out Quaker testimonies. And closely connected to this vision are ideas of the nature of the Quaker family.

Marriage and the Family

Early in the nineteenth century, Thomas Clarkson, an English abolitionist who worked extensively with Quakers, wrote that "domestic bliss" was "Friends' chief source of enjoyment." As long as Quakers were a "peculiar people," the goal of Quaker child rearing was to bring up consistent Friends. How much impact this had on the larger American society is debatable, although one historian, Barry Levy, argues that Quakers pioneered the domesticity, growing respect for women, and child-centeredness that would eventually become the norm in American society.[23]

It is more difficult to generalize about Quaker families today. Virtually all Friends consider the family a fundamental institution. All think that strong families are vital for the health of Quakerism and agree on many characteristics of a strong family. But as Friends have come to mirror the diversity of American society, so have their views on marriage and family life.

Until the late twentieth century, Friends of all persuasions assumed that marriage would be the starting point of family formation; most still do. Until the late nineteenth century, in order to marry, Quaker couples had to have the approval of their monthly meeting. That process began when the couple appeared before both the men's and the women's monthly meetings and "gave in" their intention. Committees of men and women were then appointed to be sure that the couple were "clear" of commitments to others and had parental consent; they did not judge whether they were "right" for each other. At the next monthly meeting, approval would be given and the couple "passed meeting" and were at liberty to marry, almost always at the conclusion of a midweek meeting for worship within the next month. The Quaker marriage ceremony was simple. The man and woman stood before the meeting and recited certain vows: "Friends, in the presence of the Lord, and before this assembly, I take this my Friend _____ to be my wife, promising, with divine assistance, to be unto her a loving and faithful husband, until death shall separate us." The woman repeated the same vows to her husband; in contrast to the norm in other churches, she said nothing about "obeying" him. All those present were then invited to sign the marriage certificate.[24]

Today the process of marriage for Quakers has considerable variations. Marriages where both parties are Friends are exceptional. Among pastoral Friends, the pastor performs many of the functions that the monthly meeting once had, such as counseling, and usually performs the wedding in a ceremony virtually identical to that used in most Protestant churches. Some pastoral Friends, however, choose a traditional Quaker ceremony. In unprogrammed meetings, the process begins, as it did in the past, with the couple declaring intentions to the monthly meeting and a clearness committee being appointed. Sometimes these committees make only perfunctory inquiries, but the process may go on for months, as Friends work with the couple to make sure that they are suited to each other, especially if either has had previous marriages or there are children involved. The ceremony itself will be a special meeting for worship at which those present will speak as led. Sometimes couples incorporate their spiritual or political concerns. For example, two Friends married under the care of the unprogrammed meeting in Des Moines in 1989 refused to have their ceremony in the meeting house because it had not yet sanctioned same-sex unions. They concluded the ceremony with a "purification ritual" of burning their marriage license, "sending the patriarchy in our relationship up in flames."[25]

Friends of all persuasions agree on characteristics of a good marriage: love, respect, fidelity, "mutual forbearance and trust and caring," a "covenant relationship" seeking guidance and assistance from God. But there are also points of disagreement, especially on the appropriate roles of husbands and wives.[26]

Once again, Quaker views on the subject are a continuum. At one extreme are evangelical Friends influenced by non-Quaker fundamentalism. They are clear that in a Christian marriage, the husband is the head of the family. "Your husband is the head of your house. He is responsible for the welfare of you and your children. Trust his judgment in all things," was the advice of one Evangelical Friend. "It is not hard for a woman to be subject to a man of character who is in subjection to God," writes California Evangelical Friend Charles Mylander. "Being under authority is for our own protection." These Friends always emphasize, however, that submission is not slavery, that "to submit means to always put the other person first. . . . It means we give up our rights because we love each other as Christ loved us."[27]

Probably more Friends, however, from evangelical to universalist, take the point of view that in a Quaker marriage, as one put it, "men and women are equal partners and . . . God intended it so." Leading Evangelical Friends like Jack Willcuts deplore the idea that wives are to be a "secondary authority." To those who point to the Apostle Paul's command that wives should submit to husbands, they respond that in a Christian marriage, submission will be mutual. For more liberal Friends, such New Testament strictures simply reflect the cultural limitations of ancient society. Continuing revelation has brought us to a higher standard, they argue, one that affirms the equality of all people, including husband and wife in marriage.[28]

There are similar disagreements on divorce. Until the late nineteenth century, Quakers of all persuasions made divorce a ground for disownment. Well into the twentieth century, they disapproved of divorce, and it was understood that no divorced person could be a recorded minister. We have no statistics comparing Quaker divorce rates with those of the larger American society today. Some observers think that they are higher, some lower.[29]

Today, some evangelical Friends still hold to older views. They state that "it is clear there are no 'biblical grounds for divorce.'" A few EFI pastors flatly refuse to marry divorced people. They tell couples experiencing problems that "in Christ, there are no irreconcilable differences. . . . God's truth is that the marriage vows bind us into . . . a new creation that lasts until the death of one of the spouses." From this point of view, nothing is impossible for those with faith in God, including healing seemingly shattered marriages. No yearly meeting, however, makes divorce in itself a ground for loss of membership. Eastern Region Evangelical Friends, for example, put limits on divorce only for pastors. Northwest Yearly Meeting, while labeling divorce a "tragedy," says that divorced people who "are living consistent Christian lives should not be hindered from joining the church or working in it."[30]

Other Friends are more accepting of divorce. Some Evangelical Friends argue that complete bans are overly legalistic and that Friends should recognize that sometimes the sinful behavior of a spouse, ranging from adultery to physical cruelty to "total financial irresponsibility" is justification for divorce. A few feminist Quakers even celebrate divorce as a mark of women's liberation from patriarchy, as "no cause of alarm, but . . . a measure of the level to which women's consciousness has been raised. Women can now see the subtle and personal forms of exploitation in relation to their husbands. Often, in rejecting these, women are led by the Spirit right out of their own marriages." Most unprogrammed Friends do see a divorce as an occasion for concern, in which both parties are likely to need the support of the meeting. In some cases, couples may ask their meetings to appoint clearness committees to counsel them in preserving the marriage or, if decided on divorce, to help keep the process as amicable as possible.[31]

One Friend has argued that the traditional Quaker marriage ceremony, "based on concepts of self-reliance, simplicity, and equality" is a "metaphor for Quaker family life."[32] Virtually all Friends consider families foundational for civil and religious life and want to strengthen them. In how they rear their children, and even how they define the family, however, they manifest the broad diversity of contemporary Quakerism.

All Friends agree on certain things. Parents should model the behavior that they want to inculcate in their children and, in an increasingly busy society, should make time for them. Sometimes good parenthood means setting limits, but parents must "temper their authority with grace and forgiveness so that relationships can be restored and open communication can be maintained." They affirm mothers who work exclusively in the home and those who have other careers. Family life should incorporate values important to Friends, especially worship. Meetings and churches should play important roles in the lives of children. Families that live by Christian/ Quaker values will have a positive impact on the world around them.[33]

Still, given the other differences among Friends, it is not surprising to find differences in their attitudes toward child rearing and the nature of family life. Most evangelical Friends do not see their families as different from other evangelical families. Some look back to the 1950s as an ideal time, when society "supported traditional family values." They agree that "families that pray together and read their Bibles together still stay together." Many see no harm in corporal punishment. They think that if we are obedient to God, then all will be well in our families. And they are likely to look to prominent figures in the evangelical Christian world, such as James Dobson, the founder of Focus on the Family, a leading force of the "Christian Right," for advice and guidance.[34]

More liberal Friends, both pastoral and unprogrammed, have somewhat different values. As one Friend has remarked, in some ways a Quaker home is "a smaller version of the meeting community" and reflects its distinctiveness. Thus these families place particular emphasis on modeling Quaker values, especially simplicity and peacemaking. " 'Would our children choose the nonviolent path in their own lives?' became the touchstone by which we judged all our actions," one Quaker parent remembered of her meeting in the 1950s. Such values, in turn, become a force for social change. They may also create a sense of "differentness" that can be a real trial for children, especially adolescents. Liberal Friends probably tend to be more "permissive," less inclined to corporal punishment or appeals to authority. They believe children have "That of God" and trust them to follow it. And many argue that "we worry far too much about the *form* of the family, as if, in spite of all the variations present in history, there could be one optimum pattern." Thus definitions of the family should be expanded to accommodate gays and lesbians and single parents. In some unprogrammed meetings, widowed, single, and divorced people are a majority. Others, however, assert that while Friends should be inclusive, "the best legacy we can give our children is the stability of a two-parent home that works at being deeply Christian."[35]

Are Quaker families different? Some Friends answer that families that live by the values described above are necessarily so. Others disagree. "We don't appear to have any answers because our families look like theirs and our families act like theirs," wrote two Conservative Friends. Some Friends argue that the stagnation of Quaker membership is the result of poor teaching of Quaker ways at home. One psychologist concluded that abuse, including physical violence and incest, was as common in Quaker families as in the larger society, although others have challenged her findings. Perhaps the best conclusion that can be drawn is that as American Friends have come closer to "the world," their families have necessarily come to share in the challenges and problems of that world.[36]

Conclusion

In their first two centuries, Quaker women and families were different from other religious denominations and the larger society. Friends were virtually unique in having women ministers and making a place for women in their business structure. This explains why in the nineteenth century, as the women's rights movement appeared in the United States, Quaker women supplied much of its leadership. In the last 150 years, however, society has come to accept many of the ideas of equality that Friends have long embraced, and thus Quaker women today are less distinctive.

At the same time, Friends have drawn ideas from the larger society. For self-described Quaker feminists, that means that they find inspiration not just in biblical women or Margaret Fell or Lucretia Mott but also in more contemporary feminists like Simone de Beauvoir or Mary Daly. In the case of many evangelical and fundamentalist Friends, outside ideas have had a similar impact, but have caused them to question at least some leadership roles for women, such as serving as pastors.

Similar diversity characterizes Quaker marriages and families. Some Friends see complete equality of husband and wife as sanctioned both by Quaker tradition and by God. Others, however, argue that obedience to God requires a more patriarchal pattern, in which the husband has final authority and divorce is forbidden. Similarly, some see the end of child rearing as simply bringing up good Christians, little different from other good Christians, while for others the goal is rearing young Friends who will self-consciously be apart from "the world."

In 2002 Quakers celebrated what most regard as their 350th birthday—1652 marking the emergence of Quakerism as a distinct religious movement. Their history has been paradoxical. On one hand, they were pioneers in movements that most Americans today find attractive: opposition to slavery, fair treatment of Native Americans, equality for women. On the other hand, for almost two centuries, Friends have been a divided people, often declining in numbers, their growth uneven and erratic. The separations that began in the 1820s have been only partially healed. Today, although they number only about 100,000, American Quakers are found on a wide spectrum that ranges from fundamentalist Christianity to the broadest universalism. Universalist, liberal, moderate, evangelical, fundamentalist, they have taken different paths, sometimes close enough that they can remain in sympathetic communication with each other, sometimes so far apart that encounters between different groups are disturbing and even disorienting. All are different in essential ways from George Fox and the "First Publishers of Truth" in the 1650s, but all can legitimately claim to carry forward certain elements of the original Quaker message.

Today, about a third of all American Friends are unprogrammed, still worshiping on the basis of waiting silence, broken only when someone present feels a divine leading to speak and share with the gathered meeting. Based on early Quaker practice, such worship is for these Friends absolutely foundational to a Quaker identity. They also believe in what George Fox called "That of God in Everyone," the idea that all human beings are potentially good and can be appealed to in terms of that good, because they have something of the divine in them. Theologically, some ground this doctrine in liberal Christianity; others argue that it necessarily is universalist, transcending any particular historic faith. These Friends try to transform the world from that basis. They often shape the larger American society's perceptions of Friends as humanitarians, pacifists, and social activists. Yet, with the exception of a handful of Conservative Friends, these Quakers have become largely acculturated. Their views on peace, feminism, politics, worship, and even God reflect a wide variety of non-Quaker influences and sources. Still, they have a sense of being peculiar, different from the larger American society. And they wish to be different.

In contrast, the other two thirds of American Friends are pastoral or programmed. Some are theologically liberal; more feel closer to evangelical or even fundamentalist Protestantism. Outwardly, their worship is much more like that of other Protestants, but diverse: a visitor to programmed Friends meetings and churches today would experience everything from staid mainline worship to exuberant charismatic practices. For the most part, pastoral Quakers are more comfortable with the larger American society than their unprogrammed counterparts, although there are significant exceptions. Some pastoral Friends are as committed to pacifism and social activism as unprogrammed Friends. Others have a profound sense of alienation from what they see as a sinful larger society. Their relation to it is adversarial: they try to counter its effects on their families and bring as many others as possible to saving faith in Christ before He returns and brings this world as we know it to an end. On matters of essential faith, they see no differences between themselves and other evangelical or fundamentalist Christians.

When American Quakers look at themselves, they usually reach mixed and uncertain conclusions. Unprogrammed Friends often see pastoral Friends as having given up all distinctiveness; many pastoral Friends respond that unprogrammed Friends have become so inclusive as to have lost any kind of identity at all. While differences today usually do not erupt in the ferocious conflicts that the nineteenth and early twentieth centuries witnessed, no one predicts the reunion of all Quakers at any time in the foreseeable future. And it is questionable what purpose such a reunion would serve. Moreover, while the total number of American Friends remained relatively constant or even showed a small decline over the course of the twentieth century, the numbers conceal diverse experiences. Some old Quaker strongholds, such as the Ohio Valley and the Philadelphia area, have seen steep declines. But other yearly meetings have grown significantly. And in the last half century, dozens of new Quaker congregations, both programmed and unprogrammed, have been planted. Some have failed, but many have flourished or at least found stability. Finally, Friends can point with pride to their accomplishments, whether it be more liberal Friends celebrating the world-renowned activism of the American Friends Service Committee or evangelical Friends rejoicing in a missionary impulse whose results have made Africans, Asians, and Latin Americans the majority of the world's Quakers.

American Friends are likely to continue to face problems of theology, authority, leadership, and growth. But given the tenacity of the hold of the Quaker vision on successive generations and its appeal to the converts, the convinced Friends it still attracts, Quakerism is likely to continue to exist as a small but articulate part of the American religious world.

The following biographies are not intended as a listing of the fifteen best-known Quakers in American history, nor even the fifteen Friends who have been most central to the development of American Quakerism. Instead, I have chosen Friends who exemplify three groups: those who before 1950 made an impression on the larger American society (Woolman, Hicks, Mott, Whittier, and Paul); those who have been central figures among American Friends since 1950 (Steere, Trueblood, Willcuts, Boulding, and Foster); and Friends who have become well known to the larger American society (Rustin, Michener, Simon, Turrell, and Raitt). None can be considered a "typical American Friend." As a group, they exemplify the diversity of American Quakerism, past and present.

John Woolman

John Woolman was a central figure in the birth of the antislavery movement in the United States. As historian David Brion Davis put it, when the western world made a fundamental shift away from the justification of human slavery between 1745 and 1770, this "self-effacing Quaker was a major instrument of the transformation."

Woolman was born in Mt. Holly, New Jersey in 1720. He was recorded a Quaker minister in 1743. He originally was a storekeeper, but a fear that it distracted him from his faith and growing qualms about selling the "worldly" clothing that his customers demanded induced him to become a tailor and a scribe for neighbors. He first took a public stand against slavery when he refused to write bills of sale that involved slaves.

Woolman emerged as a leading opponent of slavery with the publication of his little book, *Some Considerations on the Keeping of Negroes*. He helped move American Friends toward freeing their slaves, and his arguments influenced other, non-Quaker opponents of slavery. Woolman was also a leader of the reform movement that tightened the Discipline in the 1750s and 1760s. In the 1760s, he became known for eccentricities. Convinced, for example, that the dyes used in clothes were harmful to those who made them, he began wearing only undyed clothing. He died of smallpox on a religious visit to England in 1772.

Woolman's chief monument is his journal, which he began keeping in 1756 and which was first published in 1774. It is widely considered a spiritual classic, and has remained in print for nearly 230 years.

Edward Hicks

For many, Edward Hicks is the quintessential American folk artist. His scenes of pastoral harmony in a "peaceable kingdom" have become icons. Yet Hicks, a fiery Quaker preacher from Newtown, Pennsylvania, was profoundly ambivalent about his art.

Hicks was born in Bucks County, Pennsylvania in 1780. Young Edward became a Friend when he was taken into a Quaker family, whom he later depicted in his painting, *The Residence of David Twining*. In his twenties, Hicks made a conscious decision to live as a consistent Friend, and in 1811 he was recorded a minister. In the 1820s, he was an outspoken supporter of his distant relative Elias Hicks and was a leader of the Hicksite group in Philadelphia Yearly Meeting.

Hicks began his career painting signs, only later expanding into the scenes that would make him famous. In the 1830s he perfected his *Peaceable Kingdom*, of which he created dozens of versions. All depicted the scene in the Book of Isaiah in which leopards lie down at peace with lambs, usually with William Penn's 1682 treaty with the Indians in the background. Today his are among the most sought-after works by nineteenth-century American artists. Yet many Friends, including Hicks himself, questioned whether it was appropriate for a Quaker to live by painting, which they saw as pandering to human vanity.

In the 1840s Hicks was a steadfast conservative, and although opposed to slavery, was critical of the involvement of Friends such as Lucretia Mott in abolition and other reform activities. Hicks died in Newtown, Pennsylvania in 1849.

Lucretia Mott

Lucretia Mott was one of the influential women in the nineteenth-century United States. A Hicksite Quaker minister, she was an articulate proponent of the abolition of slavery and central to the early women's rights movement.

Lucretia Coffin was born on Nantucket Island in 1793. She attended the Quaker Nine Partners Boarding School in New York; after finishing she taught there, then married a fellow teacher, James Mott, in 1811. They moved to Philadelphia, where she was recorded a minister in 1821. In 1827 she sided with Hicksite Friends and served as clerk of the Hicksite women's Philadelphia Yearly Meeting.

In the 1830s, Mott threw herself into the antislavery cause. She attended the founding meeting of the American Anti-Slavery Society in 1833. She became a close friend of radical abolitionist William Lloyd Garrison and in 1840 went to London as a delegate to the World's Anti-Slavery Convention, only to be excluded because of her sex. On the voyage she met Elizabeth Cady Stanton. They organized the first women's rights convention in U.S. history, held at Seneca Falls, New York in 1848.

Mott's willingness to work with non-Quaker reformers and her growing liberalism outraged more conservative Hicksites, who tried unsuccessfully to silence her as a minister. Mott outlived her opponents and by 1870 was probably the most respected single Hicksite Friend. She also remained active in the women's rights movement, trying to preserve harmony among factions while refusing to compromise on the fundamental issues of legal equality and suffrage. Mott died in Philadelphia in 1880.

John Greenleaf Whittier

The best-known Quaker in the nineteenth-century United States was not a recorded minister or a central figure in the separations. He was a poet, who, Hugh Barbour and J. William Frost note, became one of the most popular authors in the United States through his "subordination of his art to religious purposes, his moralism, and his sentimentality"—qualities that do not endear him to literary critics today.

John Greenleaf Whittier was born into a Quaker farming family in Haverhill, Massachusetts in 1807. He began writing poetry as a teenager. Fascinated by politics, he became a newspaper editor in his twenties, contemplated a run for Congress in 1832, and served one term in the Massachusetts legislature.

Whittier's political horizons were limited, however, by his commitment to the abolitionist cause. He was one of the founders of the American Anti-Slavery Society in 1833, and over the next decade, through his writing and editorship of antislavery periodicals, became one of the best-known abolitionists in the United States. In the 1850s he was a founder of the Republican party in New England.

After 1850, Whittier's poetry became increasingly popular, focusing on rural New England before urbanization and industrialization transformed it. Contemporary critics acclaimed his work, and by the 1880s schoolchildren celebrated his birthday as a national event. Whittier remained an Orthodox Friend all his life, but he was open to contacts with Hicksite Friends like Lucretia Mott, and Quakers of all persuasions basked in the recognition that he brought them. Whittier died in Hampton Falls, New Hampshire in 1892.

Alice Paul

Quakers were at the heart of the women's rights movement in the United States. One of the central figures in the movement for the ratification of the Nineteenth Amendment in 1920, which gave women voting rights, was a Hicksite Friend, Alice Paul.

Paul was born in Moorestown, New Jersey in 1885, to parents whose families had been prominent Quakers for two centuries. She graduated from Swarthmore College in 1905, and went on to earn a law degree and two doctorates.

In 1907, Paul visited England, where she became involved in the women's rights movement. The English movement was militant, characterized by demonstrations and attacks on the property of opponents. Suffragettes were often jailed, and when they went on hunger strikes, force fed. Paul joined in these actions, and when she returned home, was determined to replicate them in the United States. The women's suffrage movement had previously tried to win the vote state by state, a strategy that had yielded few victories by 1912. Paul urged a shift of goals to a constitutional amendment. She and her supporters became the first protesters in U.S. history to picket the White House, which landed them in jail. Paul's campaign succeeded, however, with the ratification of the Nineteenth Amendment.

After 1920, Paul was one of the leaders of the National Woman's Party, whose goal was an Equal Rights Amendment to the U.S. Constitution. Her single-minded focus on legal equality brought criticism from those who thought that she was insensitive to other problems faced by poor women and women of color. She was an important force in adding gender to Title VII of the Civil Rights Act of 1964, which bans discrimination in employment. Until her death in 1977, she continued to advocate ratification of the ERA.

Elton Trueblood

A few Quakers have become widely read beyond the Quaker fold. Between 1945 and 1970, probably no American Friend sold more devotional books than Elton Trueblood.

Trueblood was born in Warren County, Iowa in 1900, into a family that he proudly traced back to the earliest days of the Quaker movement. After graduating from Penn College in 1922, Trueblood went east for graduate work, first at Harvard and Brown, culminating with a Ph.D. in philosophy at Johns Hopkins. He taught at Guilford and Haverford colleges before joining the faculty of Stanford University in 1935 as campus preacher. Simultaneously, he edited the venerable Philadelphia Quaker periodical, the *Friend*.

Until World War II, Trueblood was a religious liberal in the mold of Rufus Jones. Encounters with neoorthodox writers like C. S. Lewis converted him to a moderate evangelicalism. In 1946, he moved to Earlham College, where he served on the faculty in a variety of roles until his death in 1994. His appointment gave him ample time for writing and speaking. He turned out a steady stream of books that appealed especially to Cold War America, affirming traditional Christian doctrines and calling for self-discipline and sacrifice as the means to victory over communism. One fruit was the Yokefellow movement, which he founded as a nondenominational fellowship of Christians committed to such self-discipline. Trueblood's questioning of pacifism, his support for the Vietnam War, and his championship of Richard Nixon made him a controversial figure in Quaker circles after 1950.

Douglas V. Steere

Douglas Steere was one of the most influential and beloved Quaker figures of the twentieth century. His influence reached all Friends, although it was most powerful among the unprogrammed.

Steere was born in Harbor Beach, Michigan in 1901, and grew up in Detroit. His family attended a variety of Protestant churches. Having graduated in 1923 from what is now Michigan State University, he borrowed $1,000

and went off to Harvard for graduate work in philosophy. In 1925 he won a
Rhodes scholarship to Oxford, and he received his Ph.D. in philosophy from
Harvard in 1931. In 1929 he married Dorothy MacEachron. For many
Friends, their marriage, which lasted almost 66 years, was a model Quaker
union.

In 1928, Steere joined the philosophy faculty at Haverford College,
where he taught until his retirement in 1964. The Haverford appointment
confirmed his previous attraction to Quakerism, and he became an active
member of the Orthodox Philadelphia Yearly Meeting. He was also involved in numerous other Quaker organizations, like the small group that
planned the Quaker study center Pendle Hill. In 1940–1941 he worked for
the AFSC in Germany, trying to aid refugees from Nazism. He won scholarly attention as one of the first English translators of the Danish philosopher Soren Kierkegaard. Both Douglas and Dorothy Steere were leading
Quaker ecumenical figures. Their activities ranged from contacts with
Buddhists to official status as Quaker observers at the Roman Catholic
Vatican II Council from 1963 to 1965. His contemplative works on prayer
attracted a wide readership. Douglas Steere died in Haverford, Pennsylvania in 1995.

James Michener

For two centuries, Quakers were profoundly ambivalent about novels and
fiction, seeing them as distractions from the pursuit of true religion. That
opposition had disappeared by the twentieth century, when James Michener
became one of the most popular novelists in the United States.

Michener was born in New York City in 1907, and as a foundling was
taken to Doylestown, Pennsylvania, where a Quaker farm couple adopted
him. He won a scholarship to Swarthmore College, graduated with honors
in 1929, then taught in a variety of schools in the 1930s. On the outbreak
of World War II, he enlisted in the navy and served in the South Pacific.

Michener fictionalized his war experiences in a set of short stories, *Tales
of the South Pacific*, which was published to critical acclaim in 1947, winning
the Pulitzer Prize. More recognition came when Rodgers and Hammerstein
turned the book into the Broadway musical *South Pacific*. Michener produced a steady stream of books for the rest of his life, with total sales of
over 100 million. He was best known for a series of sweeping historical
novels that began with *Hawaii* in 1959. Some, most notably the autobiographical *The Fires of Spring* (1949) and *Chesapeake* (1978), have significant
Quaker characters. All reflect a Quaker aversion to racism and oppression.
Michener was a member of Swarthmore Monthly Meeting.

Michener spent his last years in Austin, Texas. On his death in 1997, he bequeathed much of his estate to Swarthmore College.

Bayard Rustin

African American Friends have been relatively few, but they have been part of Quakerism for over two centuries. One of the best known of the twentieth century was also a central figure in the civil rights movement.

Bayard Rustin was born in West Chester, Pennsylvania in 1912. His maternal grandparents were Friends, and Quakerism became his faith. After college, Rustin moved to New York City in 1937. Although he joined a Friends meeting there, he also became radicalized and for a time affiliated with the Young Communist League. During World War II, Rustin, a total pacifist, refused even to register as a conscientious objector and went to jail. After the war, he began civil rights work with the Fellowship of Reconciliation, doing jail time in the South and traveling to India and Africa to explore nonviolence further.

A relatively open gay man, Rustin was forced to keep a low profile after an arrest in 1953 on a "morals charge." He did serve as head of the War Resisters League and played an important role in the evolution of the AFSC in the 1950s. After 1955, Rustin became a key advisor to Martin Luther King Jr. He was the chief architect of the 1963 March on Washington, at which King gave his "I Have a Dream" speech. After the passage of the Voting Rights Act in 1965, Rustin pushed for African Americans to form coalitions with white liberals and working people. He was skeptical of the emerging Black Power movement and affirmative action. The emergence of the gay rights movement made him a hero to a new constituency, however. Rustin died in New York City in 1987.

Elise Boulding

Much of the Quaker impact on the larger world has been the work of remarkable Quaker women. A good exemplar over the past half century is Elise Boulding.

Elise Bjorn-Hansen was born in Oslo, Norway in 1920, and immigrated to the United States as a child to live near Newark, New Jersey. She was drawn to peace activism as a teenager, and that exposed her to Quakerism. She graduated from Douglass College in 1940, and a year later entered Syracuse University for graduate work. At a nearby Friends meeting, she met Kenneth Boulding (1910–1993), a renowned academic economist who taught at several colleges and universities, served as president of the American Economic Association, and received nominations for Nobel Prizes in both peace and economics. They were married after a courtship of only a few months. For many unprogrammed Friends, they were a model Quaker couple.

Contacts at Fisk University drew Elise Boulding to the study of sociology during World War II, and she received a master's degree in it in 1949. The births of five children, however, postponed the completion of her doctorate, at the University of Michigan, until 1969. She taught at the University of Colorado from 1967 to 1979, then became professor of sociology at Dartmouth College until her retirement in 1985.

Elise Boulding's Quakerism is reflected in her writings and activism. She has been involved in antiwar work since the 1930s, which has brought her numerous awards, including a nomination for the Nobel Prize for Peace in 1990. Much of her scholarly work has focused on questions of peace, the family, futurism, and building a nonviolent world. She has traveled widely as a speaker at Quaker conferences and workshops. Much of her Quaker writing has focused on questions of the family and the religious life of children and is collected in her book, *One Small Plot of Heaven* (1989). She today lives in Massachusetts.

Jack Willcuts

Although not well known outside the Quaker world, Jack Willcuts was a leading Evangelical Friend in the second half of the twentieth century. His influence reached a wide variety of Friends.

Willcuts was born into an old Quaker family in Burr Oak, Kansas in 1922, and received his education at Friends Bible College in Kansas and George Fox College. He alternated pastorates at Evangelical Friends churches in Oregon and Washington with two terms of missionary work in Bolivia, from 1947 to 1951 and 1954 to 1958. From 1966 to 1971 and from 1979 to 1986 he was General Superintendent of Northwest (formerly Oregon) Yearly Meeting.

Willcuts was founding editor of the *Evangelical Friend* in 1967 and served for seventeen years. Under his tenure, the magazine's evangelical commitment was unquestionable, but Willcuts was also an articulate defender of traditional Quaker testimonies, such as peace and the ministry of women, that many Evangelical Friends questioned. Willcuts was also a leader in trying to reach across Quaker boundaries, helping to organize the 1967 World Conference of Friends and serving as Friend-in-Residence at Woodbrooke, the English Quaker study center, in 1988–1989. He died in 1989.

Richard J. Foster

One admirer describes Richard J. Foster as "perhaps the best-known Quaker in the world." Certainly no other Quaker writer today has found a wider audience for works on Christian faith and life.

Foster was born in Albuquerque, New Mexico in 1942, and graduated from George Fox College in 1964. He received his doctorate in theology from Fuller Theological Seminary, a central institution for American evangelicals, in 1970. Recorded a Friends minister in 1967, he served as pastor in Friends churches in California and Oregon until 1979, when he joined the faculty of Friends University in Wichita, Kansas as professor of theology and writer-in-residence. He now lives in Colorado.

Foster first attracted attention in 1978 with his book *Celebration of Discipline*. He termed it an invitation "to explore the inner caverns of the spiritual realm." It argued for spiritual development based on disciplines of prayer, meditation, simplicity, and corporate celebration. Throughout, he blends Quaker figures and testimonies with evangelical Christian commitment. To date, *Celebration of Discipline* has sold over a million copies. *Christianity Today* magazine named it one of the top ten books of the twentieth century. Foster further developed these themes in succeeding books, especially *Freedom of Simplicity* and *Streams of Living Water*. In part trying to renew what he saw as an endangered evangelical commitment to social justice, Foster in 1989 founded the group Renovaré, "a covenant fellowship" that "seeks to articulate the heart of the Christian witness."

James Turrell

"As an artist, you seek to separate yourself to become inner directed," James Turrell said in a 1999 interview with *Friends Journal*. A well-known American artist, he sees his work as in part an attempt to translate Quaker concepts into art.

Turrell was born in Pasadena, California in 1943, into a family that belonged to the Conservative meeting there. In the 1960s, Turrell worked for a time for the AFSC, then early in the decade chose alternative service as a pilot aiding Tibetan refugees. Active in the anti–Vietnam War movement, he served time in jail for his activities. He is currently part of the unprogrammed Friends Meeting in Flagstaff, Arizona. A recent project was the design of a new meeting house for Friends in Houston.

Turrell describes himself as "a painter in three dimensions" whose art focuses on the use of light. For him, it is more than illumination. "I believe in the 'thingness' of light itself. Light, for me, is matter that exhibits phenomena and inhabits its own space." Thus his art often involves use of natural light, changing over the course of the day. In best Quaker fashion, he hopes that "the light without reminds us of the Light Within."

Bonnie Raitt

Until the late nineteenth century, one of the prohibitions that all Friends shared was a distrust of music. That disappeared in the twentieth century. Today Quaker musicians attract no comment among Friends, and some are well known to the general public.

One of them is Bonnie Raitt, who was born into a Quaker family in 1949. Her father, John Raitt, was a Broadway star whose credits included, among other shows, *Carousel*. She described her California home as equally divided between music and Quaker ideals. When she left to attend Radcliffe in 1967, her career goal was to work for the AFSC, which she refers to as the "family business."

Instead, Raitt was "discovered" by promoter Dick Waterman, who convinced her that she could combine her activism with music. She formed strong ties with blues legends like John Hurt and Muddy Waters. She gave many benefit concerts for causes dear to liberal Friends, such as opposing nuclear energy, and in 1995 founded the Bonnie Raitt Fender Guitar Project to provide music lessons for poor children. Commercial success came with her album, *Nick of Time*, which won four Grammy Awards in 1990, followed by four more awards for other works in the next four years. Still, Raitt retains her Quaker commitment to making the world a better place. "It's not about whether I'm considered great or I'm a significant artist. . . . It's how I live my life that's important."

Scott Simon

Liberal Friends usually pride themselves on their inclusiveness. In the fall of 2001, however, many were at pains to question the credentials of a self-identified Quaker who had publicly broken with the Peace Testimony, National Public Radio (NPR) correspondent Scott Simon.

Simon was born in Chicago in 1951. The son of a Jewish father and a Roman Catholic mother, he began attending Northside Meeting in Chicago as a teenager. It drew him into the anti–Vietnam War movement and confirmed his leanings toward pacifism. Soon he was a member of the AFSC Chicago office board. He resigned, however, when he became a reporter for a Chicago television station and feared a conflict of interest covering demonstrations in which the AFSC was involved. In a similar situation, he declined to cover the first legal execution in over a decade because as a Friend he felt that he would have to make some sort of protest.

Simon joined the NPR staff in 1975. In 1985 he became host of its "Weekend Edition," still a staple of its format. Today Simon is not formally a member of any Friends meeting but still considers himself a Quaker. His public support of the use of force in response to the terrorist attacks of September 11, 2001 attracted considerable attention and made him a controversial figure among Friends.

CHRONOLOGY

1624	George Fox born in England
1643–1648	Fox has his "openings"
1650	name "Quaker" first used
1652	Fox has his vision on Pendle Hill of "a great people to be gathered"
	Fox meets Margaret Fell and Swarthmoor Hall becomes headquarters of the movement
1655–1656	first Quaker missionaries reach North America
1659–1660	execution of four Friends in Boston
1662	anti-Quaker laws in England heighten persecution
1672–1673	George Fox visits America
1676	Robert Barclay publishes *An Apology for the True Christian Divinity*
1681	William Penn receives the charter for Pennsylvania, which opens the way for the migration of thousands of Friends from the British Isles
1689	Act of Toleration ends religious persecution
1691	death of George Fox
ca. 1700	Quietist era begins
ca. 1750	reform movement to tighten Discipline begins

1756	Friends begin withdrawal from the Pennsylvania Assembly
1758	Philadelphia Yearly Meeting orders members to stop buying and selling slaves
1775–1783	Friends face persecution during the American Revolution
1784	Virginia Yearly Meeting becomes the last to ban slaveholding by members
1795–1830	Friends move in large numbers into northern New England, western New York, and especially Ohio and Indiana
1827–1828	Hicksite Separation
1837–1840	Joseph John Gurney visits North America
1840–1855	Congregational Friends separate from Hicksite meetings
1844–1854	Wilburite and Gurney Friends separate from each other
1850–1865	renewal movement among Gurneyite Friends
1861–1865	Civil War isolates Southern Friends and draws many Northern Friends into the Union Army
1862	Northern Friends begin work among former slaves
1869–1879	Friends work with Indians under Grant "Peace Plan"
ca. 1870	beginning of the revival movement among Gurneyites
1877–1883	Conservative Friends separate from revivalists
1880s	pastoral system is begun
1887	Richmond Conference
1894	Rufus M. Jones begins publishing *The American Friend*
1900	Friends General Conference is formed
1902	first sessions of Five Years Meeting; first Quaker missionaries arrive in Kenya
1902–1925	Fundamentalist/Modernist controversy divides Five Years Meeting
1917	American Friends Service Committee founded
1910–1940s	independent meetings become common
1937	Friends World Committee for Consultation founded

1940—1945   Friends support Civilian Public Service during World War II

1943—1968   reunification in eastern yearly meetings

1955   *Friends' Intelligencer* and the *Friend* merge to form *Friends Journal*

1960   *American Friend* renamed *Quaker Life*

1963   Evangelical Friends Alliance formed

1965   Five Years Meeting becomes Friends United Meeting

1967   *Evangelical Friend* begins publication

1970—1977   conferences on relations among various Quaker groups

1978   Friends on Gay Concerns formed

1989   Evangelical Friends Alliance becomes Evangelical Friends International

1990—1991   realignment controversy in FUM

1994   *Evangelical Friend* stops publication

2002   FUM holds first triennial in Kenya

GLOSSARY

I am indebted to Lyn Cope-Robinson, *The Little Quaker Sociology Book, with Glossary* (Melbourne Beach, Fla.: Canmore Press, 1995); and Philadelphia Yearly Meeting, *Faith and Practice: A Book of Christian Discipline* (Philadelphia: Philadelphia Yearly Meeting, 1997). Quotations from the former are indicated by an asterisk (*); those from the latter by a pound sign (#).

—

advices   Minutes of a yearly meeting usually understood to have the weight of the meeting behind them, but not considered binding.

American Friends Service Committee (AFSC)   An organization formed in 1917, it engages in relief and social justice work on Quaker principles around the world.

birthright Friend   Originally, a child who acquired membership by birth to parents who were both members. Most yearly meetings have now abolished birthright membership, but Friends still use the term for a lifelong Quaker.

centering   "The initial stage of worship when Friends clear their minds and settle down to achieve a spiritual focus."#

clearness: "Confidence that an action is consistent with the divine will."#

clerk   The person presiding at a meeting for business.

concern   "A course of action taken under deep religious conviction."*

Conservative Friends   Friends in three yearly meetings (Ohio, Iowa, and North Carolina), and today, Friends elsewhere, who separated from Gurneyite Friends. They share a commitment to unprogrammed worship and other Quaker peculiarities. Some are strongly Christian; others are universalist.

continuing revelation   The belief that God still speaks directly to human beings without intermediaries.

convinced Friend   A convert to Quakerism.

discernment   "To see clearly; to differentiate the truth from other impressions."*

Discipline   Until the twentieth century, the common label for the body of rules and customs by which Friends govern their meetings and lives. See also *Faith and Practice*.

elders   Friends of spiritual weight. Before 1860, their function was to oversee ministry. In unprogrammed meetings, where still named, they oversee spiritual life and ministry. In pastoral meetings, they advise the pastor and perform other pastoral functions.

Evangelical Friends International (EFI):   An association of six North American yearly meetings (Eastern Region, Mid-America, Southwest, Northwest, Rocky Mountain, and Alaska) and Friends elsewhere, pastoral and strongly evangelical in theology.

Faith and Practice   A compilation of the business practices, doctrinal statements, and advices of a yearly meeting; usually includes quotations deemed appropriate from Friends over the centuries. See also **Discipline.**

Five Years Meeting: See **Friends United Meeting.**

Friends Committee on National Legislation (FCNL)   Quaker lobbying group founded in 1943.

Friends General Conference (FGC)   Overarching organizational structure for Quaker meetings formed in 1900; it embraces unprogrammed yearly meetings that are generally liberal in theology and committed to social activism.

Friends United Meeting (FUM)   A meeting formed in 1902 as the Five Years Meeting; the name was changed in 1965. Both pastoral and unprogrammed, but strongly Christian, its membership is worldwide.

Gurneyites   Orthodox Friends who in the 1840s and 1850s followed the English minister Joseph John Gurney. They were the forerunners of most of FUM and all of EFI.

Hicksites   The smaller group to emerge from the separation of 1827–1828, characterized by theological openness and opposition to what it saw as Orthodox abuse of power.

Inner Light/Inward Light/That of God   One of the most disputed of Quaker terms. Liberal Friends tend to use it to denote "the direct, unmediated experience of the divine."# Evangelical Friends see it as the influence of the Holy Spirit, showing our need for the Savior, Jesus Christ.

leading   "A sense of Divine guidance or revelation in any action; a spiritual insight."*

lay down   To discontinue or dissolve.

meeting   Both an event, such as a business meeting or meeting for worship, and an institution that others would call a church, such as "Springfield Friends Meeting."

minute "The record of a corporate decision reached during a meeting . . . for business."#

monthly meeting The basic Quaker business unit, gathering monthly to care for the business of the congregation.

overseer Traditionally, a man or woman charged with reporting to monthly meetings violations of the **Discipline.** Today, overseers provide "pastoral care and nurture" in unprogrammed meetings.#

pastoral meeting Quaker meeting in which worship centers, in a pre-set format, on a sermon by the pastor.

preparative meeting A worship group subordinate to a monthly meeting.

programmed meeting See **pastoral meeting.**

quarterly meeting A combination of two or more monthly meetings usually meeting four times a year for business purposes.

queries "A set of questions, based on Friends' practices and testimonies, . . . considered by meetings and individuals as a way of both guiding and examining individual and corporate lives and actions."#

sense of the meeting "The harmony (unity, union) reached by participants in a business meeting."* It implies discerning the will of God.

standing aside "An action taken by an individual who has genuine reservations about a particular decision, but who also recognizes that the decision is clearly supported by the weight of the Meeting."#

testimony "A guiding principle of conduct that bears witness to the presence of God in the world and in our lives." Examples for Friends include peace, simplicity, and equality.#

United Society of Friends Women International (USFWI) Mission organization, closely tied to FUM.

unprogrammed meeting Quaker meeting in which worship is based on silent, expectant waiting for guidance from God.

weight Spiritual influence, as in "weighty Friend."

Wilburites Orthodox Friends who broke with the larger body of Orthodox Friends in the 1840s and 1850s to oppose the influence of Joseph John Gurney. See also **Conservative Friends.**

yearly meeting An association of monthly and quarterly meetings and their members. Generally, among liberal Friends, yearly meetings are advisory, while in programmed yearly meetings and some Conservative ones they serve as ultimate authority under God.

1. Meeting for Worship and Meeting for Business

1. This paragraph and the following ones are based on the author's attendance at Ohio Yearly Meeting, August 17 and 18, 2001.

2. This paragraph and the following ones are based on the author's attendance at the Eastern Region Yearly Meeting, July 21–23, 2001.

3. This paragraph and the following ones are based on the author's attendance at Wilmington Yearly Meeting, July 19–20, 2001.

4. This paragraph and the following ones are based on contacts with members of the yearly meeting and Lake Erie Yearly Meeting, *Annual Records 2001*.

5. Lake Erie Yearly Meeting, *Annual Records 2001*, 25, 51–53.

6. Ibid., 78.

7. Ibid., 6–16.

8. Birthright membership was a feature of virtually all Quaker bodies until the early twentieth century—children born to Quaker parents were automatically recorded as full members at their birth, and no act of confirmation was required at adulthood to maintain membership. Few yearly meetings retain this practice today. But "birthright Friend" is a term often heard among Quakers for lifelong Friends.

9. For an excellent overview, see Arthur O. Roberts, "Paths Toward a Quaker Future," *Friends Journal* 33 (March 1, 1987): 12–17.

10. "The Meeting as Faith Community," *Quaker Life* 24 (May 1983): 9–12.

11. John Punshon, *Testimony and Tradition: Some Aspects of Quaker Spirituality* (London: Quaker Home Service, 1990), 27–28.

2. The Origins of American Quakerism, 1640–1800

1. Fox's *Journal* has gone through many editions. I have used John L. Nickalls, ed., *The Journal of George Fox* (Philadelphia: Philadelphia Yearly Meeting, 1995).

For the limitations of the *Journal* as a source for early Quaker history, see H. Larry Ingle, *First Among Friends: George Fox and the Creation of Quakerism* (New York: Oxford University Press, 1994), 251; and Rosemary Moore, *The Light in Their Consciences: The Early Quakers in Britain, 1646–1656* (University Park, Pa.: Pennsylvania State University Press, 2000), 229–30.

2. The historical literature on the English Revolution of the 1640s, its origins, and its consequences, is vast. Good starting points are Christopher Hill, *The World Turned Upside Down: Radical Ideas in the English Revolution* (Harmondsworth, Eng.: Penguin, 1976); and David Underdown, *Revel, Riot, and Rebellion: Popular Politics and Culture in England, 1603–1660* (New York: Oxford University Press, 1985).

3. Nickalls, ed., *Journal of George Fox*, 1–6.

4. Ibid., 7–8.

5. Ibid., 11.

6. Ibid.

7. Ibid., 33. The most influential treatment of Fox's understanding of the Inward Light is Hugh Barbour, *The Quakers in Puritan England* (New Haven: Yale University Press, 1964), 94–126. See also Moore, *Light in Their Consciences*, 108–11. Quakers today debate intensely whether "Inner Light" is synonymous with Fox's experience of the Light.

8. Ibid., 51–59; Barbour, *Quakers in Puritan England*, 156–59.

9. Nickalls, ed., *Journal of George Fox*, 27; Barbour, *Quakers in Puritan England*, 149.

10. Hugh Barbour and J. William Frost, *The Quakers* (Westport, Ct.: Greenwood, 1988), 25; Barbour, *Quakers in Puritan England*, 33–71; Douglas Gwyn, *Apocalypse of the Word: The Life and Message of George Fox, 1624–1691* (Richmond, Ind.: Friends United Press, 1986), 179–207.

11. Ingle, *First Among Friends*, 50; Christine Trevett, *Women and Quakerism in the 17th Century* (York, Eng.: Sessions, 1995), 16–22; William C. Braithwaite, *The Beginnings of Quakerism* (London: Macmillan, 1923), 57–58.

12. Nickalls, ed., *Journal of George Fox*, 104; Braithwaite, *Beginnings of Quakerism*, 78–110; Hugh Barbour, ed., *Margaret Fell Speaking* (Wallingford, Pa.: Pendle Hill, 1976), 8–9. For Margaret Fell's life, see Bonnelyn Kunze, *Margaret Fell and the Rise of Quakerism* (Stanford: Stanford University Press, 1993).

13. Barbour and Frost, *The Quakers*, 5.

14. For a detailed account, see Braithwaite, *Beginnings of Quakerism*, 368–400. A mass of useful material can be found in Norman Penney, ed., "*The First Publishers of Truth.*" *Being Early Records (Now First Printed) of the Introduction of Quakerism into the Counties of England and Wales* (London: Headley Brothers, 1907).

15. For a summary of persecution in this period, see Moore, *Light in Their Consciences*, 155–63. Friends kept careful records of their sufferings for their faith,

which were published in Joseph Besse, *A Collection of the Sufferings of the People Called Quakers, for the Testimony of a Good Conscience*, 2 vols. (London: Luke Hinde, 1753).

16. The leadership of women in the early Quaker movement has attracted considerable attention from scholars in the last two decades. See, for example, Trevett, *Women and Quakerism*; and Phyllis Mack, *Visionary Women: Ecstatic Prophesy in Seventeenth-Century England* (Berkeley and Los Angeles: University of California Press, 1992), 127–261. An excellent collection of primary sources is found in Mary Garman et al., eds., *Hidden in Plain Sight: Quaker Women's Writings, 1650–1700* (Wallingford, Pa.: Pendle Hill, 1996).

17. Francis Higginson, *A Relation of the Irreligion of the Northern Quakers* (1653), in *Early Quaker Writings, 1650–1700*, ed. Hugh Barbour and Arthur O. Roberts (Grand Rapids: Eerdmans, 1973), 73.

18. Mack, *Visionary Women*, 131; Kenneth Carroll, "Early Quakers and 'Going Naked as a Sign,'" *Quaker History* 67 (Autumn 1978): 69–87; Braithwaite, *Beginnings of Quakerism*, 56, 180–81; Ingle, *First Among Friends*, 78, 94–95; Barbour, *Quakers in Puritan England*, 127–59; Moore, *Light in Their Consciences*, 44, 76–77; Henry J. Cadbury, ed., *George Fox's "Book of Miracles"* (Cambridge: Cambridge University Press, 1948).

19. For Nayler, see Moore, *Light in Their Consciences*, 35–48; and Leo Damrosch, *The Sorrows of the Quaker Jesus: James Nayler and the Puritan Crackdown on the Free Spirit* (Cambridge: Harvard University Press, 1996).

20. Moore, *Light in Their Consciences*, 142–54.

21. Barbour, *Quakers in Puritan England*, 144–45; Braithwaite, *Beginnings of Quakerism*, 137–38.

22. Barbour, *Quakers in Puritan England*, 160–80.

23. Ibid. The views of Friends on peace and war in the 1650s are the subject of intense scholarly debate. For a good summary, see Meredith Baldwin Weddle, *Walking in the Way of Peace: Quaker Pacifism in the Seventeenth Century* (New York: Oxford University Press, 2001), 7–11, 245–53.

24. Bliss Forbush, *A History of Baltimore Yearly Meeting of Friends* (Baltimore: Baltimore Yearly Meeting, 1972), 1–12; Kenneth Carroll, *Quakerism on the Eastern Shore* (Baltimore: Maryland Historical Society, 1970), 7–22; Jay Worrall Jr., *The Friendly Virginians: America's First Quakers* (Athens, Ga.: Iberian, 1994), 1–41; Seth B. Hinshaw, *The Carolina Quaker Experience, 1665–1985: An Interpretation* (Greensboro: North Carolina Yearly Meeting, 1984), 3–12.

25. Barbour and Frost, *The Quakers*, 49–51.

26. Rufus M. Jones, *The Quakers in the American Colonies* (London: Macmillan, 1923), 69; Arthur J. Worrall, *Quakers in the Colonial Northeast* (Hanover, N.H.: University Press of New England, 1980), 9–15; Carla Gardina Pestana, "The Quaker Executions as Myth and History," *Journal of American History* 80 (Sept. 1993): 441–69.

27. Worrall, *Quakers in the Colonial Northeast*, 26–42; Carla Gardina Pestana,

"The City Upon a Hill Under Siege: The Puritan Perception of the Quaker Threat to Massachusetts Bay," *New England Quarterly* 56 (Sept. 1983): 323–53.

28. Jones, *Quakers in the American Colonies*, 115–18; Worrall, *Quakers in Colonial Northeast*, 7–9, 18–20; Weddle, *Walking in the Way of Peace*, 98–106.

29. Hugh Barbour et al., *Quaker Crosscurrents: Three Hundred Years of Friends in the New York Yearly Meetings* (Syracuse: Syracuse University Press, 1995), 7–12.

30. A good summary of legislation and its results is Barbour and Frost, *The Quakers*, 65–66.

31. Ingle, *First Among Friends*, 189–206; William C. Braithwaite, *The Second Period of Quakerism* (London: Macmillan, 1923), 21–115.

32. Worrall, *Quakers in the Colonial Northeast*, 14–15; Braithwaite, *Second Period of Quakerism*, 182–85. For the Quaker legal position and attempts to use the law to their advantage, see Craig W. Horle, *The Quakers and the English Legal System, 1660–1688* (Philadelphia: University of Pennsylvania Press, 1988).

33. For the text of the 1661 declaration, see Weddle, *Walking in the Way of Peace*, 234–37. For the historiographical debate, see ibid., 7–8.

34. Ingle, *First Among Friends*, 188.

35. Braithwaite, *Second Period of Quakerism*, 251–89; Mack, *Visionary Women*, 265–304.

36. Ibid., 280–86; Douglas Gwyn, *The Covenant Crucified: Quakers and the Rise of Capitalism* (Wallingford, Pa.: Pendle Hill, 1995), 317–34. For Barclay see D. Elton Trueblood, *Robert Barclay* (New York: Harper and Row, 1968). Barclay's *Apology* went through numerous editions over the past three centuries.

37. For Penn, see Melvin P. Endy, *William Penn and Early Quakerism* (Princeton: Princeton University Press, 1973).

38. Edwin B. Bronner, *William Penn's "Holy Experiment": The Founding of Pennsylvania, 1681–1701* (New York: Temple University Publications, 1962), 6–49; Barbour and Frost, *The Quakers*, 73–74.

39. Ibid., 77–78.

40. Bronner, *William Penn's "Holy Experiment"*, 59–65.

41. For good accounts of Quaker society in the Delaware Valley, see Barry Levy, *Quakers and the American Family: British Settlement in the Delaware Valley* (New York: Oxford University Press, 1988); and David Hackett Fischer, *Albion's Seed: Four British Folkways in North America* (New York: Oxford University Press, 1989), 419–603. For ties between British and American Friends, see Frederick B. Tolles, *Quakers and the Atlantic Culture* (New York: Macmillan, 1960), 1–35.

42. Bronner, *William Penn's "Holy Experiment"*, 223–34.

43. For Penn and the politics of early Pennsylvania, see Mary Maples Dunn, *William Penn: Politics and Conscience* (Princeton: Princeton University Press, 1967); and Alan Tully, *Forming American Politics: Ideals, Interests, and Institutions in Colonial New York and Pennsylvania* (Baltimore: Johns Hopkins University Press, 1994), 27–44, 68–85.

44. Braithwaite, *Second Period of Quakerism*, 457–96.

45. For quietism, see Rufus M. Jones, *The Later Periods of Quakerism*, 2 vols. (London: Macmillan, 1923), I, 67–103. For elders, see Elbert Russell, *The History of Quakerism* (New York: Macmillan, 1943), 220–23.

46. J. William Frost, *The Quaker Family in Colonial America: A Portrait of the Society of Friends* (New York: St. Martin's Press, 1973), 30–45; Tolles, *Quakers and the Atlantic Culture*, 91–113; Thomas D. Hamm, *The Transformation of American Quakerism: Orthodox Friends, 1800–1907* (Bloomington: Indiana University Press, 1988), 1–11.

47. Jones, *Later Periods of Quakerism*, I, 108–10; Richard T. Vann, *The Social Development of English Quakerism* (Cambridge: Harvard University Press, 1969), 122–57.

48. James Walvin, *The Quakers: Money and Morals* (London: John Murray, 1997), 43–120; Frederick B. Tolles, *Meeting House and Counting House: The Quaker Merchants of Colonial Philadelphia, 1682–1763* (Chapel Hill: University of North Carolina Press, 1948).

49. See, generally, Jack D. Marietta, *The Reformation of American Quakerism, 1748–1783* (Philadelphia: University of Pennsylvania Press, 1984).

50. Tully, *Forming American Politics*, 156–57; Robert L. D. Davidson, *War Comes to Quaker Pennsylvania* (New York: Temple University Publications, 1957), 113–96.

51. Marietta, *Reformation of American Quakerism*, 46–72, 203–21.

52. Fred Anderson, *Crucible of War: The Seven Years' War and the Fate of Empire in British North America, 1754–1766* (New York: Knopf, 2000), 205–7; Barbour and Frost, *The Quakers*, 126–28.

53. Jean R. Soderlund, *Quakers & Slavery: A Divided Spirit* (Princeton: Princeton University Press, 1985), 54–86; Thomas E. Drake, *Quakers and Slavery in America* (New Haven: Yale University Press, 1950), 1–33.

54. David Brion Davis, *The Problem of Slavery in Western Culture* (Ithaca: Cornell University Press, 1966), 291–332. An indispensable collection of source materials is J. William Frost, ed., *The Quaker Origins of Antislavery* (Norwood, Pa.: Norwood Editions, 1980).

55. Davis, *Problem of Slavery*, 489. On John Woolman, see Phillips Moulton, ed., *The Journal and Major Essays of John Woolman* (New York: Oxford University Press, 1971); and Edwin Cady, *John Woolman* (New York: Washington Square Press, 1966).

56. Drake, *Quakers and Slavery*, 68–84.

57. Soderlund, *Quakers & Slavery*, 173–87; Henry J. Cadbury, "Negro Membership in the Society of Friends," *Journal of Negro History* 21 (April 1936): 151–213; Sydney V. James, *A People Among Peoples: Quaker Benevolence in Eighteenth-Century America* (Cambridge: Harvard University Press, 1963), 216–39, 286–315.

58. Marietta, *Reformation of American Quakerism*, 222–48; Arthur J. Mekeel, *The Quakers and the American Revolution* (York, Eng.: Sessions, 1996), 96–128.

59. Ibid., 329–42; Jones, *Quakers in the American Colonies*, 210–12.

60. Mekeel, *Quakers and the American Revolution*, 198–216.

3. Their Separate Ways: American Friends Since 1800

1. Duck Creek Monthly Meeting Men's Minutes, 4th Mo. 28, 8th Mo. 21, 1828, Indiana Yearly Meeting Archives (Friends Collection, Earlham College, Richmond, Ind.).

2. Thomas D. Hamm, *The Transformation of American Quakerism: Orthodox Friends, 1800–1907* (Bloomington: Indiana University Press, 1988), 10.

3. See, generally, Errol T. Elliott, *Quakers on the American Frontier* (Richmond, Ind.: Friends United Press, 1969).

4. Stephen B. Weeks, *Southern Quakers and Slavery: A Study in Institutional History* (Baltimore: Johns Hopkins University Press, 1896), 265–69, 286–87; Philip S. Benjamin, *The Philadelphia Quakers in the Industrial Age, 1865–1920* (Philadelphia: Temple University Press, 1976), 3–25; Hugh Barbour and J. William Frost, *The Quakers* (Westport, Ct.: Greenwood, 1988), 154–62; Alexander Starbuck, *The History of Nantucket: County, Island, and Town* (Rutland, Vt.: Tuttle, 1969), 545.

5. The most thorough biography of Elias Hicks is Bliss Forbush, *Elias Hicks: Quaker Liberal* (New York: Columbia University Press, 1956). It has been largely superseded by H. Larry Ingle, *Quakers in Conflict: The Hicksite Reformation* (Knoxville: University of Tennessee Press, 1986). Indispensable is *Journal of the Life and Religious Labors of Elias Hicks* (New York: Isaac T. Hopper, 1832).

6. Ingle, *Quakers in Conflict*, 41.

7. Ibid., 38–61.

8. Ibid., 90–91.

9. Thomas D. Hamm, "'A Protest against Protestantism': Hicksite Quakers and the Bible in the Nineteenth Century," *Quaker Studies* 6 (March 2002): 53–55.

10. Rufus M. Jones, *The Later Periods of Quakerism*, 2 vols. (London: Macmillan, 1921), I:458–60.

11. For support of Hicksite continuity with early Friends, see Forbush, *Elias Hicks*; and Ingle, *Quakers in Conflict*. For accounts sympathetic to the Orthodox position, see William Bacon Evans, *Jonathan Evans and His Times, 1759–1839: A Bi-Centennial Biography* (Boston: Christopher, 1959); and Walter R. Williams, *The Rich Heritage of Quakerism* (Grand Rapids: Eerdmans, 1962), 164–69.

12. Hamm, *Transformation*, 15–20.

13. See, generally, Ingle, *Quakers in Conflict*; and David E.W. Holden, *Friends Divided: Conflict and Division in the Society of Friends* (Richmond, Ind.: Friends United Press, 1988), 49–68. For a socioeconomic interpretation, see Robert W. Doherty, *The Hicksite Separation: A Sociological Analysis of Religious Schism in Early Nineteenth Century America* (New Brunswick: Rutgers University Press, 1967).

14. *Memoirs of William and Nathan Hunt* (Philadelphia: Uriah Hunt, 1858), 103; *Journal of That Faithful Servant of Christ, Charles Osborn* (Cincinnati: Achilles

Pugh, 1854), 204–5; Editorial, *Advocate of Truth* 1 (1st Mo. 1828): 7; "Misstatements Corrected," *Advocate of Truth* 1 (2nd Mo. 1828): 47; P. E. Thomas to Richard Price, 3rd Mo. 27, 1841, John Jackson Papers (Friends Historical Library, Swarthmore College, Swarthmore, Pa.).

   15. Ingle, *Quakers in Conflict*, 38–61, 247–50; Hamm, "'Protest against Protestantism,'" 56–57.

   16. For Quakers and the early antislavery movement, see Thomas E. Drake, *Quakers and Slavery in America* (New Haven: Yale University Press, 1950), 133–66. For Friends and women's rights, see Blanche Glassman Hersh, *The Slavery of Sex: Feminist-Abolitionists in America* (Urbana: University of Illinois Press, 1978); and Margaret Hope Bacon, *Mothers of Feminism: The Story of Quaker Women in America* (San Francisco: Harper and Row, 1986), 120–36. For Hicksite Friends and nonresistance, see Thomas D. Hamm, "Hicksite Quakers and the Antebellum Nonresistance Movement," *Church History* 63 (Dec. 1994): 557–69.

   17. Ibid., 565–66.

   18. Ibid. One Progressive yearly meeting, at Kennett Square, Pennsylvania, survived into the twentieth century, but largely as a reunion of reform-minded Hicksites.

   19. Thomas D. Hamm, "The Hicksite Quaker World, 1875–1900," *Quaker History* 89 (Fall 2000): 17–41.

   20. Ibid.

   21. Ibid.; Deborah L. Haines, "Friends General Conference: A Brief Historical Overview," *Quaker History* 89 (Fall 2000): 1–7. For Hicksite Quaker work among the Plains Indians, see Clyde A. Milner II, *With Good Intentions: Quaker Work Among the Pawnees, Otos, and Omahas in the 1870s* (Lincoln: University of Nebraska Press, 1982).

   22. Hamm, "Hicksite Quaker World," 31–34.

   23. David E. Swift, *Joseph John Gurney: Banker, Reformer, and Quaker* (Middletown, Ct.: Wesleyan University Press, 1962).

   24. Ibid., 114–44.

   25. Hamm, *Transformation*, 20–22.

   26. Ibid., 28–34; Jones, *Later Periods of Quakerism*, I, 488–540.

   27. Hamm, *Transformation*, 28–30.

   28. Jones, *Later Periods of Quakerism*, I, 526–40.

   29. Hamm, *Transformation*, 175.

   30. Ibid., 74.

   31. Ibid., 42–63.

   32. Ibid., 63–66.

   33. Ibid., 42–66.

   34. Ibid., 66–73.

   35. Ibid., 77–87; David B. Updegraff, *Open Letters for Interested Readers* (Philadelphia: n.p., 1880), 22.

36. Hamm, *Transformation*, 87–90. For interpretations of the "Great Revival" that emphasize continuity with previous developments among Gurneyites, see Richard Eugene Wood, "Evangelical Quakers in the Mississippi Valley, 1854–1894" (Ph.D. diss., University of Minnesota, 1985); Damon D. Hickey, *Sojourners No More: The Quakers in the New South, 1865–1920* (Greensboro, N.C.: North Carolina Friends HIstorical Society, 1997), 35–47; and Carole Spencer, "The American Holiness Movement: Why Did It Captivate Nineteenth-Century Quakers?" *Quaker Religious Thought* 28 (Jan. 1998): 19–30.

37. Hamm, *Transformation*, 98–143.

38. Ibid., 92–94, 137–39; Mark Minear, *Richmond, 1887: A Quaker Drama Unfolds* (Richmond, Ind.: Friends United Press, 1987). For the record of the 1887 conference, see *Proceedings, Including the Declaration of Christian Doctrine, of the General Conference of Friends Held in Richmond, Ind., U.S.A., 1887* (Richmond, Ind.: Nicholson, 1887).

39. John Brady, *A Short History of Conservative Friends* (Richmond, Ind.: n.p., 1992), 28–47.

40. Haines, "Friends General Conference," 6–8.

41. Ibid., 8–9; Barbour and Frost, *Quakers*, 231–46.

42. Charles E. Fager, "FGC's 'Uniform Discipline' Rediscovered," *Quaker History* 89 (Fall 2000): 51–59.

43. Hamm, *Transformation*, 146; Elbert Russell, *The History of Quakerism* (New York: Macmillan, 1943), 492–95.

44. Hamm, *Transformation*, 138; Russell, *History of Quakerism*, 494–95.

45. Christina H. Jones, *American Friends in World Missions* (Elgin, Ill.: Brethren Publishing House, 1946).

46. While numerous writers have taken issue with aspects of Rufus Jones's work, he has not been the subject of a critical biography. He tells his own story in Rufus M. Jones, *The Trail of Life in the Middle Years* (New York: Macmillan, 1934). Useful is Elizabeth Gray Vining, *Friend of Life: A Biography of Rufus M. Jones* (Philadelphia: J. B. Lippincott, 1958). For English Friends in this period, see Thomas C. Kennedy, *British Quakerism, 1860–1920: The Transformation of a Religious Community* (Oxford: Oxford University Press, 2001), 86–210.

47. For modernism see William R. Hutchison, *The Modernist Impulse in American Protestantism* (Cambridge: Harvard University Press, 1976). For Jones's modernism, see Hamm, *Transformation*, 147–50.

48. Ibid., 150–60; J. William Frost, "'Our Deeds Carry Our Message': The Early History of the American Friends Service Committee," *Quaker History* 81 (Spring 1992): 1–51.

49. Hamm, *Transformation*, 162.

50. Ibid., 160–64; John Oliver, "J. Walter Malone: *The American Friend* and an Evangelical Quaker's Social Agenda," *Quaker History* 80 (Fall 1991): 63–82; John W. Oliver, ed., *J. Walter Malone: The Autobiography of an Evangelical Quaker*

(Washington: University Press of America, 1993). "Fundamentalism" is a much disputed term. The label comes from a California periodical published from 1910 to 1915, *The Fundamentals*, which saw itself as defending Protestant orthodoxy against modernist theology. It emphasized such doctrines as the Virgin Birth of Christ, the inerrancy of the Bible, and the premillennial Second Coming of Christ. "Fundamentalism" eventually became a generic term for opposition to modernist theology. See George M. Marsden, *Fundamentalism and American Culture: The Shaping of Twentieth-Century Evangelicalism, 1870–1925* (New York: Oxford University Press, 1980).

51. Russell, *History of Quakerism*, 537–41; Hamm, *Transformation*, 164–72; Barbour and Frost, *The Quakers*, 231–42; Thomas D. Hamm, *Earlham College: A History, 1847–1997* (Bloomington: Indiana University Press, 1997), 103–15, 127–39.

52. Williams, *Rich Heritage*, 206–9; Russell, *History of Quakerism*, 538–41.

53. For these developments, see Arthur O. Roberts, *The Association of Evangelical Friends: A Story of Quaker Renewal in the Twentieth Century* (Newberg, Ore.: Barclay Press, 1975).

54. A convenient compilation of membership statistics is found in Barbour and Frost, *The Quakers*, 234–35.

55. Elizabeth Cazden, " 'Wicked Hard to Herd Up': Independent Meetings and the Friends Fellowship Council," *Quaker History* 90 (Fall 2001): 1–14; Eleanore Price Mather, *Pendle Hill: A Quaker Experiment in Education & Community* (Wallingford, Pa.: Pendle Hill, 1980), 3; Herbert M. Hadley, "Diminishing Separation: Philadelphia Yearly Meetings Reunite, 1915–1955," in *Friends in the Delaware Valley: Philadelphia Yearly Meeting, 1681–1981*, ed. John M. Moore (Haverford, Pa.: Friends Historical Association, 1981), 161.

56. Elizabeth Cazden, "Rhode Island Monthly Meeting: An Evangelical Secession from New England Yearly Meeting," *Quaker History* 87 (Fall 1998): 1–16.

57. Barbour et al., *Quaker Crosscurrents*, 257–75; Hadley, "Diminishing Separation," 138–72; Bliss Forbush, *A History of Baltimore Yearly Meeting of Friends* (Baltimore: Baltimore Yearly Meeting, 1972), 149–55.

58. G. Richard Powell, "The Family of Friends in the Friends United Meeting," in *The Church in Quaker Thought and Practice: A Study in Ecclesiology*, ed. Charles F. Thomas (Philadelphia: Friends World Committee, 1979), 65. See also the essays in *Realignment: Nine Views Among Friends* (Wallingford, Pa.: Pendle Hill, 1991).

59. *Indiana Yearly Meeting, 1900 Minutes*, 42, *2000 Minutes*, 62–63; Barbour and Frost, *The Quakers*, 234–35.

60. Ibid., 242–43; Anthony Manousos, ed., *A Western Quaker Reader: Writings by and About Independent Friends in the Western United States, 1929–1999* (Whittier, Cal.: Friends Bulletin Corp., 2000), 1–12, 314–17.

61. Paul Anderson, "A People of Vision," *Evangelical Friend* 27 (March/April 1994): 4; Paul Anderson, "Probing Questions for a Forward-Looking People," *Evangelical Friend* 21 (Sept. 1987): 2; *Among Friends: A Consultation with Friends*

About the Condition of Quakers in the U.S. Today (Richmond, Ind.: Earlham School of Religion, 1999), 87.

4. Quaker Faiths and Practices

1. Howard W. Bartram, "Dimensions of the Spirit," *Friends Journal* 32 (Dec. 1, 1986): 7; Jack L. Willcuts, "New Perspectives in Mission and Service," *Evangelical Friend* 6 (Jan. 1973): 6–7, 26–27; Jack L. Willcuts, "Here and There and Now and Later All at Once," *Evangelical Friend* 21 (Jan./Feb. 1988): 11.

2. Philadelphia Yearly Meeting, *Faith and Practice: A Book of Christian Discipline* (Philadelphia: Philadelphia Yearly Meeting, 1997), 17.

3. Wilmer A. Cooper, *A Living Faith: An Historical Study of Quaker Beliefs* (Richmond, Ind.: Friends United Press, 1990), 75; Seth B. Hinshaw, *Friends Worship Today: Contemporary Concepts and Practices* (Greensboro: North Carolina Yearly Meeting and North Carolina Friends Historical Society, 1991), 26; Jones quoted in Michael J. Sheeran, *Beyond Majority Rule: Voteless Decisions in the Religious Society of Friends* (Philadelphia Yearly Meeting, 1996), 5.

4. Wilmer A. Cooper, "Friends and the Sacraments," *Quaker Life* 21 (Feb. 1980): 5–8; Del Coppinger, "Friends and the Lord's Supper," *Evangelical Friend* 28 (Jan./Feb. 1990): 8–9; Paul Anderson, *Meet the Friends* (Newberg, Ore.: Barclay Press, 1999), 19; Herman H. Macy, *What About the Ordinances?* (Newberg, Ore.: Barclay Press, 1982), 25; D. Elton Trueblood, *The People Called Quakers* (New York: Harper and Row, 1966), 128–47; Philadelphia Yearly Meeting, *Faith and Practice*, 32–33. The classic Quaker statement is found in Robert Barclay's *Apology*, books 12 and 13.

5. T. Canby Jones, "Christ in the Preaching of George Fox," *Quaker Life* 23 (Jan. 1982): 8–9; Ron Woodward, "Vitality in Worship," *Evangelical Friend* 27 (May/June 1994): 3; John Punshon, *Encounter with Silence: Reflections from the Quaker Tradition* (Richmond, Ind.: Friends United Press, 1987), 118–19.

6. Chuck Fager, "Silent Worship," *Quaker Life* 29 (Jan./Feb. 1988): 11; Silas B. Weeks, "A Regathered Society," *Friends Journal* 46 (April 2000): 23; Robert Lawrence Smith, *A Quaker Book of Wisdom: Life Lessons in Simplicity, Service, and Common Sense* (New York: Morrow, 1998), 27.

7. Mariellen O. Gilpin, "The Meaning of Silent Worship," *Friends Journal* 46 (Jan. 2000): 7; Eric Johnson, "Why I Am an Atheist," *Friends Journal* 37 (Jan. 1991): 17; Paul A. Lacey, *Nourishing the Spiritual Life* (London: Quaker Home Service, 1999), 45; Kenneth Carroll, *Touched by God in Quaker Meeting* (Wallingford, Pa.: Pendle Hill, 1998), 6.

8. Howard H. Brinton, *Friends for 300 Years: The History and Beliefs of the Society of Friends Since George Fox Started the Quaker Movement* (New York: Harper and Row, 1952), 63; Howard W. Brod, "One Unprogrammed Meeting's Experience," *Quaker Life* 36 (Sept. 1995): 7. This paragraph is based on the author's observations in visits to dozens of Friends meetings in North America.

9. Leonard S. Kenworthy, *Our Messages and Our Message-Bearers* (Kennett Square, Pa.: Quaker Publications, 1984), 14; James R. Newby, "Don't Just Do Something—Sit!" *Quaker Life* 34 (Oct. 1993): 10; Kara Newell, "What Happens in the Silence?" *Friends Journal* 43 (Sept. 1997): 14; Mariellen Gilpin, "Meditation 101," *Friends Journal* 40 (Jan. 1994): 11–12; Thomas H. Jeavons, "What Is Worship For?" *Friends Journal* 46 (June 2000): 10–11; Punshon, *Encounter*, 44.

10. Fran Palmieri, "Messages: A Personal Odyssey," *Friends Journal* 42 (May 1996): 10; Dwight Ericsson, "Silence," *Friends Journal* 44 (Jan. 1998): 8; R. Melvin Keiser, "Christ in the Mesh of Metaphor," in *New Voices, New Light: Papers from the Quaker Theology Roundtable, Fourth Month 7–9, 1995*, ed. Chuck Fager (Wallingford, Pa.: Pendle Hill, 1995), 94; John Punshon, *Reasons for Hope: The Faith and Future of the Friends Church* (Richmond, Ind.: Friends United Press, 2001), 205; Trueblood, *People Called Quakers*, 94; Punshon, *Encounter with Silence*, 12; Patricia Loring, *Listening Spirituality*. Vol. I: *Personal Spiritual Practices Among Friends* (Washington, D.C.: Openings Press, 1997), 86–87; Douglas Gwyn, *Unmasking the Idols: A Journey Among Friends* (Richmond, Ind.: Friends United Press, 1989), 20.

11. Thomas Jeavons, "The Virtue of Silence," *Quaker Life* 24 (Oct. 1983): 7; Sheeran, *Beyond Majority Rule*, 88; Claire Gorfinkel, *I Have Always Wanted to Be Jewish—And Now Thanks to the Religious Society of Friends, I Am* (Wallingford, Pa.: Pendle Hill, 2000), 26; Jones quoted in Catherine Whitmire, *Plain Living: A Quaker Path to Simplicity* (Notre Dame, Ind.: Sorin, 2001), 123; Punshon, *Encounter with Silence*, 72. For children in meeting, see Jane Wilson letter, *Friends Journal* 38 (July 1992): 5; Diane Pasta, "Raising Religious Children: The Case Against Childcare," *Friends Journal* 46 (June 2000): 12–15; and Eric W. Johnson, *Quaker Meeting: A Risky Business* (Pittsburgh: Dorrance, 1991), 60–62.

12. Mariellen O. Gilpin, "Centering," *Friends Journal* 45 (Oct. 1999): 25; Paul Buckley, "Ritual in Unprogrammed Worship," *Friends Journal* 46 (Oct. 2000): 14; Punshon, *Encounter with Silence*, 59–60; Gorfinkel, *I Always Wanted to Be Jewish*, 24–25; Sandra Cronk, *Dark Night Journey: Inward Re-Patterning Toward a Life Centered in God* (Wallingford, Pa.: Pendle Hill, 1991), 7–9.

13. Annis Bleeke and Carole Spencer, *Identity, Authority, and Community: The Experience of Two Friends at the Woodbrooke Consultation on Identity, Authority, and Community* (Philadelphia: Friends World Committee, 1999), 15; Punshon, *Encounter with Silence*, 78; J. William Frost, "A Century of Liberal Quakerism," *Friends Journal* 46 (Oct. 2000): 11; Brinton, *Friends for 300 Years*, 97.

14. Richard D. Hathaway, "Activism, Quietism, and Incarnation," *Friends Journal* 28 (Dec. 1, 1982): 7; Jay C. Rochelle, "On Worship After the Manner of Friends," *Friends Journal* 37 (Dec. 1991): 20; Punshon, *Encounter with Silence*, 80–81; Lloyd Lee Wilson, *Essays on the Quaker Vision of Gospel Order* (Wallingford, Pa.: Pendle Hill, 1993), 37, 76.

15. Brinton, *Friends for 300 Years*, 84; Whitmire, *Plain Living*, 127–28; Paul A. Lacey, *Leading and Being Led* (Wallingford, Pa.: Pendle Hill, 1985), 13–14.

16. Gertrude P. Marshall, "AFSC Outside and In," *Friends Journal* 28 (May 1, 1982): 9; J. Richard Reid, "A Vocal Ministry," *Friends Journal* 33 (July 1/15, 1987): 4–5; Patrick J. Nugent, "On Speaking in Meeting for Worship," *Friends Journal* 42 (May 1996): 7–8; Brinton, *Friends for 300 Years*, 85–86; Punshon, *Encounter with Silence*, 5, 74; Buckley, "Ritual," 16. For the explanation from San Francisco Meeting, see www.geocities.com/WestHollywood/2473/worship.html.

17. Johnson, *Quaker Meeting*, 19; Fran Palmieri, "Messages: A Personal Odyssey," *Friends Journal* 42 (May 1996): 10; Ralph Slotten letter, *Friends Journal* 45 (Feb. 1999): 5; Lacey, *Nourishing the Spiritual Life*, 47; Douglas V. Steere, *On Speaking Out of the Silence: Vocal Ministry in the Unprogrammed Meeting for Worship* (Wallingford, Pa.: Pendle Hill, 1972), 11.

18. Judith Brown, "Building Community in Conflict," *Friends Journal* 36 (Dec. 1990): 23; Smith, *Quaker Book of Wisdom*, 22; C. J. Swet, *The Wounded Meeting: Dealing with Difficult Behavior in Meeting for Worship* (Philadelphia: Friends General Conference, 1993), 12–14, 16, 24–25; Johnson, *Quaker Meeting*, 16–17.

19. Swet, *Wounded Meeting*, 9–11, 23; Johnson, *Quaker Meeting*, 17. For the functions of such a committee, see Philadelphia Yearly Meeting, *Faith and Practice*, 180–81.

20. David H. Albert, "Some Notions on Why Friends Meetings Do Not Attract Minorities," *Friends Journal* 42 (Oct. 1996): 16; Claudia Lair, "How Will Liberal Quakerism Face the Twenty-First Century?" *Friends Journal* 43 (Jan. 1997): 12; Leonard S. Kenworthy, "The Crucial Role of Spoken Ministry," *Friends Journal* 29 (Aug. 1/15, 1984): 11; Johnson, *Quaker Meeting*, 52; *Among Friends: A Consultation with Friends About the Condition of Quakers in the United States Today* (Richmond, Ind.: Earlham School of Religion, 1999), 31.

21. Marshall Massey, "Covered Meetings," *Friends Journal* 44 (Sept. 1998): 16–17; Trueblood, *People Called Quakers*, 88; Palmer, quoted in Whitmire, *Plain Living*, 11.

22. Esther Schrader, "A Glitzy Spin to a Gentle Faith," *Los Angeles Times*, Aug. 17, 1997, A1.

23. "Friends Meeting for Worship," *Quaker Life* 28 (March 1987): 40; J. Stanley Banker, "Growing the Friends' Way," *Quaker Life* 29 (Dec. 1988): 2.

24. The Richmond Declaration can be found in the disciplines of virtually all of the pastoral yearly meetings. Here I use Friends Church Southwest Yearly Meeting, *Faith and Practice (Book of Discipline)* (Whittier, Calif.: Friends Church Southwest Yearly Meeting, 1997), 20. See also Jim LeShana, "Worship in a Large Programmed Friends Church," *Quaker Life* 29 (Jan./Feb. 1988): 12; and Hinshaw, *Friends Worship Today*, 47.

25. Mary Green, ed., *A Part of My Heart Left Here . . . Renewal Messages of Donald A. Green* (Newberg, Ore.: Barclay Press, 1986), 144; Anderson, *Meet the Friends*, 12–13; Jack L. Willcuts, *Why Friends Are Friends (Some Quaker Core Convictions)* (Newberg, Ore.: Barclay Press, 1992), 4.

26. This description of Friends churches and meeting houses is based on the author's observations over thirty years.

27. David Phillips, "Local Meeting, Rise Up and Walk," *Quaker Life* 37 (Oct. 1996): 5, 30; Ron Ferguson, "It Happened Again This Morning,"*Evangelical Friend* 18 (March 1985): 2–3; Roy P. Clark, "Do I Really Worship?" *Evangelical Friend* 19 (Sept. 1985): 12–13. For a good analysis of a typical programmed meeting's worship, see Deborah Suess, "Out of the Not-So-Silent Gathering: Meeting for Worship as Pastoral Care," in *Out of the Silence: Quaker Perspectives on Pastoral Care and Counseling*, ed. J. Bill Ratliff (Wallingford, Pa.: Pendle Hill, 2001), 76–101.

28. Lacey, *Nourishing*, 19; Hinshaw, *Friends Worship Today*, 81–91; Kenneth More letter, *Quaker Life* 15 (Sept. 1974): 29; David Hagen, "The Certification of Music Ministers," *Evangelical Friend* 12 (May 1979): 8–9; "First Day News," *Evangelical Friend* 18 (Nov. 1984): 17; Robert N. Ham, "Steps Toward Effective Music in Worship," *Evangelical Friend* 23 (Jan./Feb. 1990): 14.

29. John Carter, "O Joyful Noise," *Quaker Life* 29 (Jan./Feb 1988): 18–19; "The Fire Escape," *Quaker Life* 34 (Oct. 1993): 23; David J. Howard, "Music Belongs in Our Worship," *Evangelical Friend* 23 (Jan./Feb. 1990): 13; Cary Youmans, "Festival or Carnival," *Evangelical Friend* 27 (May/June 1994): 7; Hinshaw, *Friends Worship Today*, 85–86; Schrader, "A Glitzy Spin," A1, 38.

30. Evangelical Friends Church, Eastern Region, *Faith and Practice: The Book of Discipline* (Canton, Ohio: Evangelical Friends Church, 2000), 75; Punshon, *Reasons*, 10; Hinshaw, *Friends Worship Today*, 48–49; *Among Friends*, 38; Jack L. Willcuts, "Can Quakers Preach Directly?" *Evangelical Friend* 12 (Oct. 1978): 11; Lon Fendall, "To Clap or Not to Clap," *Evangelical Friend* 22 (March 1989): 4. For an evocative account of evangelical worship in a Friends Church, see Haven Kimmel, *A Girl Named Zippy: Growing up Small in Mooreland, Indiana* (New York: Doubleday, 2001), 60.

31. Paul Anderson, "Embracing the Silence," *Evangelical Friend* 24 (July/Aug. 1991): 7; Craig Hayes, "Open Worship: God's Tool for Building the Church," *Evangelical Friend* 21 (March 1988): 14–16; David Kingrey, "Wholeness from a Pastor's Perspective," *Evangelical Friend* 17 (June 1984): 7; Stan Thornburg, "Embracing the Prophet," *Quaker Life* 29 (June 1988): 8–9; Eastern Region, *Faith and Practice*, 18.

32. T. Eugene Coffin, "The Dilemma of a Friends Pastor," *Evangelical Friend* 11 (Feb. 1978): 9; Mary Morse, "Worship: How Can We Make It Work?" *Evangelical Friend* 23 (Jan./Feb. 1990): 2–3; Mark Minear, "Letting Our Prophets Come Home," *Quaker Life* 29 (June 1988): 12; Trueblood quoted in James R. Newby, "Where Are We Going?" *Quaker Life* 32 (Nov. 1991): 3; Gwyn, *Unmasking the Idols*, 84.

33. Arthur O. Roberts, "Thoughts on Ministry," *Evangelical Friend* 15 (March 1982): 3; Paul Neville, "Our Vision as Friends," *Evangelical Friend* 22 (May 1989): 3; David Jaquith, "A Worship-Feast of Silence & Sharing," *Evangelical Friend* 22

(March 1989): 12; Jack L. Willcuts, "Oh Keep Quiet," *Evangelical Friend* 20 (April 1987): 10; Ron Selleck letter, *Quaker Life* 21 (Oct. 1980): 35; Jack Kirk, "The Changing Quaker Scene," *Quaker Life* 35 (Jan./Feb. 1994): 7; Punshon, *Reasons for Hope*, 10, 210.

34. Robert Barclay, *An Apology for the True Christian Divinity, as the Same is Held Forth, and Preached, by the People Called, in Scorn, Quakers* (London: T. Sowle Raylton and Luke Hinde, 1736), 324–25.

35. Rufus M. Jones, *The Later Periods of Quakerism*, 2 vols. (London: Macmillan, 1921), 194–242.

36. Allen C. Thomas, "Congregational or Progressive Friends: A Forgotten Chapter in Quaker History," *Bulletin of Friends Historical Society of Philadelphia* 10 (Nov. 1920): 21–32; Thomas D. Hamm, "The Hicksite Quaker World, 1875–1900," *Quaker History* 89 (Fall 2000): 19–20.

37. Trueblood, *People Called Quakers*, 113; William F. Rushby, "Cyrus Cooper's Memorial and the Free Gospel Ministry," *Quaker History* 89 (Spring 2000): 28–46.

38. For the controversy over the early development of the pastoral system, see Hamm, *Transformation*, 124–30.

39. North Pacific Yearly Meeting, *Faith and Practice* (Corvallis, Ore.: North Pacific Yearly Meeting, 1993), 134; Philadelphia Yearly Meeting, *Faith and Practice*, 181; Bliss Forbush, "On the Recording of Ministers," *Friends Journal* 31 (Sept. 1/15, 1985): 5–6.

40. Lewis Benson, *Catholic Quakerism: A Vision for All Men* (Philadelphia: Philadelphia Yearly Meeting, 1977), 71, 75; Sara Osborne letter, *Quaker Life* 34 (July/Aug. 1993): 34–35; Martha Wellons Dentiste letter, *Quaker Life* 14 (April 1973): 32; C. G. White, "The Meeting and Its Pastor," *Quaker Life* 39 (April 1998): 8.

41. *The Book of Discipline of Ohio Yearly Meeting of the Religious Society of Friends* (Barnesville, Ohio, 2001), 31; Wilson, *Essays*, 73, 95, 116–21.

42. Friends General Conference Traveling Ministries Committee, Minutes, 1st Mo. 10, 1998 (supplied by Martha Paxson Grundy, Cleveland, Ohio); Philadelphia Yearly Meeting, *Faith and Practice*, 106, 182; Ohio Valley Yearly Meeting, *Book of Discipline: A Guide to Christian Faith and Practice* (N.p., 1978), 47; Cronk, *Dark Night Journey*, 91.

43. North Pacific Yearly Meeting, *Faith and Practice*, 85.

44. Ibid., 86; Philadelphia Yearly Meeting, *Faith and Practice*, 182.

45. Frances Kinsey, "Getting a Clue About the Fine Art of Pastoring," *Quaker Life* 39 (Sept. 1998): 17.

46. Western Yearly Meeting, *Faith and Practice* (Plainfield, Ind.: Western Yearly Meeting, 1986), 128; Eastern Region, *Faith and Practice*, 76; John Ryser, "Pastor, We Need You," *Evangelical Friend* 22 (Oct. 1988): 12–13; Judith Dancy, "Call to Relationship," *Quaker Life* 38 (Nov. 1997): 7; Willcuts, *Why Friends Are Friends*, 44–45.

47. Jack Willcuts, "Out of the Silence," *Evangelical Friend* 19 (May 1986): 13; Howard R. Macy, "Discerning Gifts in Ministry," *Quaker Life* 23 (Feb. 1982): 9–10; Hugh Barbour and J. William Frost, *The Quakers* (Westport, Ct.: Greenwood, 1988), 240; John Punshon, "Visiting the 'Pastoral Majority,'" *Quaker Life* 23 (Sept. 1982): 21–22. For typical recording processes, see Western Yearly Meeting, *Faith and Practice*, 127–29; and Southwest Yearly Meeting, *Faith and Practice*, 92–93.

48. David Brock, "The ABCs of Finding a New Pastor," *Quaker Life* 39 (April 1998): 20–21; Johan Maurer, *Public Ministry Among Friends* (Argenta, B.C.: Argenta Friends Press, 2000), 28.

49. *Among Friends*, 253; Coffin, "The Dilemma of the Quaker Pastor," 7–8.

50. D. Elton Trueblood, "My Vision for the Future," *Evangelical Friend* 12 (July-Aug. 1980): 4; Trueblood quoted in Stanley Perisho, "Friends Convincement—A Leadership Style That Works," *Evangelical Friend* 15 (July/Aug. 1982): 9; Trueblood, *People Called Quakers*, 107–27.

51. Craig Hayes, "Open Worship: God's Tool for Building the Church," *Evangelical Friend* 21 (March 1988): 15; Jack L. Willcuts, "New Attitudes Toward Ministry," *Evangelical Friend* 16 (April 1983): 13; Northwest Yearly Meeting, *Faith and Practice: A Book of Christian Discipline* (Newberg, Ore.: Barclay Press, 1987), 79; *Among Friends*, 130.

52. Hinshaw, *Quaker Worship Today*, 13–14; Jack Kirk, "The Quaker Leadership Crunch: What Can Be Done About It?" *Quaker Life* 32 (March 1991): 6; Paul Neville, "Our Vision as Friends," *Evangelical Friend* 22 (May 1989): 17.

53. Robert Blake, "The Church Growth Movement Among Friends," *Evangelical Friend* 22 (May 1989): 14–15; Chuck Orweiler, "Models for Church/Pastor Relationships," *Evangelical Friend* 23 (Nov./Dec. 1989): 14–15; Charles Mylander, "Giving the Pastor Fits," *Quaker Life* 27 (Dec. 1986): 30; Ron Selleck, "Enabling or Disabling Ministry," *Quaker Life* 37 (May 1996): 21, 27.

54. Stan Thornburg, "The Friends Pastor: Between Peril and Promise," *Quaker Life* 33 (Jan./Feb. 1992): 5; James R. Newby, "Do We Really Want Pastors?" *Quaker Life* 33 (Jan./Feb. 1992): 3; Karla Minear, "Quaker Pastoral Ministry and Leadership," *Quaker Life* 30 (April 1987): 7; J. Stanley Banker, "Pastoral Scenery," *Quaker Life* 30 (April 1989): 2; Tom Spainhour, "Are Friends Equipped?" *Quaker Life* 23 (Sept. 1982): 3; Coffin, "Dilemma of a Friends Pastor," 7–8; *Among Friends*, 127, 130.

55. Howard R. Macy, "Elders," *Evangelical Friend* 17 (Sept. 1983): 3; Howard R. Macy, "Nurturing the Gift of Ministry," *Quaker Life* 23 (Feb. 1982): 13; Gwyn, *Unmasking the Idols*, 4; Robert R. Maccini, "The Quaker Ministry: Alternative to the Clergy-Laity Dilemma," *Friends Journal* 33 (Feb. 1988): 21.

56. Burrough quoted in Sheeran, *Beyond Majority Rule*, 4.

57. Ibid., 6–7; Eastern Region, *Faith and Practice*, 85–86; North Pacific Yearly Meeting, *Faith and Practice*, 74. For a good summary of the different assumptions that Friends often bring to this process, see Henry Beerits, "Maintaining a Quakerly Balance," *Friends Journal* 28 (May 15, 1982): 12–13.

58. George A. Selleck, *Principles of the Quaker Business Meeting* (Richmond,

Ind.: Friends United Press, n.d.), 9; Punshon, *Reasons for Hope*, 248; Willcuts, *Why Friends Are Friends*, 82; Benson, *Catholic Quakerism*, 37; Northwest Yearly Meeting, *Faith and Practice*, 35; Ron Selleck letter, *Quaker Life* 25 (Nov. 1984): 37; Anderson, *Meet the Friends*, 13; Richard J. Foster quoted in Whitmire, *Plain Living*, 35.

59. Cooper, *Living Faith*, 73; Damon D. Hickey, *"Unforeseen Joy": Serving a Friends Meeting as Recording Clerk* (Greensboro: North Carolina Yearly Meeting, 1987), 5; Hinshaw, *Friends Worship Today*, 110–11; Rufus M. Jones, *The Faith and Practice of the Quakers* (Philadelphia: Philadelphia Yearly Meeting, n.d.), 68.

60. Cooper, *Living Faith*, 85; Karla Minear quoted in Stanfield, *Handbook*, 13; Patricia Loring quoted in Whitmire, *Plain Living*, 148; Brinton, *Friends for 300 Years*, 115–16; Jan Greene and Marty Walton, *Fostering Vital Friends Meetings: A Handbook for Working with Quaker Meetings* (Philadelphia: Friends General Conference, 1999), 85; Barry Morley, *Beyond Consensus: Salvaging Sense of the Meeting* (Wallingford, Pa.: Pendle Hill, 1992).

61. Punshon, *Encounter with Silence*, 98; Sheeran, *Beyond Majority Rule*, ix, 55–56, 95; Bill Taber, "Ministering to the Meeting for Business," *Friends Journal* 34 (March 1988): 13; Nancy Jacob, "Learning to Listen," *Friends Journal* 33 (May 1/15, 1987): 3; Willcuts, *Why Friends Are Friends*, 75–76; Hickey, *"Unforeseen Joy"*, 4, 6.

62. Selleck, *Principles*, 10–12; Sheeran, *Beyond Majority Rule*, x, 64–66, 92–93, 97–98; Hickey, *"Unforeseen Joy"*, 7; Wilson, *Essays*, 140–41; David O. Stanfield, *A Handbook for the Presiding Clerk* (Greensboro: North Carolina Yearly Meeting, 1989), 6–7, 12; Dean Freiday, *Speaking as a Friend: Essays Interpreting Our Christian Faith* (Newberg, Ore.: Barclay Press, 1995), 24.

63. Douglas Steere, "Some Dimensions of the Quaker Decision-Making Process," *Friends Journal* 28 (May 15, 1982): 8; Sheeran, *Beyond Majority Rule*, 103.

64. Janette Shetter, *Rhythms of the Ecosystem* (Wallingford, Pa.: Pendle Hill, 1976), 16; Matthias C. Drake, *Beyond Consensus: The Quaker Search for God's Leading for the Group* (N.p., 1992), 9; Hickey, *"Unforeseen Joy"*, 17; Sheeran, *Beyond Majority Rule*, 66–69; Wilson, *Essays*, 136–37; Susan Smith, "Quaker Process," *Conservative Friend* 7 (5th Mo. 1999): 6.

65. Lacey, *Leading and Being Led*, 15, 24; Sheeran, *Beyond Majority Rule*, 24–25; Wilson, *Essays*, 186–87; Paul A. Lacey, "A Crisis for the Future of Democracy," *Friends Journal* 17 (June 1/15, 1971): 328; Julie Shaull, "Leadings, Leanings, and Other Voices," *Friends Journal* 45 (Jan. 1999): 22; Patricia Loring, *Spiritual Discernment: The Context and Goals of Clearness Committees* (Wallingford, Pa.: Pendle Hill, 1992).

66. Brinton, *Friends for 300 Years*, 108; Sheeran, *Beyond Majority Rule*, 59, 60, 111; *Among Friends*, 193; Dwight Spann-Wilson, "Strategy for Friends in the Eighties," *Friends Journal* 26 (Jan. 1/15, 1980): 9; Wilson, *Essays*, 11; Howard Macy, "The Nonsense of the Meeting," *Evangelical Friend* 13 (July/Aug. 1980): 10, 23; Punshon, *Reasons for Hope*, 292; Paul A. Lacey, *Quakers and the Use of Power* (Wallingford, Pa.: Pendle Hill, 1982), 22–23.

67. Floyd Benda, "Renewal—As Experienced by a Quaker," *Quaker Life* 37

(Oct. 1996): 6–8; Johan Maurer, "Commitments," *Quaker Life* 36 (Oct. 1995): 9; Margaret Fraser, "Learning from Friends IV: The Power of Prayer and the Business Method," London *Friend*, Sept. 25, 1992, 1236–39.

68. Whitmire, *Plain Living*, 21. For my understanding of this subject, I am greatly indebted to J. William Frost, "From Plainness to Simplicity: Changing Quaker Ideals for Material Culture," in Emma Jones Lapsansky and Anne A. Verplanck, eds., *Quaker Aesthetics: Reflections on a Quaker Ethic in American Design and Consumption* (Philadelphia: University of Pennsylvania Press, 2003), 16–40.

69. J. William Frost, *The Quaker Family in Colonial America: A Portrait of the Society of Friends* (New York: St. Martin's, 1973), 187–211.

70. Hugh Barbour, ed., *Margaret Fell Speaking* (Wallingford, Pa.: Pendle Hill, 1976), 32.

71. Hamm, *Transformation*, 5–6.

72. William P. Taber Jr., *Be Gentle, Be Plain: A History of Olney* (Barnesville, Ohio: Olney Alumni Association, 1976), 119, 175.

73. See, for example, Gerhardt Nitz, in *What Future for Friends? Report of the St. Louis Conference: A Gathering of Concerned Friends, October 5–7, 1970, St. Louis, Missouri* (Philadelphia: Friends World Committee, 1970), 50.

74. David Kingrey, "Wholeness from a Pastor's Perspective," *Evangelical Friend* 17 (June 1984): 7; Elizabeth Taylor McLaughlin, "Seeking Simplicity in a Complex World," *Friends Journal* 36 (Feb. 1990): 25–27; North Carolina Yearly Meeting quoted in Whitmore, *Plain Living*, 24; S. Francis Nicholson, *Quaker Money* (Wallingford, Pa.: Pendle Hill, 1990), 15–16; Frances Irene Taber, "Finding the Taproot of Simplicity: The Movement Between Inner Knowledge and Outer Action," in Leonard S. Kenworthy, ed., *Friends Face the Future: Continuing and Quaker Concerns* (Philadelphia: Friends General Conference, 1987), 59–72.

75. Michael Hechmer, "On Simplicity," *Friends Journal* 40 (Jan. 1994): 13–14; Daniel A. Seeger, "Gathered for Greatness," *Friends Journal* 45 (Dec. 1999): 18; Northwest Yearly Meeting, *Faith and Practice*, 16; Richard Foster, "The Lamb's War," *Evangelical Friend* 26 (March/April 1993): 19. Other good treatments of simplicity by Friends include Richard J. Foster, *Freedom of Simplicity* (New York: Harper and Row, 1981); and Frank Levering and Wanda Urbanska, *Simple Living: One Couple's Search for a Better Life* (New York: Viking, 1992).

76. Jones, *Faith and Practice*, 98; Philip W. Helms, "In the World, But Not of It," *Friends Journal* 46 (Jan. 2000): 10–12; Tom and Judy Ceppa, "Why We Dress This Way," *Friends Journal* (Dec. 2000): 24–31; Tom Goodridge, "Struggling with Simplicity: The Second Luddite Congress," *Friends Journal* 42 (Aug. 1996): 16–18; Charles E. Moran Jr., letter, *Friends Journal* 42 (Jan. 1996): 5; David L. Johns, "Keeping in Step! Ministry in a Contemporary Age," *Quaker Life* 28 (Sept. 1987): 10.

77. Thomas H. Jeavons, "Simplicity in Our Times," *Friends Journal* 26 (Dec. 1, 1980) 16–18; Eileen Bogus, "Integrating Our Lives," *Friendly Woman* 13

(Spring 1999): 1; Wilson, *Essays*, 174; Elizabeth Watson quoted by Whitmire, *Plain Living*, 36.

78. Sara Little told this story to the author in 1990.

79. Smith, *Quaker Book of Wisdom*, 57–58, 128; Frederick B. Tolles, *Quakers and the Atlantic Culture* (New York: Macmillan, 1960), 73–90; Philip S. Benjamin, *The Philadelphia Quakers in the Industrial Age, 1865–1920* (Philadelphia: Temple University Press, 1976), 49–72.

80. Johan Maurer, "On Being Possessed," *Quaker Life* 29 (Sept. 1988): 6; Catherine Coggan, "On Living Simply," *Friends Journal* 41 (May 1995): 17–18; Sheeran, *Beyond Majority Rule*, 101–2.

81. Mary Clark, "Simplicity of Focus," *Quaker Life* 39 (June 1998): 4–7; Jamie Mitchell Molitoris, "Simplicity Isn't Simple When You Have Kids," *Quaker Life* 44 (Feb. 1998): 21–24; "The Transforming Gospel," *Quaker Life* (Aug. 1998): 6; Whitmire, *Plain Living*, 14; Loring, *Listening Spirituality*, 134–36; Everett L. Cattell, *Christian Mission: A Matter of Life* (Richmond, Ind.: Friends United Press, 1981), 140; Iris-Marie Graville, "One Woman's Rantings and Ravings," *Friendly Woman* 12 (Spring 1996): 22–24.

82. A good summary of the background is Wilmer A. Cooper, *The Testimony of Integrity in the Religious Society of Friends* (Wallingford, Pa.: Pendle Hill, 1991). Several articles in the March 1998 issue of *Quaker Life* are devoted to the Harmon case. See also "Philip Harmon Sentenced," *Quaker Life* 39 (June 1998): 12; and "News Briefs," *Quaker Life* 39 (May 1998): 14.

83. Howard H. Brinton, *The Religious Philosophy of Quakerism: The Beliefs of Fox, Barclay, and Penn as Based on the Gospel of John* (Wallingford, Pa.: Pendle Hill, 1973), 21; Chuck Hosking, "Is Technology Our New God?" *Friends Journal* 44 (Nov. 1998): 9–12; Peter Saint James, "Traffic Noise and Quaker Silence," *Friends Journal* 44 (Dec. 1998): 5; Alla Podolsky letter, *Friends Journal* 46 (Jan. 2000): 5; Osborn Cresson letter, *Friends Journal* 47 (July 2001): 4; Smith, *Quaker Book of Wisdom*, xv; David Morse, *The Iron Bridge* (New York: Harcourt Brace, 1998); Goodridge, "Struggling with Simplicity," 16–18; "The Second Luddite Congress," *Plain* 12 (4th Mo. 1996), 1–47.

84. Wilmington Yearly Meeting, *Faith and Practice* (Wilmington, Ohio: Wilmington Yearly Meeting, 1977), 50; Tom Springer, "God's Grandeur Revisited," *Evangelical Friend* 26 (July/Aug. 1993): 19; David Kingrey, "Friends—Our Stewardship of the Whole Creation," *Evangelical Friend* 10 (Jan. 1977): 8–9; Eastern Region, *Faith and Practice*, 31; Raymond J. Barnett, "Home-Grown Environmentalism," *Friends Journal* 38 (Feb. 1992): 26; Lynda Goin, "Unity with Nature and Quaker Tradition," *Friends Journal* 36 (April 1990): 10–11; "Witness," *Friends Journal* 47 (May 2001): 22–23; Diane Coleman, "Why Quakers Need Their Own Theology," in Fager, ed., *New Voices, New Light*, 25; Marshall Massey, *The Defense of the Peaceable Kingdom* (Oakland: Pacific Yearly Meeting, 1985).

85. Polly Test letter, *Friends Journal* 26 (Dec. 1, 1980): 19; James R. Newby,

"Where Everybody Knows Your Name," *Quaker Life* 34 (Sept. 1993): 3–4; Whitmire, *Plain Living*, 42; Smith, *Quaker Book of Wisdom*, 42–43.

86. Gwyn, *Unmasking the Idols*, 20; Merl Kinser, "You and Your Finances: Simplicity," *Evangelical Friend* 15 (Jan. 1982): 10; Thomas S. Brown, "P Is for Pocketbook," *Friends Journal* 28 (Dec. 15, 1982): 13; J. Stanley Banker, "Endangered Testimony," *Quaker Life* 29 (Sept. 1988): 2; *Among Friends*, 76.

87. Helen G. Hole, *Things Civil and Useful: A Personal View of Quaker Education* (Richmond, Ind.: Friends United Press, 1978), 5–8; W. A. Campbell Stewart, *Quakers and Education: as Seen in Their Schools in England* (London: Epworth, 1953), 46–49; Howard H. Brinton, *Quaker Education in Theory and Practice* (Wallingford, Pa.: Pendle Hill, 1949), 23; Leonard S. Kenworthy, *Quaker Education: A Source Book* (Kennett Square, Pa.: Quaker Publications, 1987), 6–7.

88. Stewart, *Quakers and Education*, 25, 27, 31; Jones, *Faith and Practice*, 149.

89. Thomas D. Hamm, *Earlham College: A History, 1847–1997* (Bloomington: Indiana University Press, 1997), 8–10; Hole, *Things Civil and Useful*, 1–38.

90. Hamm, *Earlham College*, 31–33; Christopher Densmore, "Swarthmore College: From 'Guarded Education' to a 'Tradition of Excellence,'" 2001 (in author's possession); Diana Franzusoff Peterson, "Haverford College: Connections in the Life of an Institution," 2001 (unpublished paper in author's possession).

91. Hole, *Things Civil and Useful*, 39–74; John W. Oliver, ed., *J. Walter Malone: The Autobiography of an Evangelical Quaker* (Washington: University Press of America, 1993), 61–68.

92. Barbour and Frost, *The Quakers*, 241–42.

93. Paul A. Lacey, *Growing Into Goodness: Essays on Quaker Education* (Wallingford, Pa.: Pendle Hill, 1998), 209–38; Hole, *Things Civil and Useful*, 75–96.

94. Lacey, *Growing Into Goodness*, xix; Hole, *Things Civil and Useful*, 89; Annette Breiling, "A Survey of K-12 Friends Schools," *Friends Journal* 44 (Nov. 1998): 18.

95. Jones, *Faith and Practice*, 155; Ernest Boyer, "Connections: The Challenge to Quaker Education," *Quaker Life* 29 (Nov. 1988): 8; Lacey, *Growing Into Goodness*, 57–61. For Howard Brinton's vision, see Brinton, *Quaker Education*. This is an expanded edition of a work first published in 1940.

96. Lacey, *Growing Into Goodness*, 13–14, 17–34; Johnson, *Quaker Meeting*, 68; Breiling, "A Survey of K-12 Friends Schools," 15.

97. Lacey, *Growing Into Goodness*, 20, 168–69, 255, 260–61; Parker J. Palmer, "Meeting for Learning: Education in a Quaker Context," *Pendle Hill Bulletin* 284 (May 1976): 3–4; Ron Miller, "Nurturing and Educating Our Children," *Friends Journal* 38 (Feb. 1992): 10; Marjorie Shore, "The Dialogue Process," *Friends Journal* 31 (April 15, 1985): 18–19; Christopher A. Dorrance, ed., *Reflections from a Friends Education* (Philadelphia: Friends Council on Education, 1982), 39, 41.

98. Lacey, *Growing Into Goodness*, 23–24, 65–66, 133, 242–43, 246; Bill Kashatus, "The Challenge of a Quaker Education," *Quaker Life* 28 (Nov. 1987): 6–7; Louise Wilson, "Where Have All the Young Friends Teachers Gone?"

Quaker Life 27 (March 1986): 19; William V. Vitarelli, "Quaker Schools: Elitist Education?" *Friends Journal* 30 (Sept. 1/15, 1984): 21; Kurt Brandenburg, "Elitism and Quakerism in Friends Schools," *Friends Journal* 31 (April 15, 1985): 10–11; Alfred K. LaMotte, "A Critical View of Multicultural Education," *Friends Journal* 37 (Oct. 1991): 14–16; Spencer Coxe, "Friends Schools: Two Unmet Needs," *Friends Journal* 37 (Oct. 1991): 12–13; "Quaker Education: Readers Respond," *Friends Journal* 38 (Feb. 1992): 7. For an incisive comparison, see also Kim Hays, *Practicing Virtue: Moral Traditions at Quaker and Military Boarding Schools* (Berkeley: University of California Press, 1994).

99. *Among Friends*, 103; Lacey, *Growing Into Goodness*, 104; Breiling, "A Survey of K-12 Friends Schools," 18.

100. Jess Kennison, "Christian School A + ," *Evangelical Friend* 16 (Feb. 1983): 7; Gary Townsend, "Public Schools: Christians Can Make a Difference," *Evangelical Friend* 25 (Sept./Oct. 1991): 6–7; Lacey, *Growing Into Goodness*, xix; Kate Kerman, "Living Together, Learning Together," *Friends Journal* 31 (April 15, 1985): 14–17; Sandra Brown, "Friendly Community Based Educating," *Friends Journal* 47 (Jan. 2001): 14–15; Arthur O. Roberts, *Messengers of God: The Sensuous Side of Spirituality* (Newberg, Ore.: Barclay Press, 1996), 45.

101. Arthur O. Roberts, "Friends and Their Colleges," *Quaker Life* 37 (Nov. 1996): 4, 10; Lon Fendall, "Quaker Colleges," *Quaker Life* 37 (Nov. 1996): 5.

102. This paragraph is based on my contacts with faculty at the various Quaker colleges.

103. *Among Friends*, 93–94; *Swarthmore College Bulletin*, quoted in Densmore, "Swarthmore College."

104. William R. Rogers, "Building Blocks of Quaker Education," *Quaker Life* 30 (Nov. 1989): 11; Boyer, "Connections," 8; "Church and College Growth: How Strong Is the Commitment?" *Evangelical Friend* 17 (Nov. 1983): 27. For an excellent example of an attempt at a Quaker pedagogy, see Mary Rose O'Reilley, *The Peaceable Classroom* (Portsmouth, N.H.: Boynton/Cook, 1993).

105. Jack Kirk, "The Changing Quaker Scene," *Quaker Life* 35 (Jan./Feb. 1995): 7; Norman V. Bridges, "Consider a Christian College," *Evangelical Friend* 10 (May 1977): 6–7; Ron Johnson, "The Christian College: Today and Tomorrow," *Evangelical Friend* 18 (Nov. 1984): 2–4; Lee Nash, "Extremism and Its Antidote," *Evangelical Friend* 20 (Oct. 1986): 18; Harper Cole, "Seeking and Enhancing Quaker Values," *Evangelical Friend* 18 (Nov. 1984): 9.

106. Bill Medlin, "Earlham College," *Quaker Life* 39 (Nov. 1998): 4–7; Fred Allen, "William Penn College and Iowa Yearly Meeting," *Quaker Life* 37 (Nov. 1996): 6; J. William Frost, "A Century of Liberal Quakerism," *Friends Journal* 46 (Oct. 2000): 11.

107. *Among Friends*, 211–12; Lee Nash, "Friends Colleges: Originals or Copies," *Evangelical Friend* 18 (Nov. 1984): 6; Max L. Carter, "Creating a Campus Quaker Culture," *Friends Journal* 47 (Jan. 2001): 30–35; Thomas J. Mullen, *A*

Middle Way: Another Look at Quaker Higher Education, or Will the Real Quaker College Please Stand Up? (Muncie, Ind.: Indiana Yearly Meeting, 1975), 4.

108. Thomas H. Jeavons, "Quaker Traditions and Theological Education," *Quaker Life* 21 (Sept. 1980): 13–15; *Among Friends*, 282. For the Earlham School of Religion, see Hamm, *Earlham College*, 281–84, 336–36; and Wilmer A. Cooper, *The Earlham School of Religion Story: A Quaker Dream Come True, 1960–1985* (Richmond, Ind.: Earlham School of Religion, 1985).

109. Stephanie Crumley-Effinger, "Earlham College, Western and Indiana Yearly Meetings," *Quaker Life* 37 (Nov. 1996): 8; Lacey, *Growing Into Goodness*, 255, 257.

110. Hamm, *Transformation*, 26; Carol Williams, "Allowing Your Sunday School to Grow," *Evangelical Friend* 23 (Sept./Oct. 1989): 10–11; Cliff Loesch, "A Quarter Century of Change," *Evangelical Friend* 27 (May/June 1994): 17; Tim Harding, "Beyond the Sunday School," *Quaker Life* 31 (Jan./Feb. 1990): 9–10. This paragraph is based in large part on examination of the *American Friend* between 1900 and 1960.

111. Hamm, "Hicksite Quaker World," 32–33; David Wetherill, "Teaching Faith," *Quaker Life* 24 (March 1983): 17; Rosemary K. Coffey, "Rethinking First-Day School," *Friends Journal* 44 (March 1998): 21–22; Donna McDaniel, "Friends from Small Meetings Gather at Yearly Meeting," *New England Friend* 55 (Fall 2000): 7; Greene and Walton, *Fostering Vital Friends Meetings*, 67–69. For FGC religious education curriculum, see Shirley Dodson, *Quakerism 101* (Philadelphia: Philadelphia Yearly Meeting, 1994); and Mary Snyder, *Opening Doors to Quaker Religious Education* (Philadelphia: Friends General Conference, 1999).

5. Contemporary Quaker Debates

1. See, for example, Robert Wuthnow, *The Restructuring of American Religion: Society and Faith Since World War II* (Princeton: Princeton University Press, 1988).

2. For anti-Quaker books, see Joseph Smith, *Bibliotheca Anti-Quakeriana; or, a Catalogue of Books Adverse to the Society of Friends* (London: Joseph Smith, 1873). For the last work, see Samuel Hanson Cox, *Quakerism Not Christianity: or, Reasons for Renouncing the Doctrine of Friends* (New York: D. Fanshaw, 1833).

3. Gurney quoted in John Punshon, *Reasons for Hope: The Future of the Friends Church* (Richmond, Ind.: Friends United Press, 2001), 111–12; "Pacific Yearly Meeting," *Friends Journal* 31 (Nov. 1, 1985): 16.

4. See, for example, Indiana Yearly Meeting, *Faith and Practice* (Muncie, Ind.: Indiana Yearly Meeting, 1998), 37.

5. Northwest Yearly Meeting, *Faith and Practice: A Book of Christian Discipline* (Newberg, Ore.: Barclay Press, 1987), 10; Charles Mylander, "Litmus Test," *Evangelical Friend* 22 (March 1989): 9.

6. Rufus M. Jones, *The Faith and Practice of the Quakers* (Philadelphia: Philadelphia Yearly Meeting, n.d.), 78; Noel Stern letter, *Quaker Life* 35 (Sept. 1994):

29–30; Catherine Whitmire, *Plain Living: A Quaker Path to Simplicity* (Notre Dame, Ind.: Sorin, 2001), 108.

7. Richard J. Wood, "Faith and Friends Higher Education," *Quaker Life* 26 (Nov. 1985): 5–6; Howard R. Macy, "Worried About the Light," *Quaker Life* 32 (Nov. 1991): 5; Douglas Gwyn, *Unmasking the Idols: A Journey Among Friends* (Richmond, Ind.: Friends United Press, 1989), 30; Punshon, *Reasons for Hope*, 103–4; D. Elton Trueblood, *The People Called Quakers* (New York: Harper and Row, 1966), 70.

8. David McDonald, "A World of Beauty and Ugliness," *Friends Journal* 34 (Jan. 1988): 5; Judy Brutz, "Love and Fear," *Friendly Woman* 12 (Summer/Fall 1996): 14; *The Quaker Way* (Philadelphia: Friends General Conference, 1998), 15, 17.

9. Georgia Fuller, "Reflections on Emmanuel for the 21st Century," in *New Voices, New Light: Papers from the Quaker Theology Roundtable, Fourth Month 7–9, 1995*, ed. Chuck Fager (Wallingford, Pa.: Pendle Hill, 1995), 109; Peter Rabenold letter, *Friends Journal* 31 (March 1, 1985): 21; Daniel Liechty letter, *Friends Journal* 33 (July 1/15, 1987): 16; Karen Reynolds, "What Is God, Anyway?" *Friends Journal* 35 (July 1989): 23; Janet Ferguson letter, *Friends Journal* 44 (July 1998): 5; Daniel A. Seeger, "Gathered for Greatness," *Friends Journal* 45 (Dec. 1999): 18; Linda Chidsey, *Standing on the Rock: A Faith Conversation with Conservative Kin* (Philadelphia: Friends World Committee for Consultation, 1999), 3; Sally Rickerman, *Growing Up Quaker and Universalist Too* (Landenburg, Pa.: Quaker Universalist Fellowship, 1999), 14.

10. Michael J. Sheeran, *Beyond Majority Rule: Voteless Decisions in the Religious Society of Friends* (Philadelphia: Philadelphia Yearly Meeting, 1996), 75; Carolyn Knudsen Adams, "Let Go of Jesus Myth," *Friends Journal* 34 (Jan. 1988): 5, 37; Blanche P. Zimmerman, "The Message and the Myth," *Friends Journal* 41 (June 1995): 21; Kingdon W. Swayne, "Confessions of a Post-Christian Agnostic," *Friends Journal* 36 (Feb. 15, 1980): 6; Ray E. Stewart letter, *Quaker Life* 31 (May 1990): 35.

11. Geoffrey D. Kaiser letter, *Friends Journal* 31 (Sept. 1/15, 1985): 20; Su Penn, "Perversions," *Friends Journal* 44 (June 1998): 16; Chuck Fager, *Without Apology: The Heroes, the Heritage, and the Hope of Liberal Quakerism* (Bellefonte, Pa.: Kimo Press, 1996), 155; R. Melvin Keiser, "Christ in the Mesh of Metaphor," in Fager, ed., *New Voices*, 92.

12. Fager, *Without Apology*, 126–27; Jimmy Clifton letter, *Friends Journal* 26 (May 15, 1980): 27; Arthur Rifkin, "The Experience of Divinity," *Friends Journal* 41 (Feb. 1995): 8–10; North Pacific Yearly Meeting, *Faith and Practice* (Corvallis, Ore.: North Pacific Yearly Meeting, 1993), 12.

13. John Everhart, "Christian in a Vacuum," *Friends Journal* 33 (Aug. 1/15, 1987): 17; Jayne Maugans, "Leaving a Friends Meeting," *Friends Journal* 41 (Nov. 1995): 10; Bill Samuel letter, *Friends Journal* 42 (Feb. 1996): 5–6; John Pitts Corry,

"Jesus Among Friends," *Friends Journal* 42 (May 1996): 16–17; Lincoln Cory letter, *Quaker Life* 42 (Sept. 2001): 34; Grant Kaufmann, *The Gospel Imperative: A Message Given at the 1995 Sessions of Ohio Yearly Meeting of Friends* (N.p., 1995), 1.

14. Fager, *Without Apology*, 38; Sheeran, *Beyond Majority Rule*, 142; Wilmer A. Cooper, *A Living Faith: An Historical Study of Quaker Beliefs* (Richmond, Ind.: Friends United Press, 1990), 29–31; Lloyd Lee Wilson, *Essays on the Quaker Vision of Gospel Order* (Wallingford, Pa.: Pendle Hill, 1993), 28.

15. Willcuts, *Quakers*, 9; Wilson, *Essays*, 101.

16. Jayne E. Maugans, "Unity Through the Inward Light," *Friends Journal* 37 (Jan. 1991): 16; "Inner Light Guides," *Friends Journal* 33 (July 1/15, 1987): 17; Hall quoted in Fager, *Without Apology*, 122–26; William P. H. Stevens Jr., "Paying Attention to God," *Quaker Life* 32 (April 1991): 9; Everett A. Cattell, *Christian Mission: A Matter of Life* (Richmond, Ind.: Friends United Press, 1981), 25–28; Trueblood, *People Called Quakers*, 76–77, 278–79; Punshon, *Reasons for Hope*, 99–100.

17. Douglas Gwyn, *The Covenant of Light* (Richmond, Ind.: Friends United Meeting, 1990), 2.

18. *Among Friends: A Consultation with Friends About the Condition of Quakers in the U.S. Today* (Richmond, Ind.: Earlham, 1999), 199.

19. Paul A. Lacey, *Quakers and the Use of Power* (Wallingford, Pa.: Pendle Hill, 1982), 24–25; Greg Doudna, "Returning to Quaker Roots," *Friends Journal* 31 (May 15, 1985): 14–15; Anne Thomas, "Our Long Night of Preparation," *Quaker Life* 32 (March 1991): 15; *Among Friends*, 32, 134, 203, 216.

20. *Friends as Leaders: The Vision, Instrument, and Methods* (Wallingford, Pa.: Pendle Hill, 1980), 9, 10.

21. Ibid., 10, 22; Lacey, *Quakers and the Use of Power*, 29; Thomas H. Jeavons, "The Curious Task of Religious Leadership," *Friends Journal* 41 (Oct. 1995): 9; Robert K. Greenleaf, *Servant Leadership: A Journey Into the Nature of Legitimate Power and Greatness* (New York: Paulist Press, 1977), 13–14.

22. Douglas Steere, "Some Dimensions of the Quaker Decision-Making Process," *Friends Journal* 28 (May 15, 1982): 8.

23. Bruce Birchard, "Friends and Their Leaders," *Friends Journal* 39 (June 1993): 10; *Among Friends*, 33, 39, 143; Lacey, *Quakers and the Use of Power*, 12, 24.

24. Jack L. Willcuts, "Where Is the Power?" *Evangelical Friend* 16 (Feb. 1983): 11; Ron Selleck letter, *Quaker Life* 32 (April 1991): 35; *Among Friends*, 142–43; Alan Weinacht, interview with author, Feb. 8, 2002, and J. Stanley Banker Jr., interview with author, April 19, 2002 (notes in author's possession).

25. Jack Kirk, "The Quaker Leadership Crunch: What Can Be Done About It?" *Quaker Life* 32 (March 1991): 7; Glenn A. McNiel, "Friends Leadership Training: Questions That Won't Stop," *Evangelical Friend* 20 (Oct. 1986): 15; Lon Fendall, "Quakers Can Be Good Followers," *Evangelical Friend* 21 (April 1987): 4; Robert Blake, "The Church Growth Movement," *Evangelical Friend* 22 (May

1989): 16; Evangelical Friends Church, Eastern Region, *Faith and Practice: The Book of Discipline* (Canton, Ohio: Eastern Region Yearly Meeting, 2000), 98.

26. *Among Friends*, 127–39; Jeavons, "Curious Task of Religious Leadership," 9.

27. Bernhard Knollenberg, *Pioneer Sketches of the Upper Whitewater Valley: Quaker Stronghold of the West* (Indianapolis: Indiana Historical Society, 1945), 31.

28. Trueblood, *People Called Quakers*, 65; *Quaker Way*, 7; *Realignment: Nine Views Among Friends* (Wallingford, Pa.: Pendle Hill, 1991), 75.

29. Arthur A. Rifkin, "A Quaker Non-Creed," *Friends Journal* 31 (April 1, 1985): 9; Thomas H. Jeavons, "A Friendly Notion of Discipline," *Friends Journal* 27 (Nov. 15, 1981): 13. Baltimore Yearly Meeting took twenty years to unite on a new *Faith and Practice* after reuniting. See "Baltimore Yearly Meeting Guided to Unity," *Friends Journal* 35 (March 1989): 25.

30. Rosemary Moore, *The Light in Their Consciences: The Early Quakers in Britain, 1646–1666* (University Park: Pennsylvania State University Press, 2000), 51–59; Robert Barclay, *An Apology for the True Christian Divinity* (London: T. Sowle Raylton, 1736), 67–94. See also the essays on "The Uses of Scripture by Early Friends" in *Quaker Religious Thought* 30 (Sept. 2001).

31. Northwest Yearly Meeting, *Faith and Practice*, 10; Clare Willcuts, "Ministry Among Friends," *Evangelical Friend* 13 (Oct. 1979): 9; Myron D. Goldsmith, "Quakers and the Scriptures," *Evangelical Friend* 7 (March 1974): 6–8; Lucy Anderson, "Trinity Friends Church: A Profile," *Evangelical Friend* 18 (May 1985): 7; Edwin B. Neal letter, *Quaker Life* 21 (May 1980): 35; Susan Smith, "An Invitation to the Bible," *Conservative Friend* 2 (8th Mo. 1998): 2–3, 5.

32. Larry Costner, "God Is a Sculptor," *Quaker Life* 28 (April 1987): 15; Annis Bleeke and Carole Spencer, "Identity, Authority, and Community," *Friends Journal* 45 (Jan. 1999): 18; Cattell, *Christian Mission*, 8; Punshon, *Reasons for Hope*, 132–33, 145–51.

33. Patricia Loring, *Listening Spirituality*. Vol. I: *Personal Spiritual Practices Among Friends* (Washington, D.C.: Openings Press, 1997), 24; Joanne and Larry Spears, *Friendly Bible Study* (Philadelphia: Friends General Conference, 1990), 1; Shirley Dodson, "Theology for Each of Us," *Friends Journal* 26 (Sept. 1/15, 1980): 11; Patricia Dallmann, "Bible as Ministry," *Friends Journal* 44 (April 1998): 13; Edna J. Eisenhart, "Friendly Bible Study," *Friends Journal* 45 (April 1999): 10.

34. Gwyn, *Unmasking the Idols*, 7; *Realignment*, 76; Elizabeth Watson, *Daughters of Zion: Stories of Old Testament Women* (Richmond, Ind.: Friends United Press, 1982), passim; Annis Bleeke and Carole Spencer, *Identity, Authority, and Community: The Experience of Two Friends at the Woodbrooke Consultation on Identity, Authority and Community* (Philadelphia: Friends World Committee for Consultation, 1999), 10; Spears and Spears, *Friendly Bible Study*, 1; Eisenhart, "Friendly Bible Study," 10; Philadelphia Yearly Meeting, *Faith & Practice: A Book of Christian Discipline* (Philadelphia: Philadelphia Yearly Meeting, 1997), 30; North Pacific Yearly Meeting, *Faith and Practice*, 21–22, 58.

35. Rick Knaub letter, *Friends Journal* 47 (Jan. 2001): 5; Stanford J. Searl Jr., "Quaker Seeking: Do We Ever Find Anything?" *Friends Journal* 45 (Jan. 1999): 6; Jan Greene and Marty Walton, *Fostering Vital Friends Meetings: A Handbook for Working with Quaker Meetings* (Philadelphia: Friends General Conference, 1999), 3, 75.

36. Ibid., 75; Herb Lape, "Beyond Legalism and Ranterism," *Quaker Life* 35 (June 1994): 7.

37. Indiana Yearly Meeting, *Faith and Practice*, 97–98; Northwest Yearly Meeting, *Faith and Practice*, 35.

38. *Realignment*, 48i–v; Johan Maurer, *Public Ministry Among Friends* (Argenta, B.C.: Argenta Friends Press, 2000), 25; "Western Yearly Meeting: No Friendly Persuasion," *Friendly Letter* 20 (11th Mo. 1982): 2–3.

39. Ron Allen, "Focus Queries," *Evangelical Friend* 9 (Nov. 1975): 11; John L. Robinson, "As a Superintendent Sees It," *Evangelical Friend* 16 (Sept. 1982): 10; Jack Kirk, "The Changing Quaker Scene," *Quaker Life* 35 (Jan./Feb. 1994): 8; Alan Weinacht, interview with author, Feb. 8, 2002 (notes in author's possession).

40. Lucy Olfson letter, *Friends Journal* 32 (April 1, 1986): 16; Daniel A. Seeger, "Unity and Diversity in Our Spiritual Family," *Friends Journal* 32 (Jan. 1/15, 1986): 9–12; Steven Davison, "Friends' Use of Electronic Communications," *Friends Journal* 40 (July 1994): 11; Elise Boulding, *One Small Plot of Heaven: Reflections on Family Life by a Quaker Sociologist* (Wallingford, Pa.: Pendle Hill, 1989), 95.

41. For this and the following paragraph, I draw on an unpublished paper by J. William Frost, " 'Sex Is Not a Shortcut to Spirituality': Liberal Quakers Confront the 20th Century Sexual Revolutions" (2001, copy in my possession).

42. Evangelical Friends Church, Eastern Region, *Faith and Practice: The Book of Discipline* (Canton, Ohio: Eastern Region Yearly Meeting, 2000), 24; Tom Sine, "Waking Up to the Generational Revolution," *Evangelical Friend* 24 (Jan./Feb. 1991): 8; Stan Hinshaw, "The Birds and the Bees," *Evangelical Friend* 25 (May/ June 1992): 11.

43. Geoffrey D. Keiser letter, *Friends Journal* 32 (April 1, 1986): 18; "Sex, Truth, and God," *Friends Journal* 32 (Nov. 1, 1986): 21–22; Mildred Ringwalt letter, *Friends Journal* 28 (Dec. 15, 1982): 25; Molly Barnett and John Etter, "Toward a New Personal Relationship Ethic," *Friendly Woman* 13 (Summer 1999): 29.

44. Sheeran, *Beyond Majority Rule*, 69; "Youth Programs in Turmoil," *Friends Journal* 44 (May 1998): 24–26; Herb Lape, "Our 300-Year-Old Testimony on Sexual Expression," *Friends Journal* 32 (Feb. 1, 1986): 10–13; Herb Lape, "Sexual Expression: Discerning the Will of God," *Friends Journal* 35 (June 1989): 18–19; Herb Lape, "Beyond Legalism and Ranterism," *Quaker Life* 35 (June 1994): 6–7.

45. Frost, " 'Sex Is Not a Shortcut to Spirituality'; Bruce Grimes, "Made to Feel Welcome," *Friends Journal* 46 (May 2000): 27–28; Fager, *Without Apology*, 46.

46. *Realignment*, 99; Ann Clendenin, "Sanctuary of the Heart," *Friends Journal* 35 (June 1989): 17; Mary Gilbert, "The Bible and Homosexuality," *Friends Journal*

35 (July 1989): 28–30; Sally W. Bryan, "Equality and Judgment in the Society of Friends," *Friends Journal* 35 (Jan. 1989): 9–10; Anne D. Cope letter, *Friends Journal* 42 (Aug. 1996): 6; Stephen Zunes, "Friends and the Debate Over Homosexuality," *Friends Journal* 40 (Sept. 1994): 16–17; Penn, "Perversions," 16–17.

47. *A Resource Guide to Be Used by a Same-Sex Couple* (Philadelphia: Philadelphia Yearly Meeting, 1991); Monette Thatcher letter, *Friends Journal* 35 (June 1989): 5; "Reports," *Friends Journal* 35 (Dec. 1989): 30–31; Keith Fry letter, *Friends Journal* 36 (Feb. 1990): 6; Laurence Barber, "The Marriage Question(s)," *Friends Journal* 40 (Jan. 1994): 9; Patricia Campbell, "Spiritual Obedience, Homophobia, and the Religious Society of Friends," *Friends Journal* 43 (June 1997): 21; Ellen Hodge and Michael J. Fallahay, "Marriage Matters," *Friends Journal* 34 (Feb. 1988): 29; Irving Hollingshead, "To Grasp the Opportunity," *Friends Journal* 35 (Jan. 1989): 5.

48. Eastern Region, *Faith and Practice*, 23–24; "Friends Concerns," *Evangelical Friend* 11 (Oct. 1977): 21; Jim Rahenkamp letter, *Quaker Life* 25 (Nov. 1984): 37; Rosemary Carter letter, *Quaker Life* 37 (May 1996): 3; Evelyn Harriman letter, *Quaker Life* 37 (May 1996): 33; *North Carolina Yearly Meeting [FUM] Minutes, 1997*, 180–87.

49. "The Disownment of Cleveland (Ohio) Meeting," *Friends Journal* 41 (Nov. 1995): 28–30; Willie R. Frye, "The Listening Project," *Friends Journal* 42 (March 1996): 13–15; Ellen Hodge and Michael J. Fallahay, "Essential Lessons of Same-Gender Marriage," *Friends Journal* 35 (Jan. 1989): 6–8; *Realignment*, 48iv–v, 49–60; Thomas D. Hamm, *Earlham College: A History, 1847–1997* (Bloomington: Indiana University Press, 1997), 338–46; Charles Mylander, "Mind the Light," *Quaker Life* 31 (Oct. 1990): 18; "Christian Documents in the Friends Debate on Homosexuality," *Quaker Life* 38 (March 1997): 20–21; "Western Finds Redemptive Way Forward," *Quaker Life* 36 (Oct. 1995): 12.

50. "Assuring Civil Benefits for All," *Friends Journal* 43 (March 1997): 29; "RMYM Focuses on Prayer," *Evangelical Friend* 26 (July/Aug. 1993): 20; "Family of Friends," *Quaker Life* 29 (Dec. 1988): 5; *Indiana Yearly Meeting Minutes, 1995*, 27–28.

51. Thomas J. Mullen, *A Middle Way: Another Look at Quaker Education or Will the Real Quaker College Please Stand Up?* (Muncie, Ind.: Indiana Yearly Meeting, 1975), 1.

52. Fager, *Without Apology*, 110–11, 153; Leonard S. Kenworthy, "State of the Religious Society of Friends," *Quaker Life* 15 (March 1974): 7; J. Stanley Banker, "Growing the Friends' Way," *Quaker Life* 29 (Dec. 1988): 2.

53. Trueblood, *People Called Quakers*, 3; Douglas V. Steere, "The Mystical Dimension of Quakerism," *Friends Journal* 30 (Nov. 15, 1984): 8; Wilmer A. Cooper, "A Rejoinder Concerning 'That of God in Everyone,'" *Quaker Life* 22 (Nov. 1981): 21.

54. Lewis Benson, *Catholic Quakerism: A Vision for All Men* (Philadelphia: Philadelphia Yearly Meeting, 1977), 96; Jones, *Faith and Practice*, 15; Agnita Wright

Dupree, *Widening the Circle* (Philadelphia: Friends World Committee for Consultation, 1985), 4; Bleeke and Spencer, *Identity, Authority, and Community*, 3–4; Robert Lawrence Smith, *A Quaker Book of Wisdom: Life Lessons in Simplicity, Service, and Common Sense* (New York: Morrow, 1998), 18.

55. Peter Donchian, "What's Happening to Our Meeting for Worship," *Friends Journal* 32 (July 1/15, 1986): 15; David H. Albert, "Some Notions on Why Friends Meetings Do Not Attract Minorities," *Friends Journal* 42 (Oct. 1996): 16; Florence Capaldo Kimball, "A Call to Worship," *Quaker Life* 28 (Jan.–Feb. 1987): 7.

56. Art Perisho letter, *Evangelical Friend* 22 (June 1989): 15; Lon Fendall, "What It Means To Be a Community Church," *Evangelical Friend* 20 (July/Aug. 1987): 4; Howard Macy, "Convinced and Convincing," *Evangelical Friend* 14 (Sept. 1980): 7–8; Richard P. Newby, "Looking at Ourselves from the Inside Out," *Quaker Life* 22 (Oct. 1981): 15; Punshon, *Reasons for Hope*, 6–7, 361.

57. *Among Friends*, 285; David Brock, "What Are Your Chances?" *Quaker Life* 34 (March 1993): 9–10; Punshon, *Reasons for Hope*, 368; Priscilla Bergeron-Thomas, "Is It Time, Once Again, to Become a Peculiar People?" *Friends Journal* 37 (July 1991): 8–10; Larry Ingle letter, *Friends Journal* 38 (Dec. 1992): 6; Douglas H. Heath, "Wanted: A More Radicalizing Quakerism," *Friends Journal* 27 (April 1, 1981): 12.

58. J. William Frost, "A Century of Liberal Quakerism," *Friends Journal* 46 (Oct. 2000): 11–12; Renee Crauder, "Keeping and Discarding," *Friends Journal* 44 (April 1998): 8; Heather C. Moir letter, *Friends Journal* (June 1998): 5; Del Coppinger, "A Vision for Friends United Meeting," *Quaker Life* 33 (March 1992): 8–9; John H. McCandless, "Membership and the People of God," *Quaker Life* 25 (Jan.–Feb. 1984): 5–6; Jack Kirk, "A Crisis in Membership," *Quaker Life* 25 (Jan.–Feb. 1984): 4; Sheeran, *Beyond Majority Rule*, 114.

59. Wayne Evans, interview with author, Aug. 2, 2002 (notes in author's possession).

60. Brinton, *Friends for 300 Years*, 106.

61. Edward Hoare, *Deepening the Spiritual Life of the Meeting* (Philadelphia: Friends General Conference, 1995), 8; Wilson, *Essays*, 168; A. J. Ellis, "The Church: The New Extended Family," *Evangelical Friend* 22 (April 1989): 15–16; Greene and Walton, *Fostering Vital Friends Meetings*, v; "Reports," *Friends Journal* 40 (Jan. 1994): 19.

62. Bleeke and Spencer, "Identity, Authority, and Community," 17; "Visions of Renewal," *Quaker Life* 36 (Oct. 1995): 22; Cattell, *Christian Mission*, 76; William J. Kreidler, "Journey to 'The Peaceable Kingdom,'" in Fager, ed., *New Voices, New Light*, 39. Observations about FGC and yearly meeting attendance are based on accounts in various yearly meeting newsletters and minutes and in *Friends Journal*.

63. Jack L. Willcuts, "One in the Spirit," *Evangelical Friend* 10 (Sept. 1976): 11; Marlene Morrison Pedigo, "Reclaiming Our Quaker Faith," *Quaker Life* 39 (June 1998): 18; Fager, *Without Apology*, 12–16; *Among Friends*, 18.

64. *Realignment*, 104–5; Eden Grace, "A Personal Call Into Ecumenism," *Quaker Life* 39 (Dec. 1998): 19; *Among Friends*, 17–18.

65. Johan Maurer, "The Changing Religious Periodical," *Quaker Life* 35 (Jan./ Feb. 1994): 9; Gwyn, *Unmasking the Idols*, 114–15; Howard W. Bartram, "Dimensions of the Spirit," *Friends Journal* 32 (Dec. 1, 1986): 7; *Among Friends*, 78–80; Jack L. Willcuts, "Here and There and Now and Later All at Once," *Evangelical Friend* 21 (Jan./Feb. 1988): 11.

66. James Baker, "About Being a Friend," *Friends Journal* 41 (May 1995): 14; Dupree, *Widening the Circle*, 6; Eileen Bagus, "Say If She Came Again Today, Would You Still Answer to the Call?" *Friendly Woman* 13 (Summer 1998): 24; Paul Enyart, "The Message of Hope: Vital in Evangelism," *Evangelical Friend* 21 (April 1988): 8; Don Crist,"Diversity," *Quaker Life* 29 (March 1988): 17; Willcuts, *Why Friends Are Friends*, 39.

67. Benson, *Catholic Quakerism*, 91; Bleeke and Spencer, "Identity, Authority, and Community," 20; Frost, "Century," 12; Edward Elder letter, *Friends Journal* 39 (May 1993): 5; David L. Johns letter, *Friends Journal* 42 (March 1996): 5–6; Jonathan Vogel, "A Different Baptism: The World Gathering of Young Friends," *Friends Journal* 31 (Nov. 15, 1985): 26–27; Jack Kirk, "Friends—How Much Diversity?" *Quaker Life* 29 (March 1988): 14–15; *Among Friends*, 83.

68. Richard P. Newby, "Friendly Concern," *Quaker Life* 15 (Feb. 1974): 5; Richard Broughton letter, *Quaker Life* 34 (July/Aug. 1993): 34; C. W. False letter, *Quaker Life* 41 (July/Aug. 2000): 34; Hugh Spaulding letter, *Quaker Life* 35 (April 1994): 2; *Realignment*, 34; Fager, *Without Apology*, 117–20.

69. *What Future for Friends*, 37; Harold Smuck, "What Comes After Meeting for Clearness?" *Quaker Life* 33 (Sept. 1992): 18; Wilmer A. Cooper, "Friends Look to the Future," *Quaker Life* 32 (July/Aug. 1991): 44; *Realignment*, 12–13; Chuck Fager, "Dodging the 'Realignment' Bullet: The Iowa Conference Misfires," *A Friendly Letter* 125 (10th Mo. 1991): 2–4. The mission statement appears inside the front cover of current issues of *Quaker Life*.

70. Johan Maurer, "Lessons from Friends Church Southwest," *Quaker Life* 34 (Sept. 1993): 20–21; "Whittier Leaves Southwest Yearly Meeting," *Quaker Life* 35 (Jan./Feb. 1994): 10; Stan Bauer, "God's Spirit . . . Moving in a Mighty Way," *Quaker Life* 37 (Oct. 1996): 6; "Southwest Yearly Meeting Rejects Dual Affiliation," *Quaker Life* 38 (March 1997): 15; Johan Maurer, "An Open Invitation," *Quaker Life* 39 (May 1998): 15; Weinacht interview; Curt Shaw, interview with author, March 1, 2002 (notes in author's possession).

71. Punshon, *Reasons for Hope*, 286–87; Fager, *Without Apology*, 145–47; Bleeke and Spencer, *Identity, Authority, and Community*, 2; *Among Friends*, 213; Cooper, *Living Faith*, 153–55; Joel C. Schmeltzer, "The Fifth World Conference of Friends: A Reflection," *Evangelical Friend* 25 (Sept./Oct. 1991): 16; "Reports," *Friends Journal* 41 (Sept. 1995): 22. For a good account of the Friends World Committee for Consultation, see Daniel A. Seeger, "That All May Be One," *Quaker Life* 29 (Oct. 1988): 12–13.

72. Bruce Bishop, "YouthQuake—Changing the Face of American Quakerism," *Quaker Life* 39 (May 1998): 14.

73. These figures are based on comparing Barbour and Frost, *Quakers*, 234–35; and the statistics compiled by the Friends World Committee in "Numbers in Quaker Yearly Meetings and Groups" at fwcc.quaker.org/totals.html.

74. Mike Wall, "To Be or Not to Be—That Is the Question," *Quaker Life* 25 (April 1984): 18; Patty Levering, "Small Meetings Can Be Vital," *Quaker Life* 27 (July/Aug. 1986): 26–27; Mary Glenn Hadley, "Do We Care Enough?" *Quaker Life* 33 (Jan./Feb. 1992): 17; James R. Newby, "Ministering in a Different World," *Evangelical Friend* 24 (Jan./Feb. 1991): 2; *Among Friends*, 135; "Local Congregation Profile," *Indiana Friend* 23 (Nov. 1991): 1.

75. Newby, "Ministering in a Different World," 3; Dwight Spann-Wilson, "Strategy for Friends in the Eighties," *Friends Journal* 26 (Jan. 1/15, 1980): 10; Frost, "Century of Liberal Quakerism," 12; Sheeran, *Beyond Majority Rule*, 112; T. Eugene Coffin, "It's All Right to Grow," *Quaker Life* 29 (Dec. 1988): 15; Lloyd Hinshaw, "Keep the Small Country Church Doors Open," *Evangelical Friend* 15 (Sept. 1981): 9.

76. Henry J. Cadbury, *The Character of a Quaker* (Wallingford, Pa.: Pendle Hill, 1959), 7; Greene and Walton, *Fostering Vital Friends Meetings*, 43; *Among Friends*, 282; Margery Post Abbott, ed., *A Certain Kind of Perfection: An Anthology of Evangelical and Liberal Quaker Writers* (Wallingford, Pa.: Pendle Hill, 1997), 9–10.

77. "We Are About to Cross a Threshold," *Quaker Life* 26 (Oct. 1985): 20; Johan Maurer, "Towards a Quaker View of Evangelism," *Quaker Life* 28 (April 1987): 8; Kathy Hersh, "Outreach Is Just Another Word for Sharing," *Friends Journal* 47 (Feb. 2001): 14–15; Greene and Walton, *Fostering Vital Friends Meetings*, 86.

78. Wendy Ward, "'Word of Life' Radio Message," *Quaker Life* 42 (March 2001): 19; Jim LeShana, "Friends Fishing—From Fox Into the Future," *Quaker Life* 32 (May 1991): 8; Charles A. Routh, "A Bus Ministry for Your Meeting," *Quaker Life* 26 (Nov. 1985): 35; Virginia Dossey, "Let God Do It!" *Quaker Life* 21 (Jan. 1980): 3; David Brock, "What Are We Doing for the Next Generation," *Quaker Life* 28 (June 1987): 12; Robert Blake, "New Wine in Old Skins," *Quaker Life* 29 (Dec. 1988): 9; Howard W. Brod, "One Unprogrammed Meeting's Experience," *Quaker Life* 36 (Sept. 1995): 5, 7; David Purless, "Revive the Quaker Leadings: Missionary and Merchant," *Friends Journal* 34 (Feb. 1988): 5; Jane Berger, "Outreach a Moral Responsibility," *Spark* 33 (Jan. 2002): 10.

79. Fager, *Without Apology*, 153; Kirk, "The Changing Quaker Scene," 8; Maurice Roberts, "God Has an Exciting Future for Evangelical Friends and the EFA," *Evangelical Friend* 21 (Sept. 1987): 15.

80. Freiday, *Speaking as a Friend*, 1–3; Rickerman, *Growing Up Quaker and Universalist Too*, 1–2; Mariellen O. Gilpin, "An Experiential Approach to Jesus," *Friends Journal* 35 (Jan. 1989): 24; Carol Urner, "On Learning to Listen," *Quaker Life* 38 (Dec. 1997): 7; Linda Kusse-Wolfe, "Why I Am a Quaker," *Quaker Life*

28 (Dec. 1987): 24; Victor Lasseter, "Why I Am a Quaker," *Quaker Life* 28 (Dec. 1987): 11; Cathy Russell, "Why Am I Here?" *Quaker Life* 28 (Dec. 1987): 16; Roy Church, "Why Do They Come?" *Quaker Life* 28 (Dec. 1987): 15.

6. Quakers and the World

1. Spencer Thury, "Minutes from Mardi Gras," *Iowa Friend* 57 (April 2002): 1, 4.

2. "From the Editor's Desk," *PeaceWork*, May 2002, 2.

3. William Penn quoted in D. Elton Trueblood, *The People Called Quakers* (New York: Harper and Row, 1966), 261–62; Richard Foster, "A Great New Experience of God," *Evangelical Friend* 19 (June 1986): 3; Janet Hemphill Minshall, "A Clearness," *Friends Journal* 33 (July 1/15, 1987): 7–8; Wilmer A. Cooper, *A Living Faith: An Historical Study of Friends Beliefs* (Richmond, Ind.: Friends United Press, 1991), 102.

4. Marty Grundy, "The Body of Christ: A Practical Lesson," *Quaker Life* 41 (July/Aug. 2000): 12; Margery Post Abbott, ed., *A Certain Kind of Perfection: An Anthology of Evangelical and Liberal Quaker Writers* (Wallingford, Pa.: Pendle Hill,. 1997), 23; Sandy Perry, "A Return to Quakerism," *Friends Journal* 43 (Sept. 1997): 7–8; Rhoda R. Gilman letter, *Friends Journal* 39 (Jan. 1993): 4.

5. Everett A. Cattell, *Christian Mission: A Matter of Life* (Richmond, Ind.: Friends United Press, 1981), 66–67; "Church and College Growth: How Strong Is the Commitment?" *Evangelical Friend* 17 (Nov. 1983): 3.

6. Eastern Region, *2001 Yearbook* (Canton: Eastern Region, 2001), 38; "EFM News Briefs from the World of Friends," *Friends Voice* 8 (Summer 2002): 6–7. See also the information at the Evangelical Friends Mission Web site at www.friendsmission.org and Friends United Meeting at www.fum.org.

7. Jack L. Willcuts, "New Perspectives in Mission and Service," *Evangelical Friend* 6 (Jan. 1973): 27; Norval Hadley letter, *Quaker Life* 39 (Dec. 1998): 33–34; John Punshon, *Reasons for Hope: The Future of the Friends Church* (Richmond, Ind.: Friends United Press, 2001), 330–31; Stan Perisho, "Friends Have a Future, If , . . ." *Evangelical Friend* 24 (March/April 1991): 12; "Church News," *Friends Evangel* 55 (Feb. 2002): 6; Wayne Evans, letter to author, Aug. 8, 2002 (in author's possession). For premillennialism, see Paul Boyer, *When Time Shall Be No More: Prophecy Belief in Modern American Culture* (Cambridge: Belknap, 1992).

8. Stephen Zunes, "Making an Active Witness," *Friends Journal* 36 (June 1990): 24–25; Ward C. Miles letter, *Friends Journal* 43 (May 1997): 4–5; John Brinton Perera obituary, *Friends Journal* 44 (Aug. 1998): 29; George Lakey, "Quakers and the New Activists," *Friends Journal* 46 (Dec. 2000): 7–8; Rob Callard, "Serving God and Man," *Friends Journal* 47 (Aug. 2001): 11. For NGOs, see Elise Boulding and Kenneth Boulding, *The Future: Images and Processes* (Thousand Oaks, Calif.: Sage, 1995), 202.

9. Edward F. Snyder, *Witness in Washington: Fifty Years of Friendly Persuasion* (Richmond, Ind.: Friends United Press, 1994), 12–13, 186–87.

10. Mark S. Cary, "Friends' Attitudes Toward Business in the USA," *Classical Liberal Quaker* 40 (March 28, 2002), http://www.clq.quaker.org; Cynthia Miles-Lewis letter, *Classical Liberal Quaker* 42 (April 10, 2002), http://www.clq.quaker.org; Ray Stewart letter, *Quaker Life* 42 (April 2001): 29, 34; Gregory P. Hinshaw letter, *Quaker Life* 43 (June 2001): 34; Mary Louise Bruneau letter, *Quaker Life* 29 (Nov. 1988): 39; Dick Henry letter, *Evangelical Friend* 18 (Nov. 1984): 20; "Rocky Mountain Yearly Meeting Prayer Opportunities," *Evangelical Friend* 21 (April 1988): 20; Alan Weinacht, interview with author, Feb. 8, 2002 (notes in author's possession); Curt Shaw, interview with author, March 1, 2002 (notes in author's possession). For evangelicals and politics, see Michael Lienesch, *Redeeming America: Piety and Politics in the New Christian Right* (Chapel Hill: University of North Carolina Press, 1993).

11. Lee Nash, "Extremism and Its Antidote," *Evangelical Friend* 20 (Oct. 1986): 3; Arthur O. Roberts letter, *Evangelical Friend* 22 (Oct. 1988): 10; Johan Maurer, "'Cry for Renewal' Next Steps," *Quaker Life*, 36 (Sept. 1995), 9; Alfred K. La Motte, "I Am a Quaker; I Am Not a Member of the Society of Friends," *Friends Journal* 30 (Feb. 15, 1984): 11; Jack Powelson, "Why I Am Leaving Quakers," *Friends Journal* 48 (April 2002): 16; Jack Powelson, *Seeking Truth Together: Enabling the Poor and Saving the Planet in the Manner of Friends* (Boulder: Horizon Society Publishers, 2000).

12. See, for example, Sandra L. Cronk, *Gospel Order: A Quaker Understanding of Faithful Church Community* (Wallingford, Pa.: Pendle Hill, 1991), 14–15.

13. Trueblood, *People Called Quakers*, 187; Robert Lawrence Smith, *A Quaker Book of Wisdom: Life Lessons in Simplicity, Service, and Common Sense* (New York: Morrow, 1998), 83.

14. For a good overview, see Peter Brock, *The Quaker Peace Testimony, 1660–1914* (York, Eng.: Sessions 1990). For Indiana Yearly Meeting, see Thomas D. Hamm et al., "The Decline of Quaker Pacifism in the Twentieth Century: Indiana Yearly Meeting of Friends as a Case Study," *Indiana Magazine of History* 96 (March 2000): 45–71. For Friends who served in World War II but later came to be pacifists, see George Rubin, "Autobiography of a Pacifist," *Friends Journal* 26 (Feb. 1, 1980): 15–16.

15. Hugh Barbour and J. William Frost, *The Quakers* (Westport, Ct.: Greenwood, 1988), 250–58; Leonard S. Kenworthy, "The Impact of Civilian Public Service," *Friends Journal* 38 (Jan. 1992): 15–16; Maya Wilson, "Quaker Peace Witness in the Twentieth Century: A Preliminary Overview," in *Sustaining Peace Witness in the Twenty-First Century*, ed. Chuch Fager (Wallingford, Pa.: Pendle Hill, 1997), 19–92.

16. Indiana Yearly Meeting, *Faith and Practice* (Muncie, Ind.: Indiana Yearly Meeting, 1998), 34; Philadelphia Yearly Meeting, *Faith and Practice* (Philadelphia: Philadelphia Yearly Meeting, 1997), 85.

17. Irene Lape, "Responding to 'Ten Queries,'" *Friends Journal* 31 (Nov. 1,

1985): 19; Arthur Rifkin, "Pacifism: The Core of Quakerism," *Friends Journal* 32 (March 1, 1986): 13–14; Judith L. Brutz, "Development of Pacifism in Quakers" (Ph.D. diss., Iowa State University, 1988), 27–28; Samuel R. Levering, "Viewpoint: Lessons from the Gulf (and Other) Wars," *Quaker Life* 32 (May 1991): 20.

18. David Zarembka, "An Exciting Possibility," unpublished article, 2002 (in author's possession); Margery Post Abbott to author, Aug. 6, 2002 (notes in author's possession); Elise Boulding, "Peace Culture: The Vision and the Journey," *Friends Journal* 46 (Sept. 2000): 6–8; Ralph Levering, "Remembering Miriam and Sam Levering," *Friends Journal* 40 (June 1994): 7–9; "News of Friends," *Friends Journal* 39 (April 1993): 28; Jack L. Willcuts, "A New Call to Peacemaking," *Evangelical Friend* 10 (Jan. 1977): 2–3; James R. Lynch, "Christian Peacemaker Teams: Opportunities for Active Peacemaking," in Fager, ed., *Sustaining Peace Witness*, 263–304; Andrea Cole, "Journey to Palestine Seeking Peace," Richmond, Ind., *Palladium-Item*, April 7, 2002, E-1, 6; Leah Green, "Just Listen," *Yes! A Journal of Positive Futures* (Winter 2002): 20–21. For Alternatives to Violence, see www.avpusa.org.

19. Steve Fretzmann, "I Am Not Paying for War," *Quaker Life* 39 (April 1998): 16–17; Jeremy Mott letter, *Quaker Life* 41 (May 2000): 34; Helen Woodson, "Letter from Prison," *Friendly Woman* 13 (Summer 1999): 31–32; Vern Rossman, "Quaker with a Hammer," *Friends Journal* 31 (May 15, 1985): 6–8; Charles G. Santora, "Animal Exploitation," *Friends Journal* 33 (Feb. 15, 1987): 19; Robert F. Tatman, "A Proposed Minute Concerning Participation in War and Preparation for War," *Friends Journal* 30 (March 1, 1984): 7; Mark E. Dixon letter, *Friends Journal* 41 (May 1995): 6; William Durland, *God or Nations: Radical Theology for the Religious Peace Movement* (Baltimore: Fortkamp, 1989), 142–43; North Carolina Yearly Meeting Peace Committee, *Faith Into Action: A Program on Christian Peacemaking* (N.p., 1985), 9, 12, 30; Sandra Cronk, *Peace Be With You: A Study of the Spiritual Basis of the Friends Peace Testimony* (Philadelphia: Tract Association of Friends, n.d.), 3.

20. Arthur O. Roberts, "Holding Fast to What Is Good," *Evangelical Friend* 9 (Feb. 1976): 9; Durland, *God and Nations*, 167; Mary Ellen McNish, "Toward a Just Peace in the Middle East," *Friends Journal* 47 (March 2001): 6–8; Arthur Rifkin letter, *Friends Journal* 43 (June 1997): 4; Stephen G. Cary, "New Winds Blowing to Our South," *Friends Journal* 36 (May 1990): 8–11; Val Liveoak, "Joy, Hope, and Faithfulness—A Visit to Friends in Cuba," *Friends Journal* 39 (Feb. 1993): 7–11; Jim Fine, "The Iraq Sanctions Generation," *Quaker Life* 41 (Jan./Feb. 2000): 17–21; "Quaker Agencies Work Toward Bosnia Peace," *Quaker Life* 37 (Jan./Feb. 1996): 12. It should be noted that many pastoral Friends also share Palestinian sympathies because of the long-established Quaker school at Ramallah. See, for example, Stephen Main, "U.S. Evangelicals and Middle East Relations," *Evangelical Friend* 17 (July/Aug. 1984): 6–7.

21. Fay Honey Knopp et al., "Crime Is a Peace Issue," *Friends Journal* 28 (March 1, 1982): 9; Deborah Fink, "On Truth and Bananas," *Friends Journal* 37

(Aug. 1991): 25; Hope Luder, "Quaker Testimonies and the Third World," *Friends Journal* 45 (June 1999): 11; David Morse, "The Message of Seattle," *Friends Journal* 46 (March 2000): 12–23; Staughton and Alice Lynd, *Liberation Theology for Quakers* (Wallingford, Pa.: Pendle Hill, 1996), 31; David Morse, *Testimony: John Woolman on Today's Global Economy* (Wallingford, Pa.: Pendle Hill, 2001), 9–11, 19–20. A good overview of these themes is Val Liveoak, "Living the Peace Testimony Today: One Friend's Journey and Reflections," in *A Continuing Journey: Papers from the Quaker Peace Roundtable*, ed. Chuck Fager (Wallingford, Pa.: Pendle Hill, 1996), 100–23.

22. E. Erick and Christina Rizzo Hoopes, "Are Friends Seeking a Third Alternative?" *Friends Journal* 32 (Oct. 15, 1986): 27; Fred D. Baldwin, "With Friends Like These , . . ." *Friends Journal* 35 (July 1989): 27; Ben Richmond, "J. E. McNeil: A Skeptical Advocate for Peace," *Quaker Life* 40 (Nov. 1999): 15; Spencer Coxe letter, *Quaker Life* 41 (Jan./Feb. 2000): 2; J. William Frost, "The Christian Religion and War: An Evaluation," in Fager, ed., *Continuing Journey*, 179–81. Cf. J. William Frost, "AFSC and the Terrorist War," *Friends Journal* 48 (Jan. 2002): 6–11.

23. Northwest Yearly Meeting, *Faith and Practice: A Book of Christian Discipline* (Newberg, Ore.: Barclay Press, 1987), 101; Jack L. Willcuts, *Why Friends Are Friends (Some Quaker Core Convictions)* (Newberg, Ore.: Barclay Press, 1992), 64–65; Paul Anderson, *Meet the Friends* (Newberg, Ore.: Barclay Press, 1999), 26; Wayne Cole, "So You Want to Be a Peacemaker! Are You Ready to Be a Child of God?" *Evangelical Friend* 12 (Sept. 1988): 6; Stephen Main, "Faith and Peace," *Quaker Life* 21 (Dec. 1980): 4; Shane Kirkpatrick letter, *Quaker Life* 41 (March 2000): 2; *Let Your Lives Speak: A Report of the World Gathering of Young Friends, 1985, Greensboro, North Carolina* (London: Friends World Committee for Consultation, 1986), 118.

24. Abbott to author, Aug. 6, 2002 (notes in author's possession); Willcuts, "New Call to Peacemaking"; Norval Hadley, "To Freeze or Not to Freeze," *Evangelical Friend* 16 (Sept. 1982): 27; Lon Fendall, "Another New Call to Peacemaking," *Evangelical Friend* 19 (Sept. 1985): 6–7; Willcuts, *Why Friends Are Friends*, 57, 59; Jack L. Willcuts, "The Family of Friends Within the Evangelical Friends Alliance," in *The Church in Quaker Thought and Practice: A Study in Ecclesiology*, ed. Charles F. Thomas (Philadelphia: Friends World Committee for Consultation, 1979), 62; Jennifer Frick, "Whittier Friends Peace Camp," *Quaker Life* 43 (March 2002): 17; J. Stanley Banker, interview with author, April 19, 2002 (notes in author's possession).

25. Howard Macy, "Good News and Peace," *Evangelical Friend* 18 (July/Aug. 1985): 14; Helen Monette letter, *Evangelical Friend* 6 (May 1973): 19; Charles Jandecka, "No Conscience in Christendom," *Evangelical Friend* 14 (Nov. 1980): 14; Lauren King letter, *Evangelical Friend* 25 (July/Aug. 1992): 18; George Robinson, "Peace, Peace . . . When Do We Talk About It?" *Evangelical Friend* 25 (March/April 1992): 9; Willcuts, *Why Friends Are Friends*, 65; Marvin Miller letter, *Quaker*

Life 37 (Jan./Feb. 1996): 34; C. G. White, "A Visit from Mr. Angell," *Quaker Life* 41 (March 2000): 16; J. M. Maurer, "Rethinking the Peace Testimony," *Quaker Life* 41 (June 2000): 4; Richard N. Van Nostrand letter, *Quaker Life* 36 (May 1995): 30.

26. Trueblood, *People Called Quakers*, 196; Evangelical Friends Church Eastern Region, *Faith and Practice: The Book of Discipline* (Canton, Ohio: Eastern Region, 2000), 30; Howard Brinton, *Friends for 300 Years: The History and Beliefs of the Society of Friends Since George Fox Started the Quaker Movement* (New York: Harper and Row, 1952), 28; Smith, *Quaker Book of Wisdom*, 97; Warren A. Witte, "Actions Reshaping Our Beliefs," *Friends Journal* 44 (Jan. 1998): 10–13.

27. Arnold A. Bernstein letter, *Friends Journal* 47 (Dec. 2001): 5; Scott Simon, "Reflections on the Events of September Eleventh," *Friends Journal* 47 (Dec. 2001): 16–20; Susan Corson-Finnerty, "Choose Life," *Friends Journal* 47 (Nov. 2001), 2; "Finding Our Way: Friends Respond to the Events of September 11, 2001," *Friends Journal* 47 (Nov. 2001): 4ff; Carolyn Stuart letter, *Friends Journal* 48 (Jan. 2002), 4; David Chandler, "Hijacking the American People," *Friends Bulletin* 73 (Jan. 2002): 21; "News from Friends United Meeting," *Quaker Life* 42 (Nov. 2001): 4; "Excerpts from Statements and Letters Sent to *Quaker Life*," *Quaker Life* 42 (Dec. 2001): 21; "Dunkirk Friends," *Friends Evangel* 55 (Nov. 2001): 8; "Dunkirk Friends," *Friends Evangel* 55 (Dec. 2001), 7; William Vance Trollinger Jr., "Nonviolent Voices," *Christian Century*, Dec. 12, 2001, 20–21; Natasha Hunter, "Rethinking Pacifism: The Quakers' Dilemma in a Time of War," *American Prospect*, Dec. 3, 2001, 14–16; Evans interview.

28. Larry Ingle, "Can We Be Friends? Quakers and the AFSC," *Christian Century*, April 19, 1995, 413.

29. Rayner Wickersham Kelsey, *Friends and the Indians, 1655–1917* (Philadelphia: Associated Executive Committee of Friends on Indian Affairs, 1917), 1–161.

30. Clyde A. Milner II, *With Good Intentions: Quaker Work Among the Pawnees, Otos, and Omahas in the 1870s* (Lincoln: University of Nebraska Press, 1982); Kelsey, *Friends and the Indians*, 162–233; Flossie Fullerton, "Indian Affairs Committee," *Interchange*, March 2001, 3; Arthur O. Roberts, *Tomorrow Is Growing Old: Stories of the Quakers in Alaska* (Newberg, Ore.: Barclay Press, 1978). The current work of the Associated Committee of Friends on Indian Affairs can be found in its journal, *Indian Progress*. For other Quaker missionary work, see Esther Nelson, "Native American Centers," *Advocate* 112 (July-Aug. 1996): 6.

31. See, generally, Henry J. Cadbury, "Negro Membership in the Society of Friends," *Journal of Negro History* 21 (April 1936): 151–213; and the articles in the spring 2001 issue of *Quaker History*.

32. Jean R. Soderlund, *Quakers & Slavery: A Divided Spirit* (Princeton: Princeton University Press, 1985), 173–87; Thomas D. Hamm et al., "Midwestern Quakers and African Americans, 1800–1870," paper presented at Conference of Quaker Historians and Archivists, June 22, 2000 (in author's possession); Linda Selleck, *Gentle Invaders: Quaker Women Educators and Racial Issues During the Civil War*

and Reconstruction (Richmond, Ind.: Friends United Press, 1995); Richard K. Taylor, *Friends & the Racial Crisis* (Wallingford, Pa.: Pendle Hill 1970), 14–25. The attraction of Indiana Friends to the Ku Klux Klan in the 1920s was probably due to its commitment to Prohibition. See Thomas D. Hamm, *Earlham College: A History, 1847–1997* (Bloomington: Indiana University Press, 1997), 150–52.

33. Hamm, *Earlham College*, 202–9; John Oliver, "J. Walter Malone: *The American Friend* and an Evangelical Quaker's Social Agenda," *Quaker History* 80 (Fall 1991): 73; Emma Lapsansky, "New Eyes for the 'Invisibles' in Quaker-Minority Relations," *Quaker History* 90 (Spring 2001): 4–5; Clarence E. Pickett, *For More Than Bread: An Autobiographical Account of Twenty-Five Years' Work with the American Friends Service Committee* (Boston: Little, Brown, 1953), 369–87; Faith B. Bertsche, "The Augusta Open Door Kindergarten," *Friends Journal* 43 (March 1997): 20–22; Gordon Browne, "And Your Neighbor as Yourself," *Quaker Life* 40 (March 1999): 6–9; Lynd and Lynd, *Liberation Theology for Quakers*, 12.

34. Marlene Morrison Pedigo, *New Church in the City: The Work of the Chicago Fellowship of Friends* (Richmond, Ind.: Friends United Press, 1988), 56; Smith, *Quaker Book of Wisdom*, 101–2; James A. Fletcher, "Gathering of Friends of African Descent," *Friends Journal* 37 (Feb. 1991): 24–26; Deborah Saunders, "Send Me," *Friends Journal* 44 (May 1998): 15–17; Frances L. Peacock, "The Opposite of Fear Is Love: An Interview with George Sawyer," *Quaker Life* 38 (Sept. 1997): 4–6.

35. K. and Bill Brown, "Report on Quakers and Racial Justice Conference," *New England Friend* 57 (Winter 2002): 3; "Epistle from the Quakers and Racial Justice Conference," *New England Friend* 57 (Winter 2002): 3; Johan Maurer, "Clinton's Challenge," *Quaker Life* 39 (Jan./Feb. 1998): 17; Vanessa Julye, "Diversity Within the Religious Society of Friends: Do We Really Want It?" *Quaker Life* 40 (March 1999): 9–10; James A. Fletcher, "Toward a Truly Multiracial Family of Friends," *Friends Journal* 29 (May 15, 1983): 5–8; Catherine Daniel, "Epistle Urges Racial Diversity," *Friends Journal* 38 (Jan. 1992): 36; John L. Johnson, "Looking Beyond Light and Dark," *Friends Journal* 41 (March 1995): 16–17; Vanessa Julye, "The Underground Railroad Game," *Friends Journal* 42 (Oct. 1996): 10–11; David H. Albert, "Some Notions on Why Friends Meetings Do Not Attract Minorities," *Friends Journal* 42 (Oct. 1996): 15–19; Paul Ricketts, "A Call for Racial Justice Among Friends," *Friends Journal* 43 (July 1997): 17–18; "Reports and Epistles," *Friends Journal* 45 (July 1999): 24; "News," *Friends Journal* 47 (March 2001): 32.

36. Northwest Yearly Meeting, *Faith and Practice*, 96, 101; Marlene Morrison Pedigo, "From Corn Fields to the Inner City," *Evangelical Friend* 21 (July/Aug. 1988): 2–3, 17; Jennifer Frick, "Bear One Another's Burdens," *Quaker Life* 43 (May 2002): 12–13; Eastern Region, *2001 Yearbook*, 60; Pedigo, *New Church in the City*, passim.

37. The best account of the founding of the AFSC is J. William Frost, "'Our Deeds Carry Our Message': The Early History of the American Friends Service

Committee," *Quaker History* 81 (Spring 1992): 1–51. For subsequent years, see Pickett, *For More Than Bread*; and Mary Hoxie Jones, *Swords Into Ploughshares: An Account of the American Friends Service Committee, 1917–1937* (New York: Macmillan, 1937). Eleanor Roosevelt donated her radio broadcast fees to the AFSC. See Joseph P. Lash, *Eleanor and Franklin: The Story of Their Relationship Based on Eleanor Roosevelt's Private Papers* (New York: Signet, 1971), 551. There is a great need for a general history of the AFSC.

38. Allen Smith, "The Renewal Movement: The Peace Testimony and Modern Quakerism," *Quaker History* 85 (Fall 1996): 1–23; H. Larry Ingle, "The American Friends Service Committee, 1947–1949: The Cold War's Effect," *Peace and Change* 23 (Jan. 1998): 27–48.

39. Allen, "Renewal Movement," 7–11; American Friends Service Committee, *Speak Truth to Power: A Quaker Search for an Alternative to Violence* (Philadelphia: AFSC, 1955), esp. 50.

40. Chuck Fager, ed., *Friends & the Vietnam War: Papers and Presentations from a Gathering for Recollection, Reappraisal, and Looking Ahead* (Wallingford, Pa.: Pendle Hill, 1998), 14–17, 79–83; Tom Wells, *The War Within: America's Battle Over Vietnam* (New York: Holt, 1994), 89–91, 165–68; Guenter Lewy, *Peace & Revolution: The Moral Crisis of American Pacifism* (Grand Rapids: Eerdmans, 1988), 37–45.

41. This paragraph is based largely on AFSC annual reports from 1975 to 1990, supplemented by an interview with Mary Ellen McNish on Sept. 9, 2002, and comments from J. William Frost of Swarthmore College, a careful student of the AFSC's history. Also helpful was Gilbert F. White, "Quaker Volunteer Service for the Future," *Friends Journal* 44 (Jan. 1998): 14–15. For different views of the AFSC, U.S. foreign policy, and Third World liberation movements, see John Sullivan, "An AFSC Reflection on Guenter Lewy's *Peace and Revolution: The Moral Crisis of American Pacifism*," in Chuck Fager, ed., *Quaker Service at the Crossroads: American Friends, the American Friends Service Committee, and* Peace and Revolution (Falls Church, Va.: Kimo Press, 1988), 69–83, esp. 80–81; Peter Brock, *Pacifism in the Twentieth Century* (Toronto: University of Toronto Press, 1999), 341–45; and Lewy, *Peace and Revolution*, 157–68, 175–77, 183–85. For the work camps, see "AFSC and Youth: Shades of Yesterday, Shades of Today," *Friends Journal* 40 (Oct. 1994): 24–25. The work camps fell victim to perceptions of frequent sexual activity and drug use by participants.

42. Thomas D. Hamm, "The Elephant in the Living Room: The American Friends Service Committee and the Society of Friends in the Vietnam Era," unpublished article, 2000 (in author's possession); Chuck Fager, "Peacemaking and the 'Humanitarian Industrial Complex," in Fager, ed., *Continuing Journey*, 79; Harold Confer letter, *Friends Journal* 41 (Feb. 1995): 5; David Finke, "Friends and the A.F.S.C.," *Quaker Life* 35 (Nov. 1994): 4–8, 22–23; Lewy, *Peace and Revolution*, 27–55; *Indiana Yearly Meeting Minutes, 1991*, 35–36; Allan Kohrman, "Quak-

ers, Anti-Semitism, and the Middle East," *Friends Journal* 37 (Jan. 1991): 13–15; "Forum," *Friends Journal* 37 (March 1991): 4–5; Ingle, "Can We Be Friends?" 412. For a good collection of essays, pro and con, on the AFSC in the 1970s and 1980s, see Fager, ed., *Quaker Service at the Crossroads*. This was a response to Lewy's *Peace and Revolution*, which was highly critical of the AFSC.

43. McNish interview; AFSC *Quaker Service Bulletin* 87 (spring and fall 2001). See also "From the Editor's Desk," *Peace Work*, May 2002, 2; and "From the Editor's Desk," *Peacework*, March 2002, p. 2. *Peace Work* is published by the AFSC New England Regional Office.

44. H. Larry Ingle, "The Politics of Despair: The Quaker Peace Testimony, 1661," in Fager, ed., *Continuing Journey*, 144; Herbert N. Lape, "What the Work of Stanley Hauerwas and Alasdair MacIntyre Can Mean for Friends," in *New Voices, New Light: Papers from the Quaker Theology Roundtable, Fourth Month 7–9, 1995* (Wallingford, Pa.: Pendle Hill, 1995), 185; "Holland Resigns, Calls for AFSC Reform," *Quaker Life* 40 (March 1999): 13; Ingle, "Can We Be Friends?" 412–13.

45. John H. Michener and John Sullivan, "A Widening Path: A Widening Circle," *Friends Journal* 28 (Feb. 1, 1982): 15; John Sullivan, "Toward Diversity," *Friends Journal* 38 (April 1992): 20–21; Robert S. Vogel letter, ibid., 44 (April 1998), 4; *Realignment: Nine Views Among Friends* (Wallingford: Pendle Hill, 1991), 64; McNish interview.

46. Snyder, *Witness in Washington*, 14–15, 29–31, 181; Edwin Bronner, "FCNL Priorities, 1943–1993," *Friends Journal* 39 (April 1993): 12–13.

47. Snyder, *Witness in Washington*, 22–23, 36–40, 57.

48. Joanne Rains, "FCNL's Sense of the Nation: Quaker Priorities for Legislative Action," *Quaker Life* 37 (Sept. 1996): 8–9, 29.

49. See "Statement of Legislative Policy," *FCNL Washington Newsletter* 660 (Nov./Dec. 2001). For comments on this section, I am grateful to Joanne Warner, the current FCNL presiding clerk.

50. "Statement of Legislative Policy," 1; Snyder, *Witness*, vii, 18–21, 46–48, 169, 178.

7. "A quarterly meeting in herself": Quaker Women, Marriage, and the Family

1. The late Seth Hinshaw, former superintendent of North Carolina Yearly Meeting, shared this anecdote with me in 1987.

2. See Phyllis Mack, *Visionary Women: Ecstatic Prophecy in Seventeenth-Century England* (Berkeley: University of California Press, 1992), 127–261; and Christine Trevett, *Women and Quakerism in the 17th Century* (York, Eng.: Sessions, 1995).

3. Mack, *Visionary Women*, 265–412, esp. 366, 412.

4. Margaret Hope Bacon, *Mothers of Feminism: The Story of Quaker Women in America* (San Francisco: Harper and Row, 1986), 42–54; Rebecca Larson, *Daughters of Light: Quaker Women Preaching and Prophesying in the Colonies and Abroad* (New York: Knopf, 1999).

5. Bacon, *Mothers of Feminism*, 86–136, 152.

6. Ibid., 137–50, 161–63; Ellen D. Swain, "From Benevolence to Reform: The Expanding Career of Rhoda M. Coffin," *Indiana Magazine of History* 97 (Sept. 2001): 190–217.

7. Bacon, *Mothers of Feminism*, 202–20; John M. Craig, "Hannah Johnston Bailey: Publicist for Peace," *Quaker History* 84 (Spring 1995): 3–16; John W. Oliver, "Emma Brown Malone: A Mother of Feminism?" *Quaker History* 88 (Spring 1999): 4–21.

8. Bacon, *Mothers of Feminism*, 222. This paragraph is based on reading Quaker periodicals from 1900 to 1960.

9. Margaret Hope Bacon, "Beyond Equal Rights: The Quaker Concern for the Rights of Women," in *Friends Face the World: Continuing and Current Quaker Concerns* (Philadelphia: Friends General Conference, 1987), 100–3; Miriam Macy Pike letter, *Evangelical Friend* 9 (Dec. 1975-Jan. 1976): 26; Lauren King letter, *Evangelical Friend* 9 (Dec. 1975-Jan. 1976): 26.

10. Bacon, "Beyond Equal Rights," 106; Margaret Hope Bacon, "Quaker Women Today," *Friends Journal* 32 (Nov. 15, 1985): 4–7. This paragraph is based largely on conversations with many Quaker women over the past two decades.

11. Margery Larrabee, "Sexism, Inclusive Language, and Worship," *Friends Journal* 34 (Oct. 1988): 6–9; Sequoia Edwards, "When Being Right Isn't Enough," *Friends Journal* 34 (Oct. 1988): 8; Frances N. Beer letter, *Friends Journal* 41 (July 1995): 4; Jean Snyder letter, *Friends Journal* 41 (Feb. 1995): 4–5; Peg Morton, "Nonpatriarchal, Nonoppressive Language: How Important Is It?" *Friends Journal* 41 (Oct. 1995): 22.

12. Elizabeth Watson, "Reconstituting the World," *Friends Journal* 31 (Oct. 15, 1985): 8–10; Elizabeth Watson, *Wisdom's Daughters: Stories of Women Around Jesus* (Cleveland: Pilgrim Press, 1997), 52, 156; Susan Merrill, "Mother Nature, My Mother and Me," *Friendly Woman* 12 (Spring 1997): 4; Elisabeth Leonard, "Gender Re-Conciliation: The Foundation for Today's Quaker Peace and Social Witness," in *New Voices, New Light: Papers from the Quaker Theology Roundtable, Fourth Month 7–9, 1995*, ed. Chuck Fager (Wallingford, Pa.: Pendle Hill, 1995), 147; Elise Boulding and Kenneth E. Boulding, *The Future: Images and Processes* (Thousand Oaks, Calif.: Sage, 1995), 187; Chuck Fager, *Without Apology: The Heroes, the Heritage and the Hope of Liberal Quakerism* (Bellefonte, Pa.: Kimo Press, 1996), 96–114.

13. Nancy M. Cocke and Laura L. Jackson, "Ten Queries: Two Feminists Respond," *Friends Journal* 31 (Aug. 1/15, 1985): 14–15; Steven Smith, "Healing Gender Hurt," *Friends Journal* 39 (Jan. 1993): 16–19; Susan Hesse, "It's Time for Action," *Friendly Woman* 13 (Winter 1999): 8; Michele Lise Tarter, "The Milk of the Word of God," in Fager, ed., *New Voices, New Light*, 79; Leonard, "Gender Re-Conciliation," 149.

14. Elenita Bales letter, *Evangelical Friend* 7 (Dec. 1973): 2; Jack L. Willcuts, "Antecedents," *Evangelical Friend* 15 (March 1982): 5; Judith K. Middleton, "Are

Quakers Feminists?" *Evangelical Friend* 17 (Oct. 1983): 28; Gregg Lamm, "Christ's View of Equality," *Evangelical Friend* 19 (Feb. 1986): 9.

15. Paul Anderson, "On the Virgin Mary, Inclusive Ministry, . . . and Christmas," *Evangelical Friend* 25 (Nov./Dec. 1991): 4; Patricia Edwards-DeLancey, "Friends Women in Vocal Ministry," *Quaker Life* 24 (Jan.-Feb. 1983): 11.

16. Bruce Bray letter, *Evangelical Friend* 15 (May 1982): 12; Judith Middleton, "Women and Ministry," *Quaker Life* 30 (Jan./Feb. 1989): 15; Patricia Edwards, "Whom God Chooses: The Theological Grounding for Women in Ministry," *Quaker Life* 30 (Jan./Feb. 1989): 10–12; Jack L. Willcuts, *Why Friends Are Friends (Some Quaker Core Convictions)* (Newberg, Ore.: Barclay Press, 1992), 48.

17. Karla Minear, "It's Time to Go Public," *Quaker Life* 28 (June 1987): 16; Ann Davidson, "Visibility in the Vineyard: The Future of Women in Pastoral Leadership Among Friends," *Quaker Life* 33 (Jan./Feb. 1992): 9–10; Richard Sartwell, "Evangelical Friends and the Richmond Declaration of Faith," *Evangelical Friend* 20 (May 1987): 8–9; *Among Friends: A Consultation with Friends About the Condition of Quakers in the U.S. Today* (Richmond, Ind.: Earlham, 1999), 214; Alan Weinacht, interview with author, Feb. 8, 2002 (in author's possession); Curt Shaw, interview with author, March 1, 2002 (in author's possession); Wayne Evans, interview with author, Aug. 2, 2002 (in author's possession).

18. "Quaker Women in Ministry Today," *Quaker Life* 21 (June 1980): 14–15; Stephen Howell letter, *Quaker Life* 28 (April 1987): 39; Middleton, "Are Quakers Feminists?" 28; Mary Katherine Morse, "Women in Leadership: The 'Fly' or the Ointment?" *Evangelical Friend* 25 (Nov./Dec. 1991): 7; Evans interview.

19. Charles Mylander, "Abortion and Compassion," *Evangelical Friend* 18 (May 1985): 28; John Oliver, "Angels of Apocalypse," *Evangelical Friend* 21 (Jan./Feb. 1988): 6–7; Nellie Logan, "Feeling the Pain of Abortion," *Evangelical Friend* 21 (April 1988), 12–13; Gregory P. Hinshaw letter, *Quaker Life* 31 (March 1990): 35; Northwest Yearly Meeting, *Faith and Practice: A Book of Christian Discipline* (Newberg, Ore.: Barclay Press, 1987), 101.

20. Don Badgley letter, *Spark* 20 (Sept. 1989): 2; Rachel MacNair, "A Consistent Pro-Life Ethic," *Quaker Life* 40 (April 1999): 4–6; Louise Hopkins letter, *Quaker Life* 38 (July/Aug. 1994): 34; Nanlouise Wolfe and Stephen Zunes, "Appreciating Our Common Faith," *Friends Journal* 36 (Feb. 1990): 13–14; Lisa Rohner Schafer, "Seeking Clearness on Abortion," *Friends Journal* 36 (Sept. 1990): 18–20; "Overground Railroad," *Friends Journal* 37 (Oct. 1991): 24–25; Jean Malcolm and Stewart Mulford, "Two Friends Look at Abortion," *Friends Journal* 44 (May 1998): 9–14; "Forum," *Friends Journal* 44 (Aug. 1998): 4–5.

21. Mary Edith Hinshaw and Ruth R. Hockett, *Growth, Development, Service, Unlimited: The Story of the United Society of Friends Women* (N.p., 1981), 1–23, 34; Carolyn Sims, "So Many Worthy Projects," *Advocate* 115 (March-April 1999): 13; Clara W. Millett, "Reflections—Quaker Women in Ministry," *Advocate* 115 (Nov.-Dec. 1999): 26–27; Ann Davidson, "Fruit That Lasts," *Advocate* 113 (May-

June 1997): 4; James R. Newby, "Ministering in a Different World," *Evangelical Friend* 24 (Jan./Feb. 1991): 19.

22. Margery Post Abbott, *An Experiment in Faith: Quaker Women Transcend Differences* (Wallingford, Pa.: Pendle Hill, 1995). I have also benefited from reading an unpublished paper by Pamela Calvert, "'How Blessed It Is for the Sisters to Meet': Historical Roots of the Pacific Northwest Quaker Women's Theology Conference," 2002.

23. Thomas Clarkson quoted in Elise Boulding, *One Small Plot of Heaven: Reflections on Family Life by a Quaker Sociologist* (Wallingford, Pa.: Pendle Hill, 1989), 84. For the history of the Quaker family, see J. William Frost, *The Quaker Family in Colonial America: A Portrait of the Society of Friends* (New York: St. Martin's, 1973); and Barry Levy, *Quakers and the American Family: British Settlement in the Delaware Valley* (New York: Oxford University Press, 1988).

24. See, for example, *The Discipline of the Society of Friends, of Ohio Yearly Meeting* (Mt. Pleasant, Ohio: Elisha Bates, 1819), 35–45. The process was uniform in all yearly meetings.

25. Howard Macy, "Let's Be Friends," *Quaker Life* 23 (July/Aug. 1982): 45; Kate Hood, "Marriage Under the Care of the Meeting," *Quaker Life* 41 (June 2000): 13–16; Tom Mullen, *Middle Age and Other Mixed Blessings* (Tarrytown, N.Y.: Revell, 1991), 53–57; Dana Harr and Barclay Kuhn, "A Ceremony of Joining," *Friends Journal* 35 (Nov. 1989): 28–29; Eileen Flanagan, "Waiting for Clearness," *Friends Journal* 45 (Nov. 1999): 7–8; Philadelphia Yearly Meeting Family Relations Committee, *A Quaker Marriage* (Philadelphia: Philadelphia Yearly Meeting, 1988), passim.

26. Neil T. Anderson and Charles Mylander, *The Christ-Centered Marriage: Discovering and Enjoying Your Freedom in Christ Together* (Ventura, Calif.: Regal, 1996), 25–29; Catherine Whitmire, *Plain Living: A Quaker Path to Simplicity* (Notre Dame, Ind.: Sorin, 2001), 56; Tom Mullen, *A Very Good Marriage* (Richmond, Ind.: Friends United Press, 2001), 38–39.

27. Anderson and Mylander, *Christ-Centered Marriage*, 98–100, 131; "A Remarriage May Succeed," *Evangelical Friend* 12 (Oct. 1978): 7; Sarah Angell, "Chain of Command," *Quaker Life* (Jan./Feb. 1999): 3.

28. Mullen, *Middle Age*, 84; Jack L. Willcuts, "The Christian Family," *Evangelical Friend* 7 (March 1974): 5; Sandra Cook-Dufield, "Chain of Command or Mutual Submission: Evangelicals Dispute Family Models," *Quaker Life* 39 (Oct. 1998): 20–21.

29. For differing views on Quaker divorce rates, cf. Earl Brightup letter, *Evangelical Friend* 11 (July/Aug. 1978): 18; and Robert Lawrence Smith, *A Quaker Book of Wisdom: Life Lessons in Simplicity, Service, and Common Sense* (New York: Morrow, 1998), 165.

30. Donald M. Joy, "Grounds for Divorce," *Evangelical Friend* 18 (April 1985): 14; Ron Woodward, "Families in Trouble—Some Reflections," *Evangelical Friend*

16 (Oct. 1982): 7; Anderson and Mylander, *Christ-Centered Marriage*, 249, 275; Northwest Yearly Meeting, *Faith and Practice*, 99; Evangelical Friends Church Eastern Region, *Faith and Practice: The Book of Discipline* (Canton, Ohio: Eastern Region, 2000), 106; Evans interview.

31. Jack L. Willcuts, "Jesus's Teaching on Divorce," *Evangelical Friend* 11 (March 1978): 2–4, 27; Woodward, "Families in Trouble," 8; Marie Ingerman, "Preserving the Vital Bridges," *Friends Journal* 33 (April 1, 1987): 18–19; Judith Baker, "Friendly Divorce," *Friends Journal* 41 (June 1995): 17; Philadelphia Yearly Meeting, *Faith and Practice: A Book of Christian Discipline* (Philadelphia: Philadelphia Yearly Meeting, 1997), 70.

32. Smith, *Quaker Book of Wisdom*, 161.

33. Cf. Elise Boulding, "Families as Centers of Peace and Love: Paradoxes and Contradictions," in Kenworthy, ed., *Friends Face the World*, 45–48; Alvin Anderson, "The Church Can Help Build Families," *Evangelical Friend* 16 (Oct. 1982): 8–9; David O. Williams, "As for Me and My House, We Will Serve the Lord," *Evangelical Friend* 24 (May/June 1991): 3; Judy and Denis Nicholson Asselin, *Simple Riches: Reflections on the Work of the Quaker Family* (N.p., 1995); and Jay W. Marshall, *Family Faults: Healing the Hurts That Threaten the Home* (New Castle, Ind.: Almond Rod, 1998).

34. Anderson and Mylander, *Christ-Centered Marriage*, 10–11, 70, 89; Sheldon Louthan and Grant Martin, "Toward Better Families," *Evangelical Friend* 9 (June 1976): 2–4; Paul Anderson, interview with author, July 26, 2002 (in author's possession).

35. Sandra Cronk, *Gospel Order: A Quaker Understanding of Faithful Church Community* (Wallingford, Pa.: Pendle Hill, 1991), 9; Nicholson Asselin, *Simple Riches*, 2; Boulding and Boulding, *Future*, 128–30, 153; Boulding, *One Small Plot of Heaven*, 148–55, 161, 203, 205–6; Mullen, *Middle Age*, 140–41; David Mace, "Violence in Quaker Families," *Friends Journal* 30 (Oct. 1, 1984): 7–8; Edward Elder letter, *Friends Journal* 37 (Feb. 1991): 4.

36. Don and Pam Harris, "We Have Come a Long Way from Days of Gray," *Conservative Friend* 9 (2nd Mo. 2000): 4; Sandy Davis, "A Firm Foundation for the Children," *Quaker Life* 42 (June 2001): 10; Judy Brutz, "Is the Peace Testimony for Families?" *Quaker Life* 28 (March 1987): 7; David L. Foster, "Violence Study Flawed," *Friends Journal* 33 (Feb. 15, 1987): 18–19.

RESOURCES FOR FURTHER STUDY

Foundational

Barbour, Hugh, and Arthur O. Roberts, eds. *Early Quaker Writings, 1650–1700.* Grand Rapids: Eerdmans, 1973. The best available compilation.

Barclay, Robert. *An Apology for the True Christian Divinity.* Glenside, Pa.: Quaker Heritage Press, 2002. The most influential single Quaker theological work.

Garman, Mary, et al., eds. *Hidden in Plain Sight: Quaker Women's Writings, 1650–1700.* Wallingford, Pa.: Pendle Hill, 1996. A unique resource on women in early Quakerism.

Nickalls, John L. ed. *The Journal of George Fox.* Philadelphia: Religious Society of Friends, 1995. Fox's journal is the basic source for early Quakerism.

Moulton, Philips P. *The Journal and Major Essays of John Woolman.* New York: Oxford University Press, 1971. After Fox, Woolman is probably the most influential and widely read Quaker.

Books

Among Friends: A Consultation with Friends About the Condition of Quakers in the U.S. Today. Richmond, Ind.: Earlham, 1999. The closest thing we have to an in-depth survey of contemporary Quakers, based on numerous focus groups conducted for the Earlham School of Religion in 1998 and 1999.

Bacon, Margaret Hope. *Mothers of Feminism: The Story of Quaker Women in America.* San Francisco: Harper and Row, 1986. The best available treatment.

Barbour, Hugh, and J. William Frost. *The Quakers.* Rev. ed. Richmond, Ind.: Friends United Press, 1995. The best single-volume history of American Quakerism.

Benson, Lewis. *Catholic Quakerism: A Vision for All Men.* Philadelphia: Philadelphia Yearly Meeting, 1966. Benson was probably the most influential Christian voice among unprogrammed Friends in the second half of the twentieth century.

Boulding, Elise. *One Small Plot of Heaven: Reflections on Family Life by a Quaker Sociologist.* Wallingford, Pa.: Pendle Hill, 1989. Elise Boulding has been a leader among unprogrammed Friends, especially on the family.

Brinton, Howard. *Friends for 300 Years: The History and Beliefs of the Society of Friends Since George Fox Started the Quaker Movement.* New York: Harper & Row, 1953. As much reflective work as history; its influence on liberal Friends has been enormous.

Cattell, Everett L. *Christian Mission: A Matter of Life.* Richmond, Ind.: Friends United Press, 1981. A Quaker vision of Christian life by a leading Evangelical Friend.

Cooper, Wilmer A. *A Living Faith: An Historical Study of Quaker Beliefs.* Richmond, Ind.: Friends United Press, 1991. An excellent presentation of a moderate view of Quaker faith.

Cope-Robinson, Lyn. *The Little Quaker Sociology Book with Glossary.* Melbourne Beach, Fla: Canmore Press, 1995. An excellent introduction to Quaker groups and terminology.

Cronk, Sandra. *Gospel Order: A Quaker Understanding of Faithful Church Community.* Wallingford, Pa.: Pendle Hill, 1991. A theme increasingly important to Friends.

———. *Peace Be With You: A Study of the Spiritual Basis of the Friends Peace Testimony.* Philadelphia: Tract Association of Friends, n.d. The title describes the work.

Fager, Chuck. *Without Apology: The Heroes, the Heritage, and the Hope of Liberal Quakerism.* Bellefonte, Pa.: Kimo Press, 1996. A biting defense of modern Quaker universalism and an unsparing critique of its adversaries.

Gwyn, Douglas. *Unmasking the Idols: A Journey Among Friends.* Richmond, Ind.: Friends United Meeting, 1989. A critical look at all persuasions of American Friends.

Hinshaw, Seth B. *Friends Worship Today: Contemporary Concepts and Practices.* Greensboro, N.C.: North Carolina Yearly Meeting, 1991. The best available survey of programmed Quaker worship.

Jones, Rufus M. *The Faith and Practice of the Quakers.* Philadelphia: Philadelphia Yearly Meeting, n.p. A classic statement of liberal Quakerism.

Kelly, Thomas R. *A Testament of Devotion.* New York: Harper, 1941. One of the most influential devotional works of the twentieth century, deeply influenced by its author's Quaker faith.

Lacey, Paul A. *Growing Into Goodness: Essays on Quaker Education.* Wallingford, Pa.: Pendle Hill, 1998. The best work available on the theory and practice of Quaker education, by a long-time Earlham College professor.

Loring, Patricia. *Listening Spirituality*. 2 vols. Washington, D.C.: Openings Press, 1997, 1999. The best work available on the spiritual lives of contemporary unprogrammed Friends.

Punshon, John. *Portrait in Grey: A Short History of the Quakers*. London: Quaker Home Service, 1984. As much thoughtful reflection as history, and valuable for both reasons.

——. *Reasons for Hope: The Faith and Future of the Friends Church*. Richmond, Ind.: Friends United Press, 2001. An articulate defense of a moderate pastoral Quakerism.

Sheeran, Michael J. *Beyond Majority Rule: Voteless Decisions in the Society of Friends*. Philadelphia: Philadelphia Yearly Meeting, 1996. Sheeran, a Jesuit, has provided the best analysis of how the Quaker business process works.

Steere, Douglas V. *On Speaking Out of the Silence: Vocal Ministry in the Unprogrammed Meeting for Worship*. Wallingford, Pa.: Pendle Hill, 1972. The best work available on its subject.

Taber, William. *Four Doors to Meeting for Worship*. Wallingford, Pa.: Pendle Hill, 1992. An excellent analysis of unprogrammed worship by a leading Conservative Friend.

Trueblood, D. Elton. *The People Called Quakers*. New York: Harper and Row, 1966. Valuable for its articulation of a Christian Quaker outlook and history.

Whitmire, Catherine. *Plain Living: A Quaker Path to Simplicity*. Notre Dame, Ind.: Sorin, 2001. An excellent collection of quotations on simplicity and its implications.

Willcuts, Jack L. *Why Friends Are Friends (Some Quaker Core Convictions)*. Newberg, Ore.: Barclay Press, 1992. The best single statement of Evangelical Friends' beliefs by one of their most important leaders.

Williams, Walter R. *The Rich Heritage of Quakerism*. 2nd ed. Newberg, Ore.: Barclay Press, 1987. Quaker history through the eyes of an influential Evangelical Friend.

Anthologies

Abbott, Margery Post. ed., *A Certain Kind of Perfection: An Anthology of Evangelical and Liberal Quaker Writers*. Wallingford, Pa.: Pendle Hill, 1997. A good collection of writings of Friends of all points of view, from the seventeenth century to the present.

Fager, Chuck. ed. *A Continuing Journey: Papers from the Quaker Peace Round Table*. Wallingford, Pa.: Pendle Hill, 1996. These essays give insight into contemporary Quaker pacifism.

Kenworthy, Leonard S., ed. *Friends Face the World: Continuing and Current Quaker Concerns*. Philadelphia: Friends General Conference, 1987. Leading Friends in the United States treat contemporary Quaker and social issues.

Let Your Lives Speak: A Report of the World Gathering of Friends, 1985. Greensboro, N.C., 1985. An excellent introduction into the diversity of Quakerism, not only in the United States but also around the world.

Manousos, Anthony. ed. *A Western Quaker Reader: Writings by and About Independent Quakers in the Western United States, 1929–1999.* Whittier, Calif.: Friends Bulletin, 2000. An excellent introduction to the activities of independent, unprogrammed meetings.

Quaker Universalist Reader Number 1: A Collection of Essays, Addresses, and Lectures. Landenburg, Pa.: Quaker Universalist Fellowship, 1986. An excellent introduction to Quaker universalism.

Realignment: Nine Views Among Friends. Wallingford, Pa.: Pendle Hill, 1991. Goes beyond the Realignment controversy to sketch starkly the issues that divide contemporary Friends.

Steere, Douglas V., ed. *Quaker Spirituality: Selected Writings.* New York: Paulist Press, 1984. Extracts from classic Quaker works.

Official Documents

Since Friends have no central authority, no one doctrinal statement speaks for all. The best way to sample official Quaker positions is by consulting the books of discipline/faith and practice for the various yearly meetings. Most have published them; a few new yearly meetings use those of others. The following is a sampling that reflects the diversity of contemporary Quakerism. The yearly meeting is the publisher unless otherwise noted.

Conservative

The Book of Discipline of Ohio Yearly Meeting of the Religious Society of Friends. Barnesville, Ohio, 2001.

EFI

Evangelical Friends Church–Eastern Region. *Faith and Practice: The Book of Discipline.* Canton, Ohio, 2000.

Northwest Yearly Meeting. *Faith and Practice: A Book of Christian Discipline.* Newberg, Ore.: Barclay Press, 1987.

FGC or Unprogrammed

North Pacific Yearly Meeting. *Faith and Practice.* Corvallis, Ore., 1993.

Philadelphia Yearly Meeting. *Faith and Practice: A Book of Christian Discipline.* Philadelphia, 1997.

FUM–Pastoral

Faith and Practice of Indiana Yearly Meeting of the Religious Society of Friends. Muncie, Ind., 2002.

Faith and Practice of Western Yearly Meeting of Friends Church. Plainfield, Ind., 1986.

FUM and FGC

Faith and Practice of New England Yearly Meeting of Friends (Book of Discipline). Worcester, Mass., 1985.

Faith and Practice. The Book of Discipline of the New York Yearly Meeting of the Religious Society of Friends. New York, 1998.

Periodicals or Serials

Friends, especially liberal Friends, publish numerous periodicals and newsletters. This is a sampling that includes those with the widest readership among American Friends.

Advocate. Monthly. Organ of the United Society of Friends Women. Contact FUM, 101 Quaker Hill Dr., Richmond, Ind. 47374.

American Friends Service Committee Quaker Service Journal. Quarterly. Organ of the AFSC. 1501 Cherry St., Philadelphia, Pa. 19102.

Befriending Creation. Quarterly. Organ of the Friends Committee on Unity with Nature. 173-B N. Prospect St., Burlington, Vt. 05401.

Conservative Friend. Quarterly. Published by Ohio Yearly Meeting (Conservative). As close to traditional Wilburism as any contemporary Quaker publication. Contact Seth Hinshaw, 713 Norwood House Road, Downingtown, Pa. 19335.

FLGC Newsletter. Three times annually. Organ of Friends for Lesbian and Gay Concerns. 143 Campbell Ave., Ithaca, N.Y. 14850.

Foundation Papers. Quarterly. Christ-centered, unprogrammed Friends. 3032 Logan St., Camp Hill, Pa. 17011.

Friendly Woman. Quarterly. Mainly unprogrammed Friends. 2794 Ft. Scott Dr., Arlington, Va. 22202.

Friends Bulletin. Monthly. Unprogrammmed Friends in the western United States. 3303 Raintree Ave., Torrance, Calif. 90601.

Friends Committee on National Legislation Washington Newsletter. Monthly. General updates on FCNL priorities with special features. 245 Second St. NE, Washington, D.C. 20002.

Friends Journal. Monthly. Generally recognized as the periodical of Friends General Conference and most unprogrammed Friends. 1216 Arch St., Philadelphia, Pa. 19107.

Friends Quarterly. Quarterly British publication, generally liberal in outlook, but often containing articles by Americans. P.O. Box 21366, London, U.K. WC1B 5LH.

Friends Voice. Quarterly EFI newsletter. 110 S. Elliott, Newberg, Ore. 97132.

Friends World News. Semiannual. Published by the Friends World Committee for Consultation, 1506 Race St., Philadelphia, Pa. 19102.

Indian Progress. Semiannual. Published by the Associated Committee of Friends on Indian Affairs. P.O. Box 2326, Richmond, Ind. 47374.

Pendle Hill Pamphlets. Several published annually by Pendle Hill, 331 Plush Mill Road, Wallingford, Pa. 19086.

Quaker History. Semiannual. Published by the Friends Historical Association. Scholarly journal not limited to North America. Care of Quaker Collection, Haverford College, Haverford, Pa. 19041.

Quaker Life. 10 issues annually. Organ of Friends United Meeting. 101 Quaker Hill Drive, Richmond, Ind. 47374.

Quaker Religious Thought. Semiannual. Published by the Quaker Theological Discussion Group. Care of Phil Smith, Religion Department, George Fox University, Newberg, Ore. 97132.

Quaker Studies. Semiannual. Refereed scholarly journal covering all aspects of the study of Quakerism. Sheffield Academic Press, 370 Lexington Ave., New York, N.Y. 10017.

Quaker Theology. Semiannual. Published by Quaker Ecumenical Seminars in Theology. Liberal in outlook. P.O. Box 1344, Fayetteville, N.C. 28302.

Southern Friend. Semiannual. Published by the North Carolina Friends Historical Society. Southern Quaker history. P.O. Box 8502, Greensboro, N.C. 27419.

Electronic Resources and Web Sites

American Friends Service Committee. www.afsc.org

Evangelical Friends International. www.evangelical-friends.org

Evangelical Friends Mission. www.friendsmission.org

Friends Association for Higher Education. www.earlham.edu/~fahe

Friends Committee on Unity with Nature. www.fcun.org

Friends Committee on National Legislation. www.fcnl.org

Friends Council on Education. www.friendscouncil.org. Information on Quaker primary and secondary schools.

Friends Disaster Service. www.nvoad.org/fds.htm

Friends for Lesbian and Gay Concerns. www.flgc.quaker.org

Friends General Conference. www.fgcquaker.org

Friends United Meeting. www.fum.org

Friends World Committee for Consultation. www.fwcc.quaker.org. Includes statistical data for Friends around the world and links to many other Quaker organizations.

New Foundation Fellowship. www.thebetternet.com/users/nff/nff.html. Christ-centered unprogrammed Friends.

Quaker Heritage Press Online Texts. www.qhpress.org. Many classic Quaker writings, including Robert Barclay's *Apology.*

Quaker Information Center. www.quakerinfo.org. Numerous links to other Quaker organizations.

Quakers Uniting in Publications. www.quaker.org/~quip

Quaker Universalist Fellowship. www.universalistfriends.org

Religious Society of Friends. www.quaker.org. The largest collection of links to Quaker Web sites.

INDEX

Note: Italic page numbers refer to illustrations.